Surgeon on Iwo

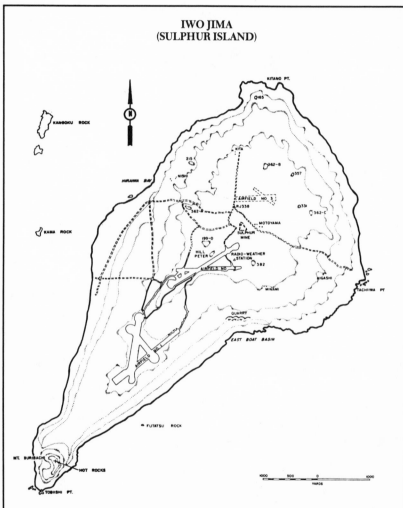

IWO JIMA
(SULPHUR ISLAND)

Showing main geographical features. Courtesy Historical Division, USMC

Surgeon on Iwo

Up Front with the 27th Marines

James S. Vedder

★
PRESIDIO

Though the action as described in the book is all true, a number of names have been changed to protect the reputations of the men who did not perform according to Marine Corps standards.

Copyright © 1984 by Presidio Press
Published by Presidio Press
31 Pamaron Way Novato, CA 94947

Library of Congress Cataloging in Publication Data

Vedder, James S., 1912–
   Surgeon on Iwo.

028951

15.95

   Includes index.
   1. Vedder, James S., 1912–   . 2. Surgeons—United States—Biography. 3. Iwo Jima, Battle of, 1945—Personal narratives, American. I. Title.
RD27.35.V43A33 1984   940.54'7573   84-6765
ISBN 0-89141-199-2

Printed in the United States of America.

Contents

Chapter One

Journey Begins

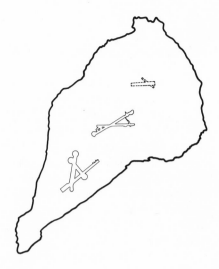

December 30, 1944, was a sparkling, clear day. During the night the snow line had moved halfway down the slopes of majestic Mauna Kea. Reveille had sounded at 0430, and after completing an early breakfast the entire reinforced 5th Marine Division of twenty thousand men was finally on the long journey from the Parker Ranch on Hawaii's western slopes to the black island of Iwo Jima. Our immediate destination was the Port of Hilo, where we would embark on our respective troop transports to start the long voyage to the western Pacific.

With a minimum of confusion, the men of our 3rd Battalion, 27th Marines, boarded the open flatcars of the narrow-gauge sugar cane railroad that connected Honokaa with Hilo on the windward side of the island. They seemed to be in an unusually somber and pensive mood. The usual banter and horseplay displayed during troop movements was conspicuously absent. As half our men were seasoned veterans from previous campaigns, I could not understand why they were taking Iwo Jima so seriously. After all, our high command was planning only a three-day operation: two days to capture the island, the third day to eliminate the remnants of enemy resistance, and a fourth day to board our transports and proceed to Okinawa.

As our tiny steam engine puffed and chugged, dragging its load of Marines through the lovely rain forest illuminated by the flaming red tulip trees, the passengers seemed oblivious of their exotic surroundings. A few men were cleaning their rifles, others were honing their trench knives

1

and bayonets, but most of them had withdrawn into their own private worlds.

At the far end of the flatcar I spotted Capt. Knute Knutson propped up against his backpack as he aimlessly whittled on a piece of koa wood. He was the commanding officer of headquarters company of the 3rd Battalion, 27th Marines and had known hard times while growing up on a farm in South Dakota during the dust bowl years.

Knutson was a muscular Scandinavian of medium height. His crew-cut blond hair, fine-textured, almost beardless, fair skin, and full, round face made him seem younger than his twenty-five years. However, instant confidence was instilled when his deep blue eyes fixed their attention on anyone seeking his help or advice. He could always be depended on to lend a hand during a time of crisis and he had a certain empathy for the new recruits who had recently joined our unit.

As I crawled over prone bodies on the swaying train toward Knute, I saw that he was not making a koa wood carving. His slashing attack on the stick that sent shavings flying in all directions was serving only to relieve inner tension.

I grabbed one of his extended legs and asked, "What's the trouble, Knute? Why are you in the dumps?"

He straightened up with a start, "Who, me? Ya, I guess I was."

"What's bugging you?"

"I was just thinking how lucky I was on Guadalcanal two times and one time on Bougainville. Will my luck run out on Iwo Jima? Yes, maybe?"

"Is that why all you old-timers are so quiet today?"

"Ya, some of them have used up their nine lives already. I still have six to go."

A few hours later when the train came to a halt, the melancholy mood of the men suddenly shifted. Joking obscenities began to flow, and I knew the Marines were functioning at their usual operational efficiency. To the strains of "Semper Fidelis," the Marine Corps hymn, and other Sousa marches played by the rear-echelon band, our 3rd Battalion marched down the pier and up the gangplank.

The PA–294 was a troop transport that could be instantly converted to an emergency hospital ship as soon as troops were disembarked on a hostile shore. She had been christened the SS *Sandoval* at launching a few months ago; she had a displacement of fifteen thousand tons and a cruising speed of twelve knots. The *Sandoval* was equipped to transport one combat battalion of a thousand men, and she was our "home" for the next fifty-one days.

The crew was as new as the ship. They had just completed their

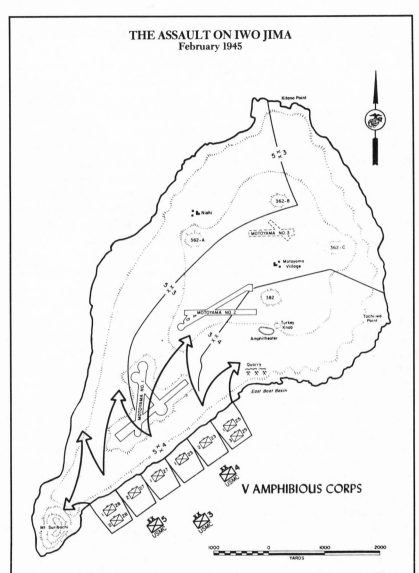

THE ASSAULT ON IWO JIMA
February 1945

The battalions that landed at H hour on D Day. The 28th and 27th Battalions are part of 5th Division. The 23rd and 25th Battalions are from the 4th Division. The rest of the troops are still afloat.
Courtesy Historical Division, USMC

shakedown cruise, and Iwo Jima was to be their first combat operation. As a result it would take several more weeks to shake out the bugs and a great deal more training before the crew would be able to operate efficiently the small landing crafts—LCVPs (Landing Craft Vehicle Personnel), forty-passenger flat-bottomed boats—scheduled to put us ashore on a hostile beach at Iwo Jima on February 19, 1945.

While waiting for the fleet to assemble, during the first part of January, we had a week of liberty on Oahu. My first mission ashore was a visit to the submarine base in the Pearl Harbor area. Most of the submarines were out on patrol. Only three were tied up at their berths, and only one of the boats showed any sign of life. A young ensign was standing at the head of the gangway directing traffic as provisions were being loaded aboard the vessel. After watching this procedure for some time, I called over to the officer and asked, "May I come aboard and see how your boat operates?"

To my delight he gave me an engaging smile and said, "Sure thing, come aboard. I'll take you down to meet the skipper."

A few moments later I was seated beside a young man who seemed no older than the ensign who had conducted me below. His insignia indicated he was a lieutenant commander, so he must be the commanding officer of this vessel. As he poured me a cup of coffee, I explained my long-term interest in submarines and hoped that someone could show me the inner workings of his underwater boat.

His ready response was, "That will be no problem. Are you headed toward Iwo Jima with the 5th Division?"

"Yes, I am. How did you know Iwo was our destination?"

"That's common knowledge from Pearl Harbor to Honolulu. Besides, we've just returned from a six-week patrol of the Volcano Islands."

"Did you get a close look at Iwo Jima?"

"We sure did. We brought home some excellent photographs taken from all sides of the island."

"Do you think we'll have an easy time cleaning up the island in three days?"

"I doubt it. The whole island is loaded with heavy artillery. Besides, they wouldn't be sending the Marines in there if it were going to be an easy operation."

"Won't the extra heavy preinvasion bombardment make a difference?"

The skipper answered, "It certainly could, and we wish you Marines all the best of luck."

Then one of the yeomen took me on a conducted tour of the submarine. I had trouble concentrating on his detailed explanations, because the ominous words of the captain kept my thoughts on Iwo Jima. About the only thing I learned was how to flush the toilets. The crowded living conditions on the boat made the accommodations on the *Sandoval* seem quite spacious.

Before leaving the submarine I stopped by the wardroom to pay my respects to the captain.

He said, "Think nothing of it, Doctor. We were glad to have you on board. We are going on a short shakedown cruise off the south shore of Oahu in a couple of days. How would you like to ship out with us?"

I said, "That sounds great. I'm sure I can get permission to go."

This was not a valid assumption. Colonel Robertson had other plans to occupy my time. He wanted his senior medical officer to accompany him on the daily briefings, which took place either at regimental or division headquarters. I never did get to see my submarine friends again.

On January 9 as we weighed anchor and headed for Lahaina Roads and Maalaea Bay off the island of Maui, I asked Dr. Charles Hely, our assistant battalion surgeon, to round up all our medical personnel on the afterdeck. Hely had just been graduated from Hahneman Medical College in Philadelphia and was eager to convert his recently acquired knowledge to practical use. For a large man he was very supple in movement. He had a head of curly black hair above wide-spaced blue eyes and a face easily provoked to a happy grin. I was fortunate to have such a pleasant colleague to work with during the coming campaign. Besides Hely and Chief Pharmacist Mate Griebe, I had forty-eight Navy corpsmen and six-teen Marine litter bearers serving under my command in the medical section of the 3rd Battalion. A few of these corpsmen were naval petty officers with ratings of pharmacist mate first class, second class, or third class. The majority of my corpsmen were hospital apprentices, a rank equivalent to that of private in the Army. I had assigned twenty-four of the more experienced corpsmen to the three combat companies that formed the spearhead of our battalion. As a result, eight corpsmen were available in each of these companies to render expert first aid to the Marines immediately after a man received an injury. Pharmacist Mates 1st Class Bukowski, Willis, and Thronson were the senior men respectively in G, H, and I companies.

The other twenty-four corpsmen were assigned to headquarters company, where they served in our battalion aid station. Maloney, Rhoe, Murphy, Allen, Smith, and Meegan were all petty officers with either a first or a second class pharmacist mate's rating and were my key men in the aid station. They were all skilled in the latest first aid procedures, and they could be depended on to direct and teach the less experienced corpsmen.

My sixteen litter bearers were all Marine privates who had been inducted into the service only a few months earlier. Because all sixteen of them had names starting with *B*, such as Blauch, Brautigen, Baldauf, Bargander, Backus, and so on, they must have been assigned en bloc to the 27th Marines from some boot camp in the states. All of them were eighteen years old, and three of them had not been allowed to graduate from high school. Because of their lack of experience and military training, I felt more than the usual sense of responsibility. My concern was augmented by the fact that these men had the shortest life expectancy of anyone in headquarters company. In order to evacuate casualties, they would have to walk upright while carrying their litters, and therefore they were fair game for enemy marksmen.

When I could hear the high-pitched, nasal voice of Chief Pharmacist Mate Griebe herding the last of my sixty-four corpsmen and litter bearers onto the open deck, I knew my meeting was ready.

"Knock it off, knock it off, you dumb bastards. Doc Vedder has some hot scoop to pass on to you birdbrains."

Griebe was one of the few petty officers in our 3rd Battalion who was a career man in the Regular Navy. Most of our men were members of the Naval Reserve who were planning to serve only for the duration of the war. Griebe could quote the naval rules and regulations verbatim. He was an expert at twisting these rules and regulations sometimes to gain an unfair advantage over his subordinates. For this reason alone he was not well liked by his fellow corpsmen.

Griebe's mannerisms did not inspire confidence. He had the disconcerting habit of avoiding eye contact during any face-to-face encounter. While talking to another, his gaze would invariably be fixed on the ground or over the other person's shoulder. A number of our corpsmen claimed he was underhanded as well as shifty-eyed. Although he was not well liked, I did not think he had been performing too badly. Besides, a superior is often not too popular with the men serving under him.

The men now waited attentively for me to pass on my latest "scoop."

"We are going to practice landing exercises on Maui with the Navy for the next three days. It will chiefly be a learning experience for the coxswains of the small boats. We want to be sure that they put us on the right beach at the right time when D day comes around. The headquarters company corpsmen will be divided among three boats. I will command the troops in one boat, Dr. Hely will be in the second, and Chief Griebe will be in the third. If one of the boats gets wiped out by a direct hit, our medical section will still be able to function. Later Griebe will give you a list of who goes in each boat."

"January 10 and 11 will be water runs only. The fully loaded small boats will circle, assemble in their correct waves, and then make mock runs for the beach. On January 12 the same routine will be repeated with one addition. We will be put ashore. There we will assemble with the rest of headquarters company and will proceed with them up the side of Haleakala, where we will camp for the night. Are there any questions?"

One timid voice spoke up, "I get so sick on those fouled-up, stinking LCVPs, I start puking as soon as I get aboard. Could I stay aboard the *Sandoval* during the practice circling?"

I answered, "The colonel says all able-bodied men will participate. Pick up a bucket in the sick bay, and hope for the best."

On January 10, as soon as we left the protection of the lee shore of Oahu, we ran into a heavy swell. Later in the morning, when the troop transports assembled off Lahaina Roads south of Maui, the waves were cresting at elevations of five to six feet. I could agree with my seasickness-prone corpsman; it would be a miserable day bobbing around in those small boats.

It took less than an hour to launch the *Sandoval's* twenty-four LCVPs and to heave the heavy hemp cargo nets over the ship's rail. Just climbing down those nets, without encumbrances, and boarding one of the LCVPs in a calm sea took considerable courage and skill. The greatest danger was getting crushed between the boat and the side of the ship. Occasionally an unlucky marine would miss the boat altogether and receive an unexpected dunking.

As I slowly climbed down the cargo net, I had instant recall of prior instructions and practice sessions. The trick of the transfer from the ship to the small boat lay in accurate timing. I must board the LCVP at the crest of a wave. If I make the leap from the net to the boat too soon, the bottom of the boat will come rushing up slamming onto my feet (usually at an odd angle), then I will topple into a heap and will be lucky to escape with only a slightly sprained ankle or a bruised shoulder.

The results would be worse if I let go of the net just *after* the crest of the wave. As the boat settled into the trough, I would suffer a free fall of anywhere from five to twelve feet. Fractured legs, an injured spine, or a concussion were the most likely injuries. So if an error was to be made, it was safer to make the leap from the net near the top of the wave while the boat was still on the way up.

As I clung to the net I watched the rhythm of the boat as it rose and fell. On the fourth wave, I watched the boat come back up from six feet below. When the rail of the boat reached the level of my boots, I made my move. The timing was perfect but the wave was larger than the others. I was thrown off balance by the rapidly rising deck of the boat. I toppled against a communications Marine who had made the leap at the same time just forward of my position. We sprawled out onto the deck in the tangle of bodies and equipment. Although I ended up on top, it was not a soft landing; my chest was bruised by the portable radio strapped to the man's back. In addition, my left shin and knee were gouged with deep skin abrasions.

While sitting propped up against the forward ramp, gently rubbing my sore knee, I was thankful that the damage had been minimal. Transfers completed, our LCVP joined nine other small boats in a circling pattern while waiting for orders to approach the line of departure for the final run to the beach.

After five hours of circling, occasionally interrupted by lining up in parallel waves for a run to the vicinity of the beach, the small boats were allowed to take their passengers back to their respective transports. Climbing back up the cargo nets was easier than the descent.

January 11 was a repetition of the day before. The sea was much calmer. We had no problem climbing down the nets to board the LCVPs. Best of all, no one in my boat lost the contents of his stomach due to seasickness. I was able to finish three chapters of Tolstoy's *War and Peace* and take a noontime nap while the Navy made numerous practice runs at the beach.

On January 12 the LCVPs again assembled while circling. At the appropriate time, we lined up with five other boats and then made a run for the beach two miles away. A few minutes later our boat ground to a halt as the bottom scraped over sand and gravel. When the ramp dropped down, we ran out onto the beach. The Navy had given us a dry landing.

The beach area was littered with supplies and equipment. The bulk of the milling men were elements of the 26th Marines. The only familiar faces were those men who had landed in the boat commanded by Chief Griebe. Dr. Hely, his men, and the rest of the 3rd Battalion, 27th Marines, were nowhere in sight. It soon became obvious that our two boats had been sent in from the wrong assembly point. We could now understand why the Navy needed all this landing practice.

I instructed Griebe to keep our men collected in their present location while I sought information about the whereabouts of the 27th Marines. A younger officer of the 26th Marines soon set me straight. The main body of the 27th Marines had been put ashore two miles to the east. I knew our bivouac area was to be located on the lower slopes of Haleakala at the 3,000-foot level.

I returned to my men waiting on the beach and told them that the Navy had fouled us up good. "They put us ashore two miles west of our regiment. We can take a shortcut up to the bivouac area, which is located right here on the situation map. Who has a compass?"

One of the radiomen handed me his compass, and soon we set an angular course up the side of the mountain. Our direct course was interrupted many times by deep ravines and thickets of brush. We did not rejoin our 3rd Battalion comrades until after 1700. Hely greeted us warmly, and Colonel Robertson was glad to have his medical section restored to full strength.

When the sun dropped behind the shoulder of Haleakala, the air at this 3,000-foot elevation became uncomfortably cold. As we were on the Kona side of Maui, the dried brush burned well and gave off a comfortable amount of heat. As dusk settled in, the side of the mountain was dotted with hundreds of individual fires.

Our aid station soon had a roaring fire going. I dispatched half the men to gather a reserve supply of wood to last through the night. Griebe worked out a watch schedule for the rest of the men to keep this fire going. Suddenly a roaring bellow erupted from the regimental headquarters area, which was located three-hundred feet below us on the mountainside. The voice belonged to Col. Louis Plain, the regiment's second in command.

The message was clear: "OK, all you dumb bastards, you'd better take this war business seriously. We're operating under blackout conditions, so put out those goddamned fires right now."

Within twenty minutes, the last of the fires was extinguished. We shivered through the long night, wrapped in our single blankets.

We left Oahu for the last time on January 27 and headed out for the western Pacific. Our 5th Division convoy consisted of twenty-two large assault troop transports guarded by six destroyers and destroyer escorts. The old battleship *New York* brought up the rear of the convoy. It followed us only as far as Eniwetok, where it proceeded on ahead to partake in the preinvasion bombardment of Iwo Jima.

Shortly after Oahu dropped below the horizon, our high command issued a manifesto of encouragement over the loudspeaker system.

"Hear this, hear this. Before landing, intensive air strikes and surface bombardment will smash this tiny two-and-a-half-by-five-mile island with nine thousand tons of hot steel. To date no other island target has been so favored. The enemy will be so demoralized that it will be an easy task to secure the island in three days or less. Then we'll reboard our transports and proceed to Okinawa."

Except for the blackout conditions imposed between sunset and sunrise, we had a pleasant cruise sailing through the central Pacific. Because all the portholes had to be closed and covered, the troop compartments became insufferably hot, so most of the men spent the bulk of the night on the topside decks. As we crossed the international date line, we enjoyed a full moon in a cloudless starlit sky.

Two days later Colonel Robertson called us back to the harsh realities of the impending struggle. He scheduled a meeting of all the battalion officers, to be held in the wardroom at 1330. Everyone was waiting expectantly when he entered the compartment followed by Major Mix.

Donn J. Robertson was a handsome man in his late twenties, well over six feet tall, graceful and assured in movement. His unruffled exterior promoted confidence and trust, and he earned the affection of his junior officers by listening patiently to our problems. Even when exasperated, he never employed the common profanities.

The colonel began with: "Gentlemen, I have received some unsettling information today. The fourteen thousand enemy troops on the island have been recently reinforced with nine thousand new men. The other bad news is that our chief adversary will be Lt. Gen. Tadamichi Kuribayashi. He is one of the foremost artillery experts in the Imperial Army. It is not likely that he will order any foolish banzai charges. They will lay back and blast us with their heavy weapons. Iwo Jima will be a tough nut to crack."

Robertson continued, "D day has been scheduled for February 19, if the weather permits. The 4th Division will land on the eastern beaches in the center of the island. The 27th and 28th marines will lead the assault on the beaches just to the south of the 4th Division. These beaches lie along the narrow neck of the island just north of Mount Suribachi. Both regiments will drive straight ahead until the island is cut in two. Then the 28th Marines will turn south and eliminate the enemy entrenched on Suribachi. Our 27th Marines will turn north to lend the 4th Division a hand on the western side of the island."

At this moment Captain Gray, the commanding officer of I Company, broke into the discussion. Gray was an equal in size to the colonel, but there the similarity ended. Gray was a taciturn man with a determined thrust to his jaw. When he did have something to say he always came directly to the point. I thought his personality was a bit abrasive, but his men were unreservedly devoted to him.

Gray said, "Christ, they're out of their minds up there."

Robertson shot back, "Who are the guys up there?"

"The armchair strategists in corps command."

"Let's have it. What's the problem?"

"We'll get slaughtered fighting up that steep two-hundred-foot hillside. The Nips will be banging at us from Suribachi, the crest of the hill, and the highlands to the north."

"Nonsense, the Nips will be neutralized by the prelanding air and sea bombardment."

Gray persevered, "Why not land on the gradual-sloping west beaches? We'll have a lot more maneuver room."

"Kuribayashi agrees with you. All his big guns are trained on the west beaches. What's more, we'd get blown out of the water before we ever landed."

Gray looked skeptically at the colonel, "Are you sure of that?"

As Robertson patted his briefcase he said, "Yeah, I have the latest military info in here. You can check it out after the meeting."

Gray still looked unconvinced. He grunted, chomped off the end of his unlit cigar, and spewed out the fragments of the tobacco leaf on the deck.

The colonel then continued, "The 1st and 2nd battalions of the 27th Marines will lead the assault on D day, landing in waves just five minutes apart. Our 3rd Battalion will be held in reserve and will not be committed unless there is a determined counterattack. However, we will furnish very close backup support. Our entire battalion will be ashore when the eighteenth wave lands just ninety minutes after the first Marine hits the beach. Major Mix will pass out the schedule sheets listing landing times for the different units."

Capt. Reuben Munson of G Company was the first to question the landing schedules. Munson was a recent college graduate who had assumed his first combat command only three months before when his senior officer had been transferred to another unit. "Hell's bells, Colonel, somebody has flipped his lid. The 1st and 2nd battalions will never clear the beaches before we pile in on top of them."

Captain Hall chimed in with a nervous twitching of both eyelids, "Yah, Munson is right. Bodies will be piled up like cordwood on the beach. We'll make an irresistible target for the Nips."

Captain Gray added, "Can't we hold off our landing until the other guys get started up the hill?"

These comments were greeted with many murmurs and nods of approval among the assembled officers. Hely and I both fell into this category. We did not believe that our medical section belonged ashore in the thirteenth wave only sixty-five minutes after the initial landing. We would all be ashore while half our battalion was still afloat. There would be no place available to practice our surgical skills. We could only serve as more cannon fodder for the enemy.

The colonel digested these comments calmly and, after a moment of quiet thought, said, "You men have made some good points. There may be a few foul-ups in store for us. General Rocky wants the assault battalions on the crest of the hill during the first hour. The island will be cut in two by nightfall. Our 3rd Battalion must be ashore early to lend any needed support. If all goes as planned we'll be held in reserve all through D day. I wish you men would give further thought to the problem. There may be room for some minor adjustments."

We dropped anchor in the lagoon of Eniwetok Atoll on the morning of February 6. It was a reassuring sight to see this twenty-by-thirty mile lagoon filled with American shipping. This was the crossroads of our western Pacific expansion. Part of the traffic was headed southwest to the Philippines, and the rest was being diverted northwest to the Marianas. It was too bad the Japanese high command could not share this view of naval supremacy with me. It might have encouraged them to have opted for an earlier surrender.

My musings were brought to an end when the loudspeaker blared, "Hear this, hear this. There will be no liberty ashore. The mail boat leaves in ten minutes. All authorized personnel report to the quarterdeck." I was one of the authorized personnel to go ashore, as our very nearsighted Lieutenant McCabbe had fractured his only pair of glasses a few days before. His vision was only 20/200 without glasses. I hoped to get a new lens installed at the station hospital on Engebi Island. Otherwise, McCabbe would have to make do with one lens when we landed on Iwo Jima.

I parted with my shipmates as they headed south toward the Engebi Club with their mail sacks, while I skirted the airfield on my way to the hospital. After twelve days at sea, it felt good to walk on the solid coral roadway. As I turned in at the hospital entrance, I noted the limping approach of a B–24 bomber at the far end of the runway. Part of its tail had been shot away. I wondered where they had been.

My mission at the hospital was not too successful. They had no optical shop. The only optical shop west of Honolulu was located on Kwajalein Island four hundred miles to the east. They would ship the glasses to Kwajalein for repair and ask them to forward the repaired glasses to the naval hospital on Saipan. If all went well, I would pick them up in one week. This seemed to be a rather dubious solution, but there was no alternative.

Just then an ambulance wheeled into the emergency room section with its sirens blaring. When I arrived in the area, they were unloading the tail gunner from the crippled B–24. The bomber had run into heavy flak on a bombing run over Ponape. The tail gunner had picked up some shrapnel in the back, shoulder, and legs. Fortunately, they were rather small slivers of steel, and eventually he should make a satisfactory recovery.

I returned to the pier, sobered by the thought that in only thirteen more days Dr. Hely and I would be responsible for the care of injured men—many more seriously wounded than the tail gunner who had just returned from Ponape.

Our convoy left the Eniwetok lagoon on February 8 and made an uneventful passage to Saipan. The *Sandoval* dropped its hook on the anchorage off the west coast on February 13, eight miles from the western beaches of the island. From this vantage point, we had a panoramic view of the huge Air Force installations on Saipan and Tinian. These islands had been secured less than eight months ago; it seemed incredible that these giant bases could have been developed in such a short time.

It was thrilling to watch the steady stream of the new B-29 bombers as they lumbered down the long runways on both the islands with full bomb loads. As soon as each plane became airborne, it would swing around Mount Tapachou on the north end of Saipan and head for the home islands of the Japanese Empire fifteen hundred miles to the northwest. In less than an hour's time forty-two of these big planes had taken off from the runways on Tinian and Saipan, each with a lethal load of explosives.

A voice on the loudspeaker brought us back to our own problems. "Hear this, hear this. Colonel Robertson wants all 3rd Battalion officers to report to the wardroom for a meeting at 1400."

The colonel started the meeting five minutes early when he ascertained that all his officers were present. "Before we settle down to battalion business, I would like to pass on friendly greetings from the Air Force commander of the Marianas' air wing. They wish us quick success at Iwo, for they desperately need these airfields for emergency landing sites. At present a lot of our B-29s cannot complete the three-thousand-mile round trip between Japan and Saipan. Too many of our planes and crews are lost at sea on the long return journey. Possession of the airfields on Iwo will permit them to make round-the-clock bombing raids on the home islands. When this happens, the war should be shortened."

The colonel continued, "Now for some slightly unpleasant news. We will spend most of the fourteenth and fifteenth at sea in the LCVPs. The Navy did such a sloppy job on Maui last month that Gen. Holland Smith wants them to have more practice. He wants to be sure we'll be put on the right beach at the right time when we land six days from now."

Captain Hall asked, "What beaches will we be landing on?"

The colonel answered, "This is a Navy show only. We'll be making mock runs at Tinian."

Captain Gray interrupted, "Why do we have to ride around? Why can't they get their practice with empty boats?"

The colonel said, "I need you men in the boats to check up on the Navy performance. For instance, Gray, when I Company makes its mock run for the beach, I want you to be sure that the boats carrying your three platoons are all traveling in the same line. You can communicate with your platoon leaders by using simple hand signals."

The fourteenth and fifteenth of February were miserably wet and seasick days for the troops. The constant thirty-five knot trade winds kicked up a choppy sea, producing a continual showering spray that thoroughly soaked everyone in the small boats within the first hour. The air temperature was just under 70 degrees Fahrenheit, but the chill factor from the wind soon had the shivering occupants of the boats huddled against the forward ramps. Here the intermittent deluges of seawater were less severe. Our ponchos were able to keep us partly dry in this location.

We rode about for six hours on the fourteenth and five hours on the fifteenth. As we lined up for our mock runs at the beach, I was happy to note that we were in the same formation with the other boats carrying headquarters company personnel. It looked like the Navy was going to put us on the right beaches on February 19.

Our corps commander had shown a certain amount of pity for his men. He allowed us to board the small boats on both days without being encumbered with full combat gear. So when I pulled up beside the heavy, rope nets hanging down the sides of the *Sandoval*, I scampered up them with great alacrity and headed for my cabin. It was great to stand under a hot shower and get the chill worked out of my system; dinner seemed like a gourmet banquet after my day-long fast.

At dusk on February 16, our convoy of twenty-two transports and eight ancillary ships weighed anchor and headed northwestward toward our target 750 miles away. Encouraging reports began coming in over the loudspeaker system.

"Hear this, hear this. Our bombardment fleet has now encircled the island at eighteen thousand yards and is closing in for the reduction of the fortress. More tons of high explosives will be used against Iwo Jima than have been used on all the other Pacific islands to this date. In addition, our carrier forces are serving as a screen between Iwo Jima and the home islands. They have just rocked the Empire with the first large-scale diversionary air raid."

That evening I dined at the head table with Colonel Robertson and the other senior officers of the battalion. While we drank our after dinner coffee, I raised the question of casualties.

The colonel was optimistic. He felt that if we could achieve our goal on the first day, cutting the island in half, we should secure the entire island in three days and chalk up a minimum number of casualties.

Our discussion was interrupted by a communique from Admiral Turner. "Hear this, hear this. The bombardment fleet has closed to within fifteen thousand yards of the island, and the volume of our fire has been intensified. All facets of the operation are proceeding according to plan."

I offered a tentative opinion, "Maybe the Nips will be so shell-shocked that they'll be overrun before the third day."

Fred Mix flashed me a crooked grin as he said, "Don't let them hand you a snow job, Doc. Right now the Nips are settled down deep in their cave system having a pleasant dinner of curried rice washed down with sake. They'll pass the evening hours sharpening their trench knives and sorting out their ammunition."

Most of the officers at the table accepted this statement with brief nods of assent. The colonel scowled momentarily but offered no rebuttal.

This discussion upset my equanimity considerably. Wanting solitude, I bypassed the usual nightly bridge game and found a secluded section of the upper boatdeck for quiet meditation. The stiff northwest wind caused an eerie vibration in the numerous wires and cables as it whistled through the *Sandoval's* superstructure. I was able to enjoy total solitude as this otherworldly recital drowned out all human sounds.

For the first time I had to admit to myself that I was afraid. Would I ever return to my loved ones back home? Would I become one of the casualties? If so, would I be killed, or end up as one of the so-called basket cases? Or maybe I would be lucky. Perhaps if I kept busy looking after my corpsmen and doing my best for the wounded Marines, I might survive with my honor intact. During all this emotional and mental activity, I kept pacing back and forth on the limited deck space.

Finally, after three and a half hours of this physical exercise in the brisk night air, I returned to my cabin in a state of total exhaustion, and fell into a deep and dreamless sleep for the first time in many days.

By the morning of February 17, the weather had moderated. The wind had died down and the temperature risen slightly. The sun was attempting to break through the dissipating clouds. The majority of the Marines were topside, and most of them were busy disassembling, oiling, and reassembling their weapons. Others were working over whetstones sharpening their knives and bayonets. Some of them repeated this activity several times during the next forty-eight hours. Just keeping busy seemed to relieve the tension.

Late in the afternoon a noisy altercation erupted in the vicinity of a recently opened forward hatch. All the company commanders had Quartermaster Sergeant Wentworth surrounded as he backed up against a ventilator. They were shouting, gesticulating angrily, and occasionally jabbing a finger into his midriff.

The angry chorus proceeded as follows, "All quartermasters are a bunch of dumb bastards."

"The pig fucker should get a drumhead court-martial."

"Hell no, he should be tossed overboard for shark food."

The usually taciturn Captain Gray was especially incensed. As he thumped Wentworth's chest for the third time, he was finally able to speak, "You stupid SOB."

"Our rifle grenade cartridges are ruined, all ruined. You let them soak in bilge water for two months, you fucked-up jughead."

As he talked, Gray's face flushed with his increasing anger. He seized Wentworth by his dungaree lapels and began shaking him violently.

"You are a fouled-up, worthless jerk. What are you going to do about it?"

Behind me a calm, authoritative voice spoke out, "Steady men, let's quiet things down a bit."

Peace and quiet were instantly restored as Colonel Robertson continued. "This has happened to the Marines more than once. Twenty-four hours of sun curing should make 90 percent of the cartridges operable."

Then Lt. Jim Gass, who was standing beside the colonel, spoke up, "As the senior quartermaster officer in this battalion, I'm asking you birds to lay off Wentworth. He is a good man. The hold was dry when we loaded the ammunition last December. If you want to make something of the seepage that has occurred, let me have it instead of Wentworth."

With the conclusion of this statement, Gass thrust his determined chin forward and fixed his challenging blue eyes on the company commanders with a defiant stare.

Before anything more could be said, the colonel broke in, "Let's knock it off and get on with the war."

During dinner, the loudspeakers announced, "Hear this, hear this. Our bombardment fleet has closed to within seven thousand yards of the island, and the enemy's counterbattery fire has been silenced. Sleep well, mates."

Major Mix directed a sly grin in my direction and said, "Looks like the top brass is trying to build up our morale."

"Why do you say that, Fred?"

"Because the Nips are well settled deep underground and are still sharpening their knives while they wait for us."

I turned to the colonel and asked, "Do you agree with what Fred says?"

"Mix is being a bit pessimistic. They've got to be suffering some damage."

This last statement by the colonel made me feel more comfortable as I proceeded to my cabin. The enemy certainly would be confused and disorganized when we landed.

Mix caught up with me just as I was about to enter the stateroom.

He said, "Hey, Doc, you have all the company officers pretty shook up."

"What for? What did I do?"

"They say you gave the company corpsmen all the medicinal brandy today."

"That's true. So what?"

"Your corpsmen have refused to turn the brandy over to their commanding officers."

"They had better not. I told the corpsmen we would stick with Navy regulations. The company corpsmen will handle the brandy and dispense it to the wounded as needed."

"Jesus, Doc, we didn't do it that way in the Solomon Islands."

"I believe you. On Iwo Jima, we are going to do it this way."

As I closed the cabin door, I could hear Mix muttering to himself as he proceeded along the passageway.

Before breakfast on the eighteenth, I hurried up to the bridge and received permission from the colonel's orderly to enter his stateroom.

"What's the trouble, Doc? You shouldn't be having problems this early in the morning."

"Brandy is the only thing that is giving me trouble at this time. The company officers are trying to take it away from my corpsmen."

The colonel chuckled briefly and then said, "So they are at it again. They usually try to pry the brandy loose from every new battalion surgeon. Sometimes they're successful, most of the time they're not."

I asked, "How do I keep them off my back?"

The colonel answered, "Just tell them that we will stick with Navy regulations. The corpsmen will keep and administer the brandy."

"Thanks much, Colonel. That's all I needed to know."

After breakfast, while taking my morning constitutional topside, the ambush was sprung on the upper boatdeck. Without warning, I was suddenly surrounded by fourteen of our company officers. Although I did not get physically manhandled as Wentworth had the day before, the feeling of hostility among these determined men was readily apparent.

Captain Hall said, "How about letting us take some of the brandy supply?"

I answered, "No way. The corpsmen will be putting the brandy to better use. They'll be the first to treat a man after he gets hit."

Captain McCahill said, "How about splitting the supply and letting us keep half of it?"

Captain Munson added, "There are only two ounces of brandy in each bottle. Two or three bottles couldn't hurt anybody."

Captain Gray then threw in the clincher. "It's a Marine Corps tradition. The commanding officer is expected to carry some spirits for emergencies."

"Sorry, men. Navy regulations state otherwise. The brandy stays with the corpsmen unless Colonel Robertson agrees with you gentlemen."

This statement introduced indecision and uncertainty into the ranks of my fellow officers. Some of them wanted to confront Colonel Robertson, but the majority advised caution. While the discussion continued, I edged over to a nearby ladder and made my escape down to the main deck.

A little later I asked Griebe to round up all the medical personnel for a final briefing at 1000.

When all sixty-four corpsmen and litter bearers were assembled, I said, "I would like to go over the landing procedures one more time. There are no essential changes from earlier briefings. The 3rd Battalion will be the reserve unit for the 27th Marines for the entire day unless an emergency develops. However, all components of the 3rd Battalion have to be ashore just ninety minutes after the first Marine touches dry land."

I continued, "The company corpsmen will land with their respective units. The medical personnel of headquarters company will all land with the thirteenth wave. As there are only five minutes between each wave, we'll all be ashore sixty-five minutes after the initial landing.

"The aid station group will be divided up equally into three boats. Hely, Griebe, and I will be commander of the troops until we hit the beach. Twelve of our corpsmen will be in each boat. In addition, twelve headquarters company Marines will be traveling in each boat with us. When we land on Red Beach 2, which is located three hundred yards north of Mount Suribachi, the Marines will locate and join their respective units. The corpsmen from the three boats will assemble and follow Dr. Hely and myself up the hill close behind the assault troops. Are there any questions?"

Pharmacist Mate Smith was the first man to gain my attention. Smith was a clean-cut young man of twenty-one who dealt with life's problems on a deliberate and mature level. He was one of my most reliable corpsmen. When given any task to perform, he could be depended on to carry out the order to the best of his ability. He never employed the rough language of the Marine Corps. When the war ended, he planned to enroll in either a medical school or a divinity college.

Smith asked, "When we land, do we break out our gear and set up an impromptu aid station after the corpsmen in Dr. Hely's and Dr. Griebe's boats find us?"

I answered, "That will not be necessary. We will not set up for business as long as we are being held in reserve. The Navy beach party medical section will be taking care of all casualties that occur on or near the beach."

Griebe then asked, "How long do we stay on the beach?"

"No longer than it takes to assemble our headquarters company medical section, two to five minutes at the most."

Smith then asked, "How fast and how far do we advance up the hill?"

I answered, "We'll keep in touch with the battalion command post. Either Major Mix or Captain Knutson will give us orders from time to time. There may be a bit of confusion on the beach, and some of us may be separated from the main body for a time. It is vital that we all dig in for the night in the same location, for we'll be one of the assault battalions on D day plus one. We'll have to be set up and ready to handle a lot of casualties early on the morning of February 20."

Corpsman Willis then raised his hand and asked, "May I change the subject?"

"You sure can, go ahead."

"Since the brandy was passed out yesterday, my company officers have been bugging me to turn it over to them."

"Navy regulations and the colonel say you are to keep it and to dole it out to the wounded only."

Willis gave me a happy smile and said, "Thanks, Dr. Vedder."

Willis was the senior corpsman in H Company. He came from the western part of Tennessee, and he was a fine young Southern gentleman. His full, round face and curly brown hair made him appear much too young to be a member of this Marine expeditionary force. His tough internal fiber belied these external appearances, however. He could hold his own with his hard-bitten comrades and still be liked and respected by these front-line troops.

I asked for further questions. As we had gone over the landing procedures at several other briefing sessions, only silence greeted this request.

I said, "Be at your boat stations at 0530 with all your combat gear. Don't forget to bring your seabags containing the plasma and medical supplies. Everyone is dismissed except Kramer, I want him to stick around for a few minutes."

When I first joined the battalion in July 1944, Kramer was an established member of the 3rd Battalion. He had been assigned the duty of keeping the records of the medical section and had done a creditable job.

He was a big man slightly on the corpulent side. He always carried out instructions at a deliberate, almost plodding, pace. On Iwo Jima he was going to keep the logbook for the aid station. For each casualty, he would enter the name, rank, and serial number. In addition, a note of the treatment given would also be logged in, as well as the final disposition of each casualty. At the end of each day, he would have to send a casualty report to regimental headquarters.

Because of his dependability, I was going to assign him an additional duty on the first day of combat. He would carry in a special seabag loaded with surgical instruments, needles, and sutures. This bag weighed fifty pounds, which was ten pounds more than the general medical supply bags carried by the other men. Kramer was a big strong man. The extra ten pounds shouldn't slow him up any.

I said, "Kramer, you are going to carry my special bag of instruments when we land tomorrow. So when the ramp goes down, we both jump out on the beach at the same time. You are to stay at my side at all times and hang on to that bag at all costs. I may need some of those instruments at any time."

Kramer answered, "I understand the problem, Dr. Vedder. You can depend on me to stick with you."

By midafternoon the weather had moderated, and the sun felt comfortably warm as I lay outstretched on one of the after hatchcovers. The marines had opened the hatch beside me and now began unloading shells for the 57mm and 75mm heavy weapons.

Soon a roar of dismay assailed my ears. All the shells were of the fragmentation type. No armor-piercing shells were available. This time the acrimony of the company officers fell upon the quartermasters supply depot back on Hawaii. Wentworth escaped any further verbal or physical abuse.

After dinner, while taking several exercise turns around the main deck, I encountered the colonel, who was doing the same thing.

He said, "I'm glad to see you are keeping in shape. We'll be needing all of our reserve strength before this operation is completed."

"Has something new come up? There have been no recent reports over the loudspeaker system."

"I have just received some confidential and disquieting news from the *Rutledge*."

"What happened? Can you tell me?"

"Doc, our bombardment fleet has run into serious difficulties. To carry out some close-in rocket demolitions, our gunboats had run up to within two hundred yards of the beaches, and the larger ships had closed to within two thousand yards. The Nips must have thought it was the real landing. They opened up with a withering fire. Within a few minutes nine of our gunboats were sunk, and two cruisers and a destroyer were knocked out of action."

I said, "Jeepers, it looks like Mix is right after all. They are just holed up underground waiting for us to come."

The colonel answered, "Let's hope for the best. You'd better turn in early. Tomorrow will be a long, rough day."

Back in my cabin, I began re-sorting my combat paraphernalia. Weight was going to be a problem. What could safely be discarded? The steel helmet was essential. My .45-caliber pistol and shoulder holster had to go with me. The two boxes of .45-caliber pistol shells seemed awfully heavy. I decided to leave one box behind. Resupply should be available.

A handgrenade in each dungaree jacket pocket caused the garment to weigh down heavily about my shoulders. I was tempted to leave both grenades behind, but I finally compromised and took one along. Two canteens of water tugged heavily at my belt; one of the canteens was discarded. My trenching shovel and gas mask were not expendable.

Some of the contents of my backpack had to be sacrificed for the sake of greater mobility. An hour later my discard pile consisted of two cartons of cigarettes, three cans of ham, one set of dungarees, one woolen shirt, one box of pistol shells, one handgrenade, one canteen of water, and volume two of *War and Peace*. I had planned to finish the book after the island was secured, while we were waiting for transportation to Okinawa.

My remaining portable property still posed a formidable weight problem in the range of fifty to sixty pounds, but it now seemed to be manageable.

After this final sorting out of my combat gear, I followed the colonel's injunction and climbed into my bunk in hopes of getting a few hours of sleep. Although physically tired, my racing thoughts would not allow me to drop off into restful slumber.

Would the battle last three days? How long would we be fighting on Iwo? The twenty-three thousand Japanese defenders on the island might never surrender. Even if they came out of their caves and died in a glorious banzai charge, it would take some doing to kill them all in just three days.

Then my overactive mind turned inward and began summing up my prior military experience. I had served fourteen months at Camp Elliott teaching Navy doctors and corpsmen the mysteries of practicing medicine under combat conditions.

After leaving Camp Elliott, I had spent another six months with the Marine Troop Training Unit. My teaching role with this organization involved working with the medical section of the 81st and 96th Army divisions making amphibious landings on the simulated hostile shores of San Clemente Island, off the coast of California. After this tour of duty, I was finally transferred to the 5th Division for a combat assignment.

Although I had been teaching combat medicine for the past twenty months, in just a few hours I would receive my first baptism of hostile fire on this island of Iwo Jima.

Chapter Two

D Day
February 19, 1945

Through the ship's loudspeaker system, reveille sounded at 0430 on February 19. I slid wearily from my bunk and found there was no rolling motion to the ship. I slipped on my skivvies and socks and hurried out on deck for a look at our surroundings. Our ship was lying still in the water, idling, and all I could see was the blinking of stars in the sky. The sky was dark, very dark, and I looked in vain for outlines of ships or island; all I could see was the water, dark and ominous. A few Marines were moving around among the Navy crew, who were standing by their general quarters stations. I could hear the rumbling of the men below stirring and gathering their gear and equipment.

Hurrying back to my cabin I bumped into Colonel Roose complaining about the racket I was making. I headed for the shower, my last shower aboard ship.

The usually brilliantly lighted dining room was in semidarkness, lighted only by the battle station lamps. The compartment was empty except for a few Marine lieutenants picking at the mounds of food resting on the central tables. All our mess attendents were at their general quarters stations helping launch the small boats. One bite of a cold tenderloin steak caused my tense, nervous stomach to rebel, ending all attempts at eating. On leaving I picked up three apples and three oranges and found they fitted very nicely into my gas mask. At least I would have fresh fruit for the three-day operation.

Soon debarkation orders were blaring out over the loudspeaker system. I lined up my twenty-four enlisted men beside the forward landing net on the starboard side waiting for LCVP Boat Number 21 to pull alongside.

My orders to these enlisted men were quite simple, "My command ends when we hit the beach. Only the corpsmen stay with me. The rest of you find your headquarters company unit and go to work." These Marines were either cooks, communications men, or members of the intelligence section.

As we stood waiting at attention, the sky brightened in the east. It was going to be a calm, clear day. A few minutes later, as the sun appeared over the horizon, we could see the silhouette of Iwo Jima clearly outlined twelve miles to the west. Mount Suribachi to the south stood out as the highest point on the island. The bare rock of Suribachi's summit, 556 feet high, reflected back the first rays of the sun. In just a few hours, we would be landing three hundred yards north of this eminence on Red Beach 2.

At this moment the debarkation officer called out, "All men in boat team 21 over the rail. Your boat is alongside."

I slid over the rail clutching the hemp strands of the net. I felt unbalanced and top-heavy. Except for my heavy boots, all the surplus weight was located above my belt. Besides my forty-pound backpack, I was encumbered by my steel helmet, my trenching shovel, one pistol plus extra shells, one handgrenade, one canteen of water, and a gas mask filled with three oranges and three apples. If I made one misstep and fell into the water, I would sink like a stone.

Fortunately, we had only a two-foot swell to contend with. All the members of Boat Number 21 embarked on their LCVP without mishap. After making an upright landing in the boat, I offered a silent prayer of thanks before depositing my backpack against the forward ramp.

I then called Smith over to my side and said, "You are the senior corpsman on this boat. Check out the seabags filled with medical supplies that are being carried by our men. See that each sixty-foot coil of rope is firmly secured to its respective bag. We don't want to lose any plasma or dressings when the men start crawling from shell hole to shell hole."

Smith answered, "I've already taken care of that detail, sir. All the lines and seabags are secure."

I then said to Kramer, "Bring your seabag up forward and park it against the ramp. As the troop commander of this boat, I have the honor of being allowed to lead the way to the beach when the ramp drops. Since you are carrying the special bag with the surgical instruments, I am going to share this honor with you. When the ramp goes down, you, I, and the instrument bag all leap out together. Then stick right with me when we get ashore. If we get separated, I'll have no tools to work with."

Kramer nodded understanding.

Our thirteenth wave of twenty-four boats reported to the rendezvous area just to the seaward side of the battleship *Tennessee* at 0830, where we held our positions with a slow circling pattern. From this vantage point, we had an excellent view of the morning's activities. The entire eastern side of the island was embraced by a double ring of American naval vessels all throwing hot steel at the enemy. The outer ring was occupied by the battleships and cruisers. The destroyers and gunboats on the inside were attacking the island from a distance of less than a thousand yards.

From time to time, the *Tennessee* would fire its formidable battery of 14-inch guns. The wrenching recoil of this action would push the venerable battlewagon broadside a few yards in our direction. This produced a wave action sufficient to splash water over our gunwales.

One hundred yards north of us, an LST hospital ship was anchored waiting to receive the injured.

Iwo Jima presented a very grim and forbidding appearance along its entire five-mile length. Except for a little greenery on the northern highlands, the island appeared devoid of vegetation. The terrain itself presented a forbidding series of terraces. We were directly in front of Red Beach 1 with its narrow strip of jet black sand.

At an elevation of 200 feet, but only six hundred yards from the waterline, the remains of some enemy planes were clearly visible in the revetments about Motoyama Airfield Number 1. The route to the airstrip was barred by a series of ten terraces, each about twenty feet high. Each terrace averaged between thirty and seventy yards in width. The natural walls separating the terraces were inclined at 60- to 70-degree angles. There was no way to reach this airfield except by direct assault.

To the south lay the cliffs of Mount Suribachi. Its sheer rock walls ruled out a flanking movement in this direction. The land to the north appeared equally difficult. Motoyama Airfield Number 2 started a thousand yards to the north at an elevation of 300 feet. The approaches to this airstrip were very similar to those of Airstrip 1. However, the extra hundred feet above sea level made the problem that much greater. Each airstrip was about two thousand yards long and equally well guarded by terrain, men, and hidden guns.

To the north of Airstrip 2 lay the rugged highlands. Three of the rocky peaks rose 362 feet above the surrounding ocean. Sparse foliage could be seen in some of the deep ravines leading to the beaches. This broken-up terrain looked like an impossible area to fight through. Even though our 5th Division objectives appeared difficult to attain, I was glad that the 4th Division had been assigned to occupy the wretched landscape to the north.

Field glasses trained on the island did not furnish much additional information. In fact, it appeared quite devoid of life. No obvious block-houses or pillboxes were visible to my untrained eyes. The Japanese, being masters of camouflage, had skillfully built their fortifications into the landscape. They were ready and waiting for us to trespass on their beaches.

At exactly 0830 the great preinvasion bombardment began. For twenty-five minutes the island was smothered in a great cloud of smoke, dust, and debris. Big chunks of Mount Suribachi would occasionally be seen flying off into space. At 0855, the island was completely blotted out by a phosphorus smoke screen as the first wave moved in toward the beach. When the smoke began clearing at 0910, it was apparent that our first amphibian tanks had penetrated to the level of the fifth and sixth terraces on the east slope of the island. Several of our tanks were lying knocked over on their sides, or showed ominous clouds of black, oily smoke issuing from their interiors. In retaliation, our flame-throwing tanks were soon in action mopping up isolated centers of enemy resistance. The forward waves of our 1st and 2nd battalion troops of the 27th Marines could now be seen advancing in close support of our armored vehicles.

A new wave was landing every five minutes. At that rate, our thirteenth wave would be put ashore at 1005, just sixty-five minutes after the initial landing. In the excitement of the battle, I forgot my resolve to conserve my fresh fruit supply as I absentmindedly slipped an orange from the recesses of my gas mask. Within a half hour, returning amphibian tanks were delivering wounded to the LST hospital ship adjacent to us. One of the less seriously wounded Marines, with a blood-soaked dressing on his head, called over to us.

"I'm one of the lucky ones. I just got a scalp wound. Two of my buddies got killed real dead."

Just then our lead boat signaled all the boats of the thirteenth wave to pull up to the line of departure, which was located three hundred yards on the landward side of the *Tennessee*. Our twenty-four boats started for the beach at exactly 0950. We were allowed to stand up and watch the island draw closer until the distance to the beach narrowed to a thousand yards. Then all hands willingly crouched down hugging the steel deckplates. My place was far forward, next to the ramp.

As I soon wearied of kneeling, I flopped down flat on the deck with my backpack propped against one of the crossbars of the ramp. Kramer was crouched beside me holding the precious seabag of surgical instruments. The sun shone warmly on us, for it was a beautiful day. The roar of the twin motors of our LCVP running at full throttle completely drowned out the noise of the battle except when a salvo from the *Tennessee*'s 14-inch guns passed directly overhead, sounding like giant thunderclaps a few feet above us. The vacuum produced by their passage caused our small boat to rock momentarily as it headed full speed for the beach.

In my supine position, I watched the gyrations of one of our naval gunfire spotting seaplanes as it circled lazily about the north end of the island. Suddenly without warning, the entire tail of the plane disintegrated, and the remainder plummeted toward the sea a smoking ruin.

No time remained to brood about this disaster, for the boat's coxswain called out the order to loosen the cotterpins holding up the ramp. The final drive for a dry landing was on. The boat's motors were roaring and throbbing at full throttle. Soon the bottom was scraping on the sand. Down came the ramp with a thud. We were greeted by all of the furies of hell.

My first impressions of Iwo Jima, as I ran down the ramp, were the jet black sand, the countless prone bodies lying against the first embankment, and the ear-shattering decibels of sound. In seconds Kramer and I crossed the six-foot strip of beach. The crisscrossing of high velocity bullets close overhead sped us along. On arriving at the eight-foot embankment, which sloped up at a sixty-degree angle, we encountered a new problem. There was no room to seek temporary sanctuary here. Every inch of ground was covered by bodies that had arrived on the previous twelve waves. Kramer and I did the best thing. We plopped down between the legs of two earlier arrivals. This gave our bodies some protection. However, our legs were stretched out on the open beach.

On taking stock of our situation, I discovered that the bag of surgical instruments I had entrusted to Kramer was nowhere in evidence. A glance back at Boat 21 showed the bag waiting on the deck just inside the ramp. Despairing of making any attempt to deliver verbal orders to Kramer, I jumped up and dashed back into the boat.

As I hoisted the fifty-pound bag onto my shoulder, a mortar shell landed squarely in the boat just to the north of us. I staggered back to the embankment while debris from this explosion rained down on all sides of me.

After finding a new pair of legs to crawl between, I looked around for Kramer. I could not see him. Either he had moved or I had taken off at a tangent on leaving the boat for the second time.

I began to feel very much alone. All the men above and around me were strangers from the 1st and 2nd battalions. I could locate no Marines or corpsmen from the 3rd Battalion.

I recalled the heated discussion on the *Sandoval* when the company officers challenged the wisdom of the regimental orders that put our reserve battalion on the beach less than an hour after the initial landing. These officers claimed our men would pile in on top of the earlier waves to make a god-awful mess. How right they were!

I remembered the colonel's order that the corpsmen in Hely's and Griebe's boats were to join up with my men. After assembling on the beach, we were to move inland with the rest of headquarters company. There was no way that I could carry out this order. I could not even locate any of the corpsmen who rode in with me on LCVP Number 21.

Indecision stayed my progress only momentarily, since staying on the beach seemed like a sure way to get maimed or killed. It might be safer to move inland behind the attacking Marines. By taking this course I would be carrying out the colonel's orders even though I had no men to follow me.

After undoing the sixty-foot length of line attached to my surgical bag, I jabbed and poked two Marines who were blocking my exit from the beach. They rolled over on their sides so that I had room between them to crawl up the eight-foot embankment. At the top of this bank, a level plain forty yards wide greeted me before the next twelve-foot-high terrace took off at a seventy-degree inclination.

Spotting a shell hole thirty feet away, I jumped up and made a dash for its safety while my right hand clutched the end of the line attached to the seabag. Bullets cracked past me from the left, front, and right. I had to leap over one dead Marine as I dove into the relative safety of this shell hole.

I then started the laborious task of pulling in the line and bringing the fifty-pound surgical bag forward to my new position. When the bag came up over the parapet, I was surprised to see Sergeant Becker of headquarters company crawling along right behind it. At last I had found one of the Marines who had come in with me in Boat 21. He waved and gave me a nervous smile.

As he came closer I could see blood running down both sides of his face. His head began weaving in an aimless manner. A bullet fired from Suribachi had penetrated the base of his nose, causing considerable damage to his facial bones. After slapping on a hurried compress, I rolled him down to the beach into the waiting arms of a beach party corpsman. Then I sprinted back to my advanced shell hole and finished pulling my bag in with me.

A glance to the south showed Corpsman Smith forty feet away wriggling forward on his abdomen with a rope trailing along behind. He soon slid into a small depression and began pulling his seabag forward. I was so happy to see one of my corpsmen that I shouted words of encouragement in his direction. The roar of detonating high explosives drowned out my attempts at verbal communication. I then tried gestures and hand signals, but they went unnoticed. Smith was undoubtedly concentrating on his own survival problems.

The murderous enfilade of the enemy soon drew my attention back to my own precarious position. A Marine a few feet to my right had been hit in the lower back, so I crawled over to lend him a hand. His spinal cord must have been damaged, as he had no motor power remaining in his lower extremities. He still had full use of his arms, which he used effectively as I helped him crawl back to my shell hole.

After packing gauze into the wound, I looked back at the long row of heads peering over that eight-foot embankment just beyond the beach. I gave several frantic arm signals requesting help in moving this man back to the beach. Much to my surprise, two men in blue helmets came charging up into view carrying a litter. They were corpsmen attached to the naval beach party section. It took them only seconds to place him on the litter and whisk him out of sight back down to the beach.

Meanwhile, another marine who had crawled a few feet ahead of my temporary shell hole sanctuary suddenly crumpled in a heap. A cursory examination showed he was beyond all help. A bullet from Suribachi had punched a neat hole in the left side of his helmet, penetrating his brain.

My attention was then diverted by a half-track that had stopped a few yards to my right. Its 75mm cannon began firing at the enemy cave entrances on Suribachi only a quarter mile away. This action called for immediate retaliatory machine gun fire. The .30-caliber bullets were soon ricocheting off the steel sides of the half-track in a lively fashion.

Instinctively, I huddled up against the dead body of the Marine who lay just to my left. Its close proximity afforded me more comfort than real protection. Fortunately, the half-track soon moved off to the north, drawing the hostile fire along with it.

As I lay beside my dead comrade, I began to consider my options. It still seemed that the safest place to go was inland away from the beach. The concentration of targets there would keep the bulk of the enemy's guns pointed there.

Creeping and crawling was too slow. The longer I stayed near the beach, the greater was the danger of being picked off by the sharpshooters on Suribachi. The only alternative was to get up and run for it.

So after standing up in full view of the enemy with the surgical bag on my shoulder, I headed inland, staggering more than running. I covered the first thirty yards of flat terrain with little difficulty but fell smack on my face when I tried to climb the next embankment, which was twelve feet high and sloped upwards at a seventy-degree angle. I left the bag at the base of the incline but kept a tight grip on the end of its line as I scrambled to the top on all fours. It took only a short time to pull the surgical bag up to my level. With the bag on my shoulder, I wobbled off over twenty yards of flat land before I encountered the next embankment, which was twenty-five feet high. This time I scooted up the slope using both hands and feet. At the top I again pulled the bag up to my level.

It took me about five minutes to complete this process three more times. By the time I reached the fifth terrace level, the violent exertion was taking its toll. My heart was pounding, and my respiratory rate was out of control.

It is a medical fact that, if anyone breathes at a rate of sixty times a minute or more for a period of time, he will blow off enough carbon dioxide to lose consciousness, and that is exactly what happened to me.

After I hauled the surgical bag up to the fifth level, things became blurry. As I turned landward toward a shallow trench, the last thing I recall before the lights went out was rolling into a depression with my bag of surgical instruments.

Moments later, as my senses started clearing, I was horrified to find myself looking into the staring eyes of a Japanese soldier who lay only two feet away. Fortunately, these were sightless eyes. Close inspection showed blistered, peeling facial skin with one half of his mustache singed away. The stench of freshly burned flesh informed me that a flamethrower had recently ended his career. The pungent odor of burned meat was augmented by three of his comrades lying in the same trench just to our north. The same flamethrower must have wiped them all out at the same time.

As my senses continued to clear, I lay quietly in the trench hoping to regain my physical strength quickly. I felt even more alone and abandoned than I had back there on the beach a short while ago. What if I had advanced too far and was now lying out in no-man's-land? Would Japanese reinforcements come to reclaim this trench? I quickly removed the waterproof covering from my pistol. In my haste to get it operable, I jammed the weapon by sliding the magazine in backwards.

At that moment someone grabbed my boot. I shut my eyes and braced myself for the thrust of cold steel that I expected to pierce my vitals. Instead, Colonel Robertson slid into the trench beside me. Mix, Kennedy, and some communications Marines were accompanying him.

The colonel shouted into my ear, "Doc, what in hell are you doing up here? You are not supposed to lead the advance of our battalion."

I yelled back in order to be heard above the battle din, "Am I ever glad to see you, Colonel. My corpsmen all disappeared during the confusion on the beach. I thought some of them would follow me if I moved inland. Besides, I thought it would be safer up here. I really don't want to be the advance guard."

"You're OK, Doc, but stay right where you are. Knutson will be bringing headquarters company along in a short while."

"I'll be glad to do that, Colonel. I'll stay right here until Knute comes along."

The colonel, using arm signals, then directed his men to follow him farther into the interior. In a few seconds, they had all climbed the next embankment and disappeared onto the terrace immediately above me. It was comforting to know that an important part of the 3rd Battalion was now operating between the enemy and me.

A few minutes later, elements of H Company began passing through my position in the trench containing the four roasted Japanese. I spotted Captain McCahill a few yards away as he ascended the steep incline below me. He recognized me after I flashed a *V*-for-victory hand greeting. He changed course and climbed into the trench beside me.

He shouted, "What are you doing up here, Doc? All your men are milling around back on the third terrace."

I said, "I'm waiting for Knute to bring them up. The colonel told me to wait here until they arrive. How is it going so far?"

McCahill answered, "Not too bad. Today we cut the island in two. Tommorrow we mop them up."

"That sounds great, Mac. We'll have a big celebration when we get back to Honolulu."

H Company moved on and disappeared over the top of the next embankment. Again I was left by myself, and that lonely feeling began to return. There was some comfort in knowing that friendly troops were now functioning on all sides of me. Twenty minutes later, more men appeared coming up from below. As they ascended the embankment up to my position on the fifth terrace, I could recognize a number of familiar faces belonging to Marines and corpsmen of headquarters company.

I welcomed Corpsman Rhoe as he climbed into my shallow trench and joined me. Rhoe was one of my favorite corpsmen. He came from a small town in Minnesota where he had worked as an auto mechanic before joining the Navy. He always had a friendly smile and did his best to be helpful. Although he had had no prior medical training in civilian life, he became quite skilled at handling the military first aid procedures.

He would move slowly and deliberately but performed his assigned tasks efficiently without wasted motions.

I said, "I'm sure glad to have you fellows up here with me. By the way, do you know where Kramer can be located?"

Rhoe gave me a worried smile, saying, "He's a few yards to the north with Hely and Griebe. He's scared that you will lower the boom on him."

"Would you tell him to come over here? I promise not to take him apart."

A short time later Kramer crouched down beside me in our shallow trench on the fifth terrace. Rather than look in my direction, he kept his eyes fixed on the dead enemy with the burned face and singed mustache.

I shouted in his ear, "Why did you leave my surgical bag in the boat when the ramp went down?"

"I'm sorry, Doc. I got so scared that I just forgot."

"OK for that, but why did you run away and leave me?"

"Honest, Doc, I didn't run away."

"You sure did. When I came back with the instrument bag, you were nowhere around."

"I hadn't moved an inch. When you came out of the boat the second time, you headed up the beach to the north a good ten yards before you plopped down out of sight. I just stayed where you left me because I was afraid I couldn't find you. Besides, I was too scared to move."

This was all true. I decided to forgive and forget. I said, "Kramer, do you see that bag lying propped up against that dead Nip? Do you recognize it?"

"I sure do, Dr. Vedder. I just packed it yesterday."

"I'll give you one more chance. If you lose it again, I'll see that you get thrown in the brig."

"Thanks, Doc. I won't let you down again."

In the meantime, Dr. Hely, Griebe, and the other senior corpsmen had come over to give a brief report on our medical section.

In order to be heard above the roar of the battle, I had them gather close around while Hely bellowed, "We got by real lucky. Only two guys got nicked by tiny shell splinters and didn't need evacuation."

I answered, "That's great. The colonel just passed by a few minutes ago. He wants us to stick with Captain Knutson, Lieutenant Familo, Lieutenant Pope, and the rest of headquarters company as we work our way up to the spine of the island."

For the next three hours, our medical section mingled with the other headquarters company personnel as we inched our way up to the tenth terrace just at the south end of Airfield 1. Our low profile attracted no enemy shellfire. We were harassed only by occasional snipers. The enemy was venting his wrath at the front lines and the beaches.

We held our reserve position at 200 feet above sea level, just at the southern edge of Airfield 1. Our assault troops of the 27th Marines had already crossed over to the western side of the island and were making slow progress in uprooting a stubborn enemy.

From the vantage point of this high ground, we could observe the unfolding battle action as it progressed in three directions. To the north, the 4th Division troops had landed in force. Although they had not penetrated very far inland, and shell bursts were frequently appearing in their midst, they seemed to have the situation under control. To the east, the beach area was littered with supplies. At the surf line, a number of broached and damaged boats could be readily identified.

At 1530 I spoke to Hely, "Charlie, I'm going to work my way over to the command post and ask Knute how things are going. Stay with the men and keep them together. We'll have to move into our night bivouac area pretty soon."

A few moments later, I crawled up to Captain Knutson's position in the battalion command post and found him sitting on some ammunition boxes staring glumly off to the north with both hands holding up his chin. To gain his attention I tapped him on the shoulder.

"Hi, Knute, how are things going?"

He gave me a distressed look, "Terrible."

"What do you mean by 'terrible'? Aren't we making good progress?"

He slowly removed his hand supports from his chin as he said, "Good God, Doc, see those 4th Division regiments off to the north? They are getting massacred. Notice those multiple shell-burst geysers erupting among the men and machines. After attacking all day, they have penetrated inland barely two hundred yards from the beach. They are still getting badly mauled, and their casualty rate must be awfully high."

"But, Knute," I insisted, "isn't our 5th Division doing a lot better?"

"Ya, but not too much better. Look at the two red beaches we crossed this morning. Didn't you see all the wrecked boats and equipment littering the area? The yellow beaches to the north are in even worse shape."

To lend force to this gloomy evaluation, two of our landing craft disintegrated from direct shell hits on Red Beach 2 just as their ramps were being lowered for unloading.

I gulped twice and managed to ask how long he thought it would take to secure the island.

He thought awhile before answering, "It will take many days or maybe never. If the casualties get too high, the top command may call it a bloody repulse and let us retire to our ships."

A short time later, I presented a detailed summary of Knutson's evaluation to Hely and the senior corpsmen in my section. I was pleased to note that this bad news was accepted in a rather matter-of-fact way.

At 1600 the 26th Marine regiment landed on the two red beaches we had crossed seven hours earlier. They were put ashore to serve as the reserve regiment for the 5th Division. Our high command wanted them dug in before nightfall; they would then be available to lend us a hand in fending off the banzai attack that often occurred on the first night after a landing.

While our regiment had spent the entire day creeping and crawling to our present position at the south end of Airfield 1, the 26th Marines came milling up the hill as a disorganized cluster of men thirty-six hundred strong. In less than ten minutes they were wandering about among us in an aimless fashion. Many of them were busily gathering up various battlefield souvenirs. Because they presented such an excellent target, the inevitable had to happen.

The first large shell crashed down a hundred yards to the north of us. Three seconds later the second shell erupted a hundred yards to the south.

The battle-wise Marines of headquarters company screamed in unison, "Hit the deck and take cover. We are going to be clobbered by a box barrage."

It took me less than ten seconds to dive into a convenient shell hole. During that short period of time, a half dozen 155mm to 240mm heavy artillery shells made roaring geysers as they exploded in my immediate vicinity.

I had a soft landing when I came to rest at the bottom of my shell hole. Another body had preceded me into this temporary refuge. I had come to rest on this man's upper back and neck. His face had been mashed down into the black sands of Iwo Jima. As I rolled off his body, he raised his head and began spewing sand and dirt in my direction. As I helped him wipe the grit from his eyes and nose, I recognized my shell hole mate. I was sharing my immediate future with Father Calkins, the Catholic chaplain of the 27th Marines, a reserved young man who had only recently been ordained. After spitting out the last of the sand and dirt, he said, "What should we do, Doc? Should we get up and run for it, or should we just stay here?"

While he asked these questions, several more heavy artillery shells exploded very close by. The violent earth tremors and air concussions set off by these detonations jolted us into complete immobility.

Placing my mouth adjacent to his ear, I said, "Padre, we'd better stay where we are. If a shell lands in our hole, we'll never know it. Near misses can only shake us up. If we try to run for it, we're almost sure to get picked off."

So we hugged the ground in the deepest recesses of our temporary haven. During this period of forced inaction, we learned a great deal about shrapnel. The smaller fragments buzzed by like swarms of angry bees. The medium-sized pieces sounded like a flock of purple grackles moving from one clump of trees to another. Some of the largest chunks were the size of dinner plates and made a soft sighing sound as they passed by. They were also clearly visible as they floated close by overhead. These large fragments could readily cut a man in half if he were to get in their way.

When a searing pain on my posterior left thigh induced me to investigate, I discovered how hot spent shrapnel is. A ragged chunk of red-hot steel the size of a fifty-cent piece had burned through my trouser leg and was starting to cook the skin underneath. After I hurriedly brushed this fragment away, close inspection showed that several other smaller fragments were smoking on our clothing. After brushing the hot steel fragments off, we kept alert watching for and removing new pieces as they rained down upon us. This activity had a salutory effect, for it gave us something positive to do. Just lying helpless in our shell hole had been unnerving.

In less than ten minutes, the shelling ceased as quickly as it had started. As we cautiously poked our heads over the rim of our shell hole, we could see countless other heads doing the same thing. The recent souvenir hunters were keeping well out of sight. Two mangled American bodies lay in the next shell hole to the east of us. There seemed to be no other casualties in our immediate vicinity.

I shook hands with Father Calkins and wished him a safe trip up to the regimental command post.

In parting I said, "Father, don't forget to include me in your future prayers."

He smiled and said, "That will be no problem. I can easily take care of that request."

A rapid check showed that none of my men had become casualties. It was quite a relief to find that we had been so lucky. I made a quick trip to the battalion command post to get new orders from Captain Knut-son. Knute was up forward with the colonel and his staff. Lieutenant Familo of the intelligence section had been left in charge.

Familo was an amiable, easygoing young man who had graduated from Western Reserve University in Cleveland before enlisting in the Marine Corps. He was one of the few officers that had a minor problem with obesity. For his height and age, he would have done better if he had carried twenty-five pounds less. He had jet black hair and twinkling brown eyes, and when he smiled, which was quite often, dimples appeared on both chubby cheeks, giving him a look of small-boy innocence.

Familo said, "Hi, Doc, they left me in charge of the rear echelon. Knute just called in. He wants you to bring up the whole medical section to the new command post on the west side of the island."

I said, "That sounds great, but how do we get there?"

"That's easy. Just head west along the south end of Airfield 1. On the spine of the island you'll pass through regimental headquarters. Then just keep going and you'll run into our 3rd Battalion people a couple of hundred yards farther west."

"How about sending a guide with us? There's an awful lot of confusion around here."

Familo gave me one of his happy, carefree smiles and said, "Sorry, Doc, none of us here know the way any better than I told you. If you keep the revetments between you and the enemy to the north, you won't get lost or hurt."

With that encouragement, I rounded up my men and passed the new orders along to them. As we approached the summit, we could for the first time see most of our encircling fleet on both the east and west sides of the island. It was a comfort to know that they would be standing by to lend us a hand if a banzai attack should be staged during our first night ashore.

As we moved along the southern border of Airfield 1, we soon encountered our first revetment, containing a disabled Japanese Zero fighter plane and a scene of carnage. The recent artillery barrage had caught five men of the 26th Marines in this enclosure. Only two of the shattered bodies were still living. Their recently acquired souvenirs were lying close by.

A piece of shrapnel had shattered the left jaw and face of one of the living. He was lying on his abdomen with both legs stretched out making aimless twitching movements. These movements gave very little relief, for his upper airway remained partially obstructed.

The other man was sprawled on his back in deep coma with several square inches of bone missing from the side of his head, leaving the brain covered only by the dura membranes. Another piece of shrapnel had sliced off all the upper muscles of his left shoulder.

As Hely and my twenty-four corpsmen rushed in to help these wounded, I shouted, "Hold it men, keep on moving up the hill to the west side."

Hely said, "What the hell. Have you blown a gasket?"

"Hell, no. We have to get bedded down before dark. I'll keep Griebe, Rhoe, and Maloney back here to help me."

"Can't I stay here? You take the gang to the bivouac area?"

"No."

As Hely reluctantly led our aid station group up the hill, I said, "Rhoe, cover the head and shoulder wounds with sterile dressings. Maloney, start a unit of plasma on the same guy." I then turned to Griebe, "You help me with the mangled face."

"What should I do?"

As I reached in my surgical bag for a rat-toothed forceps and a curved-bladed scissors, I said, "Get a handful of surgical sponges and roll him over on his back."

When the man lay on his back, thrashing about as he struggled to overcome his airway obstruction, I was at last able to locate a large fragment of jaw bone wedged in the back of his throat. The bone fragment was readily grasped by the rat-toothed forceps and removed, while the soft tissue to which it was still attached was snipped through. The patient gratefully took several unimpeded lungfuls of air. His shattered facial structures presented a grotesque appearance and I wondered how our plastic surgeons would ever restore this man's identity.

The other casualty was also soon ready for transport, even though his pupils were dilated and his condition comatose. Rhoe had deftly covered the head and shoulder wounds with sterile dressings. Maloney had started a unit of plasma, which was entering the man's veins at sixty drops a minute.

I sent Rhoe out to round up some transportation and Maloney to search the wounded man's backpack for warm clothes. He was still in deep shock.

Maloney was another of my dependable corpsmen, a quiet, sandy-haired lad who had more medical knowledge than the average corpsman. He had finished his course in chiropody before joining the Navy.

Just after Maloney started a second unit of plasma on the patient, Rhoe returned with an empty weasel that had just deposited a load of ammunition farther to the west. Our two wounded men were quickly placed aboard. The assistant driver was instructed in the proper handling of the plasma bottle, so the life-giving fluid would continue to run until he was received aboard one of our hospital ships.

By now it was getting quite dark, and Griebe was getting apprehensive. His sense of alarm was justified. The division orders stated, "All movement shall cease one half hour after sundown. Unless the correct password is given promptly, anyone walking about after dark shall be considered an enemy and shall be shot forthwith."

The password for D day was a rapid listing of American cities; the next night American automobiles would be used; and on the third night, individual states would be named. We started on our trek.

As we passed various groups of Marines already dug in for the night, the four of us kept up a lively chant of different American cities. One trigger-happy Marine frightened us unduly when he accidentally slipped the safety catch from his BAR and fired several rounds into the air.

While shouting, "Chicago, Louisville, Atlanta, New Orleans, San Diego," et cetera, we stumbled into the fourth revetment, which lay on the southwest corner of Airfield 1. It happened to be the command post for our 27th Marines. Colonel Warnham was hunched over his field telephone with his back to a fourteen-foot mound of earth as he delivered orders to his battalion commanders. A persistent enemy gunner was bouncing 75mm shells off the top of the parapet at thirty-second intervals. The colonel seemed oblivious of the sand and dust that showered down upon him with each blast.

In a nearby foxhole I spotted Dr. Schultz, our regimental surgeon. I climbed in with him and shouted, "Hi, Schultz. How do I find the 3rd Battalion's command post?"

He answered, "Just keep going west about two hundred more yards, and you'll run right into them. However, you'll have to work a detour around that battery of 105mm howitzers you see firing behind us a little over to the west."

I said, "Thanks for the information, Doctor. How did the 1st and 2nd battalions make out today?"

"They cut the island in two, but they paid dearly for it. Besides that, the regiment's command suffered a big loss. Colonel Plain got an arm half shot off when he charged a pillbox this afternoon."

I was sorry to hear that. We were going to miss him before this operation was over.

As we passed behind that battery of 105s, it was reassuring to see our heavy weapons hurling all that steel at the enemy off to our north.

All this time we were shouting the names of cities. Our four voices were quite ineffective, for I am sure that we could not be heard.

We finally located Colonel Robertson and his staff just beyond the southwestern corner of the airfield. All of headquarters company was dug in for the night.

The colonel said, "I'm glad to see you made it up here with your rear echelon. Hely tells me you have been busy back there patching up 26th Marines."

"Most of them were dead. We got the two live ones sent back to the beach. Where can I find Hely and the rest of my men?"

The colonel answered, "You'll find them dug in around the edges of a giant crater made by a 16-inch shell from one of our battlewagons about fifty yards to the southwest. Check out their foxholes when you get there. I don't want anyone located down in the middle of that big shell hole. If anyone has holed up more than two feet below the surface, have them start over closer to the rim of the crater. If too many men get bunched up in that deep pit, a well-placed mortar round could wipe out most of our medical section."

We had no trouble finding our resting place for the night. The crater made by the 16-inch shell was over thirty feet in diameter, and the center of the pit was fifteen feet below the surface. All of my men had followed orders correctly. No one was required to change the location of his foxhole.

While I was digging my foxhole on the north rim of the crater, Corpsman Robert Gass approached me, saying, "I don't have a buddy. I'm the odd man."

Gass was another recent high school graduate. He was a skinny little fellow who weighed less than 120 pounds.

I said, "That's great, Bob. You help me dig this hole, and we'll bunk here together."

While we were busy enlarging the foxhole, the flares started popping off at a lively rate. For seconds at a time we would have almost daylight illumination. Then we would be plunged back into temporary darkness. When the next flare burst, it was a comfort to see our battery of 105mm howitzers still blasting away at the enemy at a rapid rate. With this heavy artillery fire, and the almost constant light of the flares, I did not see how the enemy could possibly mount a successful banzai attack against us. I expressed this reasoning to young Bob Gass. It seemed to have a toniclike effect on the young man, for he relaxed, and we both became less jittery.

We were soon settled down for the night in our foxhole just below the north rim of the big shell hole. We had spread Gass's poncho on the ground, and mine was used to cover both of us. The chill night air caused us to huddle close together for warmth and reassurance. At this point I remembered my supply of fresh fruit. Since landing on the island, I had eaten no food or water. Both thirst and hunger had been obliterated by the tight-knotted sensation that had gripped my midriff all day. Now an apple or an orange might taste good.

I said, "Bob, how would you like a surprise?"

He answered, "I'm not too sure I can stand any more surprises."

"This happens to be a good one. Would you like a fresh orange or an apple?"

"Gee, Doc, you've got to be kidding, aren't you?"

"Not at all, Bob. I stowed three of each in my gas mask before leaving the ship this morning."

"Gosh, that's great. I'd like an orange if you can spare it."

My anticipation turned to complete chagrin when I opened the gas mask container. The day's activities—creeping, crawling, diving, and falling—had reduced the fruit to a sticky mess of apple sauce and orange pulp. Part of one orange was still edible; I shared equally with my foxhole buddy.

I flung the useless gas mask away hoping the Nips didn't resort to chemical warfare.

Eventually we were able to develop enough body warmth; the cramps eased off; and finally sleep overtook me, even though the tempo of the continuing battle increased all about us.

Chapter Three

D Day Plus 1

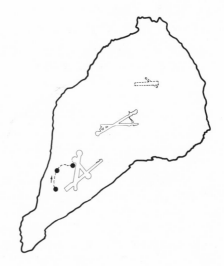

The crescendo of artillery fire kept rising as the night wore on. Being combat neophytes, we had not yet learned to tell in which direction the shells were traveling. Being blissfully unaware of the true situation, we both slept quite well. We were only roused to wakefulness when a large shell exploded within a few yards of our foxhole. This event occurred with routine regularity.

In truth, the enemy was no longer handicapped by our air observation. When the moon finally set, leaving complete darkness relieved only by occasional flares, the enemy was able to wheel out the heavy guns from the protection of caves in the northern highlands. With little danger of retaliation, they used these big guns to work us over with great ferocity. Without our knowing, they came close to blowing us loose from our fragile foothold on the island.

My first real recollection of February 20 was the frantic high-pitched voice of Corpsman Gass as he shook me awake.

"Look, Doc, look. See what they did to our howitzers."

Gass was not being an alarmist. Our fine battery of 105mm howitzers, one hundred yards to our rear, had been reduced to a shambles. Only two pieces were still firing back at the enemy. The only reassuring sight was our Navy, which still encircled the island. As there was now enough light, our spotter planes could pinpoint targets for the ships to fire at.

I said, "It doesn't look too good does it, Bob? Find Hely and Griebe and tell them to get the men ready to move out. I'm going to battalion headquarters for the latest dope."

As Colonel Robertson was checking out the front-line troops, Major Mix was in charge.

"Fred, what's going to happen today?"

"We are going to attack the bastards at 0800. After what they did to us last night, I hope we run them clear off the map."

"Besides wrecking our howitzers, what else did they do to us?"

"Christ, Doc, they clobbered us good. Besides dealing us a lot of casualties, they wiped out all of H Company's headquarters personnel, including Captains Hall and McCahill. They are all dead."

This came as a real shocker. I managed to gulp out, "How did they come to get it all at one time?"

"It happened shortly before dawn. They were all huddled up in a big shell crater studying the battle plans for today. A large mortar shell landed on them and it got every one of them."

It seemed unbelievable that both Hall and McCahill were dead! To cover my confusion, I asked, "Who is going to take over the command of H Company?"

Mix answered, "That's what the Colonel is doing now. He'll select one of the senior lieutenants." He continued, "By the way, Doc, our attack jumps off at 0800 from our present position. Set up your aid station for business in the same place where you camped last night. You can expect a lot of casualties after the troops move forward."

I returned to our medical section to pass on the latest battle plans fresh from the command post. "When the attack starts at 0800," I told my men, "we take care of the casualties right where we are. So break out our gear right now and get prepared to handle an overflow of business."

I continued, "If the attack proceeds as planned, we will have to follow close behind the advancing troops. That means we'll have to proceed in two echelons. I will lead the forward echelon, which will consist of Griebe, eight corpsmen, and six litter bearers. Griebe will designate the men who will accompany me. When Hely's group gets all the casualties treated and evacuated, they will come forward and join us. Kramer and his casualty book will stay with the rear echelon. Are there any questions?"

Before any voices could be heard, all hope of conversation was drowned out by the clash, clanging, and rumble of many friendly tanks that were assembling just to the west of our giant shell hole. They were going to lead the attack at 0800.

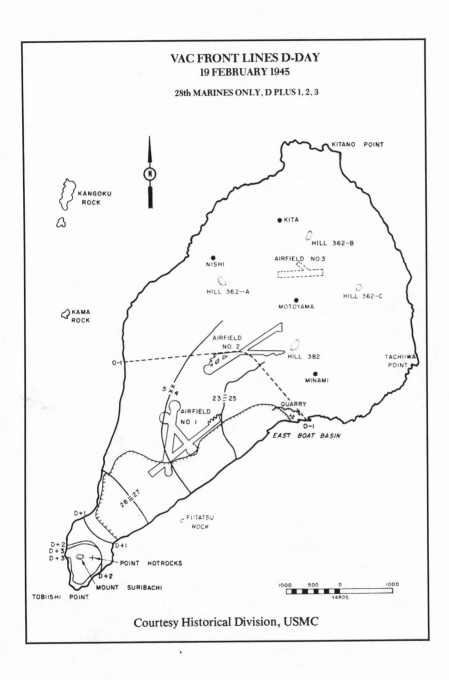

VAC FRONT LINES D-DAY
19 FEBRUARY 1945

28th MARINES ONLY, D PLUS 1, 2, 3

KITANO POINT

N

KANGOKU
ROCK

KITA

HILL 362-B

AIRFIELD NO.3

NISHI

HILL 362-A

HILL 362-C

KAMA
ROCK

MOTOYAMA

AIRFIELD
NO. 2

HILL 382

TACHIIWA
POINT

O-I

5 X 4

23 ≡ 25

MINAMI

AIRFIELD
NO I

QUARRY

O-I

EAST BOAT BASIN

28 ≡ 27

D+I

FUTATSU
ROCK

D+2
D+3
D+3

D+I

POINT HOTROCKS

D+2

MOUNT SURIBACHI

TOBIISHI POINT

1000 500 0 1000
YARDS

Courtesy Historical Division, USMC

The enemy found them an immediate and lucrative target. Soon we were bracketed by a barrage of shellfire, just as murderous as the one we had experienced the afternoon before. Today we were even more vulnerable, because most of us were bunched up in our aid station site in our huge shell hole. The tankmen were not at all concerned. They merely battened down their hatches and prepared to wait out the storm right where they were.

I grabbed Corpsman Rhoe and said, "Get over to the battalion command post and tell Major Mix what the tanks are doing to us. Ask him to radio orders for the dumb bastards to move forward a few yards before we all get killed."

Just five minutes later, the assembled tanks gunned their motors and lumbered one hundred yards over to the northwest of us. The barrage of artillery fire obediently followed the tanks over to their new rendezvous area.

During this time we were feverishly working to set up our aid station in the bottom of our 16-inch naval shell crater fifteen feet below the surface. The sounds of battle above became a jumbled but undiminished roar. Communication was limited to loud shouts at close range. Looking up from our sanctuary, the world consisted of steeply sloping black sands on all sides and a patch of blue sky above. The acrid odor of the exploding shells had the taste of death as it drifted down to our subterranean level.

All our corpsmen were digging flat niches in the sides of our crater large enough to hold one casualty on a litter. In less than fifteen minutes we had spaces ready to accommodate sixteen wounded men at one time below ground level.

Four feet from the bottom of the crater two larger platforms were carved on opposite sides of our deep pit. These spaces would serve as improvised operating tables for Hely and me. We would be working back to back on the most seriously wounded while standing in the bottom of our surgical amphitheater.

At 0757 the first request for a litter-bearing team came from I Company. By 0815, all of our litter bearers were out on the battlefield gathering up casualties. By 0830, our shell hole aid station was filled with casualties, about equally divided between walking wounded and stretcher cases.

The walking wounded were tagged and treated by the corpsmen. After being logged into the casualty book by Kramer, they would be sent to the rear on their own power.

The stretcher cases soon became too numerous for Hely and me to treat individually. We had to delegate treatment authority to our more able corpsmen. The multitude of maimed and mangled men soon became faceless blurs as the morning wore on. As soon as one casualty was sent back to the beach, another battered Marine would quickly take his place. Rapid evacuation of these badly wounded men soon became the name of the game, because any casualty's chances for survival would be greatly improved if he could get early care aboard a hospital ship, where whole blood would be available.

Later during the morning, a memorable case was deposited on my surgical table. The left trouser leg was soaked with fresh blood from the knee to just above the ankle. Corpsman Murphy, who was acting as my first assistant, exposed the wound by cutting away the blood-drenched clothing. The knee joint had been laid open by a chunk of shrapnel, exposing the shiny, smooth joint surfaces. Spurts of bright red blood keeping accurate time with each heartbeat were squirting out from behind the glistening condyles of the right thighbone. The main artery to the lower leg must have been cut and was now retracted up behind the thigh bone. It would be a difficult task to secure this artery and tie it off.

My first inclination was to bind up the wound quickly and send him back to a hospital ship, where a trained surgeon could do a proper job. But I could not follow this course with a clear conscience, since he might bleed to death beneath the dressings. I would have to staunch the blood flow first.

"Murphy, hand me the large curved hemostatic clamp, get Smith to start a unit of plasma, and then keep sponging the blood out of the knee joint so I can see what I'm doing."

It took three tries and finally Murphy said, "You got the bleeder, Doc, the wound is dry."

Using a small, curved needle threaded with a silk suture held by my slenderest needle holder, I was able to place the ligature under the hemostat's blades and around the end of the torn artery, which was firmly in the grasp of the instrument. I had just completed tying the vessel off with a secure knot when a shell burst on the lip of our crater above and in front of me. Seconds later a free-falling body rolled down the steep incline of our shell hole and landed on top of my patient, pinning my hands, which were still holding the silk suture against the injured Marine's knee joint. Being sedated by a large dose of morphine and the early stages of shock, the patient was able only to utter a feeble groan of protest.

Murphy pulled this freshly created corpse off my patient, dropping him behind us on the floor of the shell hole. This dead man was a straggler from the 26th Marines. A few minutes earlier he had begged me to send him out as a combat fatigue casualty. I had told him to wait on the rim of the crater and we'd talk about it later. How I wished that I'd sent him away earlier!

Murphy and I turned our attention back to our patient. Examination of his wound was a disheartening experience. Small twigs, sand, and small pebbles had liberally seasoned the open knee joint. Fortunately, the suture had not been torn loose from its moorings, for the wound was dry. Using thumb forceps we carefully picked out the larger objects from the recesses of the knee joint. Then using all the water in Murphy's canteen, we carefully rinsed out the smaller foreign particles. The wound was soon dressed and the leg immobilized in a plywood molded splint.

The patient was now ready for his trip to the beach. An amphibian tractor, returning to its ship for another load of ammunition, was flagged down. My casualty, plus two others, were laid on the steel deck of the vehicle for the start of their journey back to friendlier shores.

A short time later our litter bearers placed another casualty on our shell hole operating table.

Murphy exploded, "God help us. What can we do for this guy?"

"He's about had it, but we'll give it a try."

The man's right arm had been blown off just below the elbow. Another piece of shrapnel had opened up the right shoulder joint. Worst of all was the extensive damage to the left anterior chest wall, leaving the heart and upper lobe of the lung exposed.

I shouted, "Murphy, put a tourniquet on the arm stump and bandage the shoulder and arm wounds. Smith, take the aspirator and suck out his upper airway. Then get plasma going in as fast as it will run."

I fished a large darning needle threaded with a heavy silk suture from my surgical bag. I had to cover this ghastly chest wound. The patient's own skin lying at the margins of the wound was the only material available. Starting from the top I threaded the darning needle through the skin edges and then pulled them tightly together before tying a secure square knot. It took five of these sutures to cover the lung and contain it within the chest cavity. It took eight more of these sutures to pull a layer of skin over the exposed heart.

Twenty minutes later the chest wound was temporarily closed, the shoulder and arm wounds were dressed, the obstructed upper airway had been cleared, and Smith was starting a second unit of plasma. The patient's respiratory efforts were no longer impeded, and the alarming cyanosis had disappeared.

Kramer, who was making the rounds logging the new casualties in the book, stopped to check his dog tags.

He blurted out, "This guy is Corpsman Giese from G Company."

Murphy grabbed a water-soaked dressing and began cleaning the dirt, dried blood, and spittle from the patient's face. He soon cried out, "It really is Giese."

The face washing roused Giese to consciousness. He opened his eyes and focused on Murphy as he said, "Tell Hely that Finnigen is dead."

He started to struggle up to a sitting position in hopes of being able to breathe with less difficulty and speak with less strain.

I said, "Easy, Giese. You have told us enough. I'll give your message to Hely. Save your strength for the trip back home."

I continued, "Boys, load him in the next amphibian tractor heading for the beach. Smith, you ride along with him and keep the plasma running."

Later on I asked Hely, "Why did Giese want you to know of Finnigen's death?"

"His mother contacted me back in California. He was her only son. She asked me to look after her boy. I said I would. Now I have the painful duty of writing her a letter, if we ever get out of this mess."

A different type of casualty came crawling into our shell hole aid station at 0925. He was a corporal still wearing his tank helment. The injuries were limited to his feet, which were shapeless, swollen blobs covered by overdistended, but still unbroken, skin. An enemy infiltrator had tossed a satchel charge under his tank. The damage had been caused by the violent buckling of the deckplates against his feet. Although we had no x-rays to confirm the diagnosis, I felt certain that every bone in both feet had been fragmented by the blast. The additional evidence of subcutaneous bleeding indicated serious damage to ligaments, tendons, and muscles.

The pain had not been relieved by 30 mg of morphine sulphate. He was still writhing in agony as we loaded him into an amphibian tractor. We sent him off after injecting him with another Syrette of morphine. I often wondered how his feet looked and functioned after his eventual hospital discharge.

Next was my second contact with combat fatigue. This became more of a problem in later weeks. Sergeant Brown, a veteran, came stumbling into our shell hole at about 1000 hours in a state of abject disorganization. Between his choking sobs, he poured out his litany of woes.

"Doc, my nerves are gone. I just can't take it any more. I got by

Guadalcanal, Vella Lavella, and Bougainville OK. It's a lot different here. I've seen more hot steel flying around in the last twenty-four hours than we encountered during nine months in the South Pacific."

"Get a grip on yourself, Brown. You can't let your men down. Settle down here for a while, and then get back to your outfit."

An hour later he was still wracked with despair. I called Kramer over and said, "Log Brown in as a combat fatigue case, and get him shipped off the island."

The majority of our men with similar combat records performed with great valor. All of us were terrified, but we concealed our feelings. Esprit de corps was probably the greatest motivating factor keeping us facing death or mutilation on an almost constant basis. Probably the psychiatrists have a better explanation. At any rate, I did not feel guilty about sending Brown away.

At 1100 another problem was brought to me. We were rapidly running out of litters needed to retrieve the wounded from the front lines. The personnel aboard the hospital ships had forgotten to make the automatic exchange of sending one litter to the beach for every casualty and litter brought aboard. Fortunately, each of the wounded carried a poncho. After treating them in the aid station, they would be rolled out of the litter onto their outspread ponchos. Four men, each grasping a corner of the poncho, could easily lug the patient over to a returning amphibian tractor.

Major Mix stopped by to check on us at 1200. He placed his chin within inches of my ear before attempting to be heard above the increasing din of battle. "Get your crew on the move right now."

"What's the big rush?"

"We need you guys up closer."

"What for?"

"Our troops have pushed ahead twelve hundred yards."

"Sounds great, but we need time to get ready."

"How much time?"

"At least a half hour."

"That's too much. Headquarters company leaves in five minutes."

As I broke out my situation map, I said, "Show me where we're supposed to go."

Mix studied the map briefly and poked his finger at the escarpment that protected Airfield 2 off to the northeast.

"Our front-line troops are stalled at the base of this escarpment, and the Nips are holding the top in force."

"Yeah, but where do we locate our new aid station?"

Mix's finger drifted off a few hundred yards to the southwest toward

Airfield 1. "See those revetments on top of the bank at the northwest corner of Airfield 1? They are loaded with busted-up Jap planes."

"Will you locate headquarters company up there?"

"Naw, we'll be dug into the bank down on the flats below the planes."

"OK, Fred, we'll see you up there soon."

I found Chief Griebe on the outer perimeter of our shell hole aid station shouting orders at our litter bearers. When only a few feet away, I screamed, "Come here real close, I want you to hear what is going on."

"Aye, aye, sir. What do you want?"

"We got to move up closer right now. Get our forward echelon organized."

"Gosh, Doc, that will take a little time."

"Meet me right here with our men in fifteen minutes."

I then dropped down into the bottom of the shell hole where Hely was applying a plywood splint to a casualty with a fractured leg. Positioning myself close to his left ear, I shouted, "We've got to move our aid station up to the north end of Airstrip 1."

"No way, Jim, we can't leave right now. We've got casualties lying all over the place."

"Don't worry, I'll just take Griebe and the twelve men of the forward echelon. You and the rest of the gang will finish the job here first."

"How do we get there, Jim?"

"Break out your situation map and I'll show you."

After repeating Mix's instructions, Hely asked, "Do you want to take our aid station shotgun along?"

"Sounds like a good idea. Who's had any shotgun training?"

"Nobody."

"We'll give Corpsman Allen a chance. Show him how to operate the gun."

Each battalion aid station was equipped with an automatic 12-gauge shotgun. Double O ammunition was the standard issue for this weapon. Each cartridge contained nine shiny little steel balls that were designed for close-in work. We hoped these steel balls would discourage the enemy if they ever broke into our aid station, either during infiltration at night or during a banzai attack.

When our small party of thirteen men left the confines of our shell hole aid station, we immediately felt naked and exposed. The open country to the north seemed more desolate than ever. The shattered branches of a few shrubs furnished the only vegetation. The leaves had been blown away long ago.

In the distance, about a half mile to the northeast, the elevated revetments at the north end of Airfield 1 could occasionally be seen. Though obscured from view by earth geysers produced by constantly bursting shells, it was obvious that the bulk of the artillery fire was being directed at our advancing front-line troops. So our chief concern, traveling up to our new aid station, would be the danger of being picked off by a by-passed hidden sniper. It was disconcerting to know that this heavily shelled area was to be the site of our next aid station. We hoped the enemy would lose interest in this position as our forward troops advanced.

The route to our goal presented a typical lunar landscape. Craters of all sizes and depths encompassed the entire area. The remnants of the road we were to follow was still discernible even though some segments had been completely obliterated. About two miles to the north, the jagged, forbidding highlands overlooked and dominated the entire battle arena. Was this where the Nips' big guns were located?

Our little band straggled north along this fractured road, careful to follow prior instructions. We were to keep well separated and were never to bunch up under any circumstances. Thus, any concealed sniper would have difficulty picking off more than one man at a time. Because the enemy preferred officers for targets, I attempted to make myself look like an unrated corpsman by slogging along with a litter precariously balanced on my right shoulder. Even though it was not permissible, seeking sanctuary in any of the deep shell holes we passed was a very tempting thought, and I wondered how many of my men were considering the same idea. At any rate, no one put such thoughts into action.

After proceeding about four hundred yards, we entered a small grove of shattered scrub trees. Only their trunks and larger branches were still preserved. Suddenly our battalion shotgun blasted off twice just inches below my left ear. I whirled around to face Corpsman Allen only three feet away. He too had stopped walking. His mouth was open with his tongue licking his upper lip, a startled expression on his face. He was pointing the barrel of the gun straight up, his finger still on the trigger.

I yelled, "For God's sake, Allen, what are you trying to do? Those steel balls whizzed by too close for comfort."

Allen said, "I'm sorry, Doc, I didn't mean to fire the gun. I was checking the safety and the thing just went off."

Allen seemed to be genuinely apologetic for this accidental discharge and I decided not to make a big issue of it. Besides, Allen was one of my key corpsmen and a licensed chiropracter. He was a bright, outgoing young man, who had helped a number of our men overcome their psychosomatic complaints while we were stationed back in Hawaii at our training camp. In addition, he had picked up the rudiments of first aid very quickly and was good in instructing our new men who had less skill in these procedures.

I said, "No harm's been done. Just be more careful in the future. Until you get better acquainted with the weapon, we'll let you lead the way for the time being."

"Which way do you want me to go?"

I pointed to the northeast and said, "See that high bank about five hundred yards away, with the wrecked planes on top? We're going to camp near there tonight."

We proceeded in that direction for only a few yards before we encountered Major Mix, Lieutenant Familo, and a few enlisted men operating a temporary command post; they had direct radio communication with the front-line troops. Both Major Kennedy and Colonel Robertson were up forward working with the company commanders.

They were situated behind a man-made earthen embankment that protected them from direct observation by the enemy on the high ground to the north. In addition, two wounded men from the 1st Battalion were lying in their midst waiting for treatment and evacuation.

Mix said, "Glad to see you, Doc. I just called the 1st Battalion command post and asked them to send corpsmen to take care of these guys. Colonel Butler doesn't know what happened to his battalion medical section. They got lost yesterday right after they hit the beach."

The word soon got out that medical help was available. Within a half hour, nine other casualties from the 1st Battalion were brought into our temporary aid station.

At 1400 Lieutenant Familo said, "We are moving our command post up to the north end of Airfield 1. When you finish with these guys from the 1st Battalion, come up and join us."

We evacuated these wounded at a rapid rate, but new casualties kept taking their place. At 1430 we received five new 1st Battalion casualties, just as Dr. Joe Duer and about half of his 1st Battalion corpsmen came straggling into our temporary aid station.

My first remarks were, "Joe, am I ever glad to see you. Where in the hell have you been? We've been swamped by your 1st Battalion casualties."

Duer answered, "We're glad to be here too."

As he blew his nose and wiped dust particles from his eyelids and lashes, he continued, "We got pinned down in an abandoned enemy bunker right near the beach after we landed yesterday. We just got out a few hours ago. They hammered us with heavy mortar fire. We lost a lot of our corpsmen via the casualty route before we made our escape."

"I'm glad to see you made it up here. How about taking over these casualties?"

"Why not, they all seem to be 1st Battalion men. It will be great to work out in the open for a change. That bunker was a real dungeon."

Duer gave the orders, and his men proceeded to take over the care of the wounded men.

While this activity was getting under way, I asked Duer, "What happened to Big Weber?"

Before he could answer, a voice spoke in a low monotone directly behind me, "Here I am, Jim. I'm doing all right."

I wheeled around to face Dr. Weber. He was standing stiffly upright. His face was a frozen mask, and his blank stare was fixed on the horizon.

It took only a few minutes for my men to secure our equipment in preparation for our next forward movement. We moved out into the open country, and I noted that Weber had not moved or spoken. His hands were still jammed into his pockets, and his immobile face was pointed in the direction of the western horizon.

A short while later we again caught up with Mix, Familo, and the rest of our 3rd Battalion command post personnel. They were dug in at the base of a sixty-foot-high man-made embankment at the northwest side of Airfield 1. In leveling off the airstrip, the Japanese had shoved the excess earth in this direction. The slope ran up at a seventy-degree angle. On top of this embankment was a large flat space that was divided into several revetments containing numerous partly demolished enemy planes. It was not safe to peer over the top of the embankment, because the wrecked planes were inhabited by snipers.

We felt more secure in this location because the enemy on the high ground to the north no longer had us under direct observation. They did keep us off balance, though, by occasionally lobbing a mortar round into our area.

My twelve men unloaded their equipment on the flat sand near the steeply sloping bank leading up to the airstrip. As we hurriedly dug our foxholes, I noted that we were surrounded by our cooks, naval gunfire people, and communications men all dug into the steep bank. We would have to treat our new casualties out on the open ground. There were no large shell holes into which to haul them.

At this moment one of the radio operators approached me. As most of the shells were crisscrossing by overhead, I could hear clearly from a distance of three feet.

He said, "G Company just called in. They got a litter case that needs hauling out."

"We have no litter bearers. They are all in the rear echelon with Hely."

"What shall I tell them?"

"We'll send a litter up with one of the cooks. Volunteers can then haul him back here."

Before this plan could be carried out, the headquarters company of the 27th Marines settled in to the south of us. I sent Griebe over to request help from Chief Pharmacist Mate Pepper. As they had seen little action so far, they were glad to help out. Beside furnishing a litter team to G Company, their corpsmen pitched in and helped us with the wounded that came straggling in. Most of the casualties came from the 3rd Battalion, 26th Marines.

Late in the afternoon Sergeant Tassone came hobbling into our dressing station. He had a nasty gash in his left calf. His right hand firmly gripped his carbine while the left hand clutched a beautiful, fully jeweled samurai sword.

As he slid onto the litter lying beside me, I said, "What happened to the colonel?"

"Nothing. He doesn't know I got slashed."

"How come he doesn't know?"

"The colonel had me run a message up to H Company."

"Tell me where this sword came from."

"As I ran past a small cave, a little Nip charged out swinging his sword. He caught me by surprise and cut my leg with the first lunge."

"How did you get away?"

"I didn't. I just brained him with the butt end of my carbine and picked up his sword."

I called Allen over to tie the knots of the sutures as I placed them in the skin edges. During this procedure, Tassone kept up a running commentary concerning his extended family of Greek origin back in Chicago. After three years he felt it would be nice to get home to see them all again. Besides, Iwo Jima was the worst of all his combat experiences. In less than two days he'd seen more hot steel flying around than during his entire tour of duty in the Solomon Islands.

As I put the last suture in place, I said, "We'll soon have you on your way to a clean bed aboard ship."

Tassone's gay mood suddenly shifted as he choked out his reply, "Jesus, Doc, I can't go back."

"What in the hell are you talking about?"

At the same time I glanced up to look at my patient. He was attempting to hold back gulping sobs. The tears were flowing down both cheeks, washing clear channels through the accumulated layers of Iwo Jima's powdery dust. His handsome face was contorted with anguish, and attempts to answer my question were choked off by his convulsive sobbing.

"Tell me, Tassone, what's eating your guts out?"

He gained control of his emotions in a few seconds and blurted out, "I can't ship out. You've got to send me back to duty."

"Why?"

"I can't let the old man down. He needs me to look after him."

"Your wound will fall apart if you start chasing around with him."

"Please, Doc, send me back to duty."

"No. You can come back when the gash heals up."

Just then Allen succeeded in flagging down a weasel that was returning to the beach. I handed Tassone a lighted cigarette, placed his recently acquired sword by his side on the litter, and wished him a speedy trip back to his family in Chicago.

Just as the weasel gunned its motor for the takeoff, Tassone made one final attempt, "Send me back to duty. Ship me out later if I can't cut the mustard."

As they roared away, Allen and I shouted, "Goodbye and good luck."

Shortly after dusk we cleared out our last casualty. A growing concern for Hely and the rest of my corpsmen became a nagging worry. We had split our medical section at noon, almost five hours ago. They should have joined us here by now. The artillery shelling around us had been very severe, which made traveling in our area dangerous. What could have happened to them?

My concerns were diverted by the sudden appearance of Captain Munson of G Company. He had drifted back from the front lines to check up on the condition of some of his wounded men at the time of their evacuation.

After speaking briefly with Griebe, Munson approached me with his usual jaunty, debonair gait and treated me to one of his affable smiles.

"Griebe tells me that the battalion casualty logbook is back in the rear echelon with Kramer."

"Yah, that's right."

"Can you log me in as a casualty when the book arrives?"

"That depends. Are you combat fatigue or what?"

"Never that. I want to claim a Purple Heart medal."

"You look pretty healthy for a wounded Marine."

"Honest, Doc, I got hit by a chunk of shrapnel this morning."

"Really? Let me see where."

"OK, I'll show you."

With that, Munson slipped his dungaree trousers down to display a tiny splinter puncture about one fourth of an inch long in the mid right thigh.

"Reuben, that's no real wound."

"A sliver of shrapnel made this tiny hole, and you've got to log it in so I get the Purple Heart."

"OK, Munson, you win."

"Thanks, Doc. Don't forget to return me to duty after you treat the wound."

"I hope the Navy doesn't scare your folks too bad when they report you wounded in action."

"For a Purple Heart I'll take that chance."

After Munson left, I absentmindedly opened a box of K rations and began to gnaw on one of the hard, dry biscuits. It was difficult to bite chunks off. When I finally chewed a biscuit, the sticky glutinous mass clung to the tongue, palate, and pharynx. Copious quantities of water were required to wash this material down, and water had become a scarce commodity. We had received no resupply of this precious fluid since we had left the ship the day before. Our canteens were nearly empty. The resupply vehicles coming ashore from the ships were loaded down with ammunition and other war materials. There was no room for water.

We did find a temporary solution for the water shortage. As we evacuated each wounded man, we would relieve him of his canteen and distribute the contents among my corpsmen. This procedure did not deprive the wounded in any way, because they would be taken aboard a hospital ship in less than an hour.

After borrowing some water from one of Allen's canteens, I was finally able to wash down two K ration biscuits. It was the first solid food I had eaten since leaving the ship. I had only sucked out the juice of the sections of orange that Gass and I had shared the night before. I now understood why the Marines called those K ration biscuits "dog bones." They not only looked like commercial dog bones, but they tasted so bad that they must not have been meant for human consumption. As I examined the small tins of cheese and ham that lay in the bottom of the K ration box, heartburn and upper abdominal cramps returned with a vengeance, and so, for D day plus one my food intake consisted of two "dog biscuits" from a K ration box.

By now it was almost dark, and my corpsmen were starting to move off to their foxholes for the night before Hely and the rest of our medical section came drifting into our area. It was a relief to know they had made it through the barrage.

I said, "It sure is good to see you, Charlie. Did any of our men get ambushed?"

"We lost two of our litter bearers. They got clobbered by a mortar burst. Everyone else made it."

"What took you so long to get up here?"

Hely said, "One of the medical sections of the 26th Marines wandered off, and we got stuck with all their casualties."

"Hurry up and pass the word along to your men to get dug in pronto."

"What's the hurry, Jim? What do we get for supper?"

I tossed him a K ration box and said, "This is it. We are surrounded by trigger-happy Marines who are all dug in for the night. See that row of heads lined up on the top of the bank sixty feet above us?"

"Yah, what are they doing up there?"

"Those are boys from A Company. They are our front-line troops. They will try to intercept any infiltrators from the wrecked planes in the revetments above us."

"By the way, Jim, what is the password for tonight?"

"It will be American automobiles. Encourage our men to keep their heads down. I don't want anyone shot by friendly troops."

"OK, we'll use the password if we have to move about topside tonight."

"Hurry up and get bedded down. It's too dark to see the end of your nose from where I'm standing."

"See you in the morning, Jim."

By the time I rolled into my foxhole, Hely and his men had disappeared below ground. My men had prepared this foxhole for me earlier in the day, but the day's casualties had left me without a buddy. This sand-walled apartment was much too large to accommodate just one man. It had been hastily constructed by enlarging a crater from a 90mm mortar burst, and then my men had enthusiastically dug it far too deep. The bottom was nearly three feet below the surface. If another shell should land close by, I could get buried alive. It was damn lonely and frightening to be left in this alien environment without human companionship.

Why should I stay here all alone? Why not pull rank on my corpsmen and move into one of the nearby foxholes? With these thoughts, I sat up in my solitary bedroom and stared out into the dark night.

I knew that my men were all dug in around me within twenty to fifty feet of my present location, but how would I find them in this absolute blackness? I would find a friendly foxhole if I crawled out in any direction. However, I could not be sure of a friendly reception, even though I would be shouting the names of American automobiles, for my voice might not be heard over the Japanese artillery fire, which always picked up after daylight failed. If my corpsmen felt as nervous and jumpy as I, it would not be safe to move around tonight.

Soon the flares were popping off at irregular intervals. For the few seconds they lighted up the landscape I strained my eyes in all directions. This eerie, orange-red light seemed to be absorbed into the gray-black sands of Iwo without showing distinct images. Staring out for the next seven flares, I could not identify any of the terrain features except the silhouetted heads of A Company standing guard on the bank sixty feet above me. At this point I resigned myself to spending the night alone in my oversized foxhole.

As I lowered myself to the cold, damp floor, an exposed tree root painfully poked itself into my right side. A hasty flip to my left caused a half bucket of sand to descend onto my helmet and face. After shaking off the sand and finding a somewhat comfortable position, I became aware of the chill night air. My feet had become painlessly numb, but the violent shivering of my body soon had me sitting bolt upright searching through my backpack. Near the bottom I located the all wool, navy blue sweater that had been hand knitted by my mother-in-law. After buttoning both the sweater and dungaree jackets tightly about my neck, I wrapped my poncho in a spiral fashion around my body and again lay down. From sheer exhaustion I drifted off into sleep until a nearby shell burst jarred me awake with a shower of sand. As I glanced up at the sixty-foot bank, an orange flare outlined A Company men still up there standing guard.

This was repeated several times, until finally emotional and physical exhaustion supervened. Deep sleep ended a long, grueling day.

Chapter Four

D Day Plus 2

At 0300 I was abruptly roused by a firm grip violently shaking my shoulder. In my semistuporous condition, I pulled the pistol from my shoulder holster and began fumbling with the safety catch. Before I could fire, another arm reached down into my foxhole and snatched the weapon away. Just then a flare momentarily lighted the sky and my assailant. The helmeted head of Major Mix was staring back at me. His right hand was clutching my .45-caliber pistol.

He said, "Hey, Doc, wake up and get ready."

"What for?" I shook my head trying to get oriented.

"Munson got hit bad in the thigh."

"Is he bleeding much?"

"Not now. Corpsman Bokowski stuffed bandages in the hole and wrapped it up tight."

"When is he coming in?"

"Real soon."

"OK, Fred, would you wake Griebe and have him bring a lot of plasma along?"

"Sure thing. Where do I find him?"

"He's holed up a few yards to the south."

As he turned to leave I shouted, "Hold it Mix. I want my pistol."

He stopped, reset the safety catch, and then tossed the weapon on top of me.

"Sure, Doc, now that you're really awake, it should be safe to let you have it."

Getting out of my foxhole proved to be a difficult operation. When I tried to rise to a sitting position, every vertebra in my lower spine screamed in protest. The long sojourn on the cold, damp ground made it impossible to flex my spine.

The problem was solved by rolling over on my abdomen and pushing up on all fours then crawling out on my hands and knees. By the time I was up, working the kinks out of my back, I saw a figure crawling toward me from the south. He was shouting, "Buicks, Studebakers, Fords, Chevrolets, Chryslers," and so on. Griebe had arrived lugging several units of plasma.

In a tense voice he said, "By God, Doc, I made it. Rifle bolts were slamming home all around me."

"At least you didn't get shot. Get busy and restore three units of plasma."

When the next flare lighted the landscape, we could see four men stumbling over the rough ground with a prone figure on a litter. A fifth man with a carbine held in the ready-to-fire position was leading the group. The litter bearers were chanting a litany of American automobiles as they carefully placed their casualty at the edge of my foxhole.

A new flare showed the man on the litter very different from the dapper, self-confident Captain Munson who had demanded the Purple Heart citation for an insignificant wound only a few hours earlier. His skin was a ghastly, ashen color, and his breathing was so shallow that for a moment I thought he might be dead. His skin was still warm to my touch, and I could detect a rapid thready pulse. I rolled him over on his back and waited for the next flare to give me light. Several well-placed battle dressings covered the wound site in the upper right thigh. No blood was seeping through the dressings. Bokowski had done a good job with his primary treatment.

The problem was to estimate the nature of Munson's injuries. What was the cause of his surgical shock? It could be due to a shattering of the thigh bone with muscle disruption, a severing of a major artery, or a combination of the two. If an artery was torn, I should go in and ligate it. It would be hard to find in the dark. Because there was no continuing blood loss, I elected to treat him as a compound fracture of the femur and leave Bokowski's dressings undisturbed. If active bleeding should recur—well, I'd worry about that later.

I said, "Griebe, Munson is hearing the angels sing right now. He needs whole blood, but plasma should keep him alive until he gets the blood aboard ship."

I placed a tourniquet around Munson's arm, "OK, Griebe, shine the light on his forearm while I place the needle inside a vein."

Griebe complied, but no light issued from the flashlight. He had followed blackout instructions by placing two pieces of carbon paper behind the lens.

I said, "Take those damn papers out, I can't see anything."

Griebe answered, "I can't, Doc. The Marines have been ordered to shoot out any light that gets turned on."

"Take one of the carbon papers out. Maybe we'll have enough light."

The flashlight with only one carbon over the lens still gave a very feeble light. Because of Munson's state of shock, the veins did not distend and become clearly visible. Two tries with the needle were not successful. I was about to try for a third time when I heard a corpsman babbling beside me. On glancing up, I saw him pointing his rifle at the row of heads lining the top of the hill, now lighted up by a newly exploded flare.

He said, "See those Nips. They're coming after us."

I grabbed the weapon, realizing the state of his nerves. I said, "Give me your rifle. You need to lie down for a while."

Without protest he allowed me to deposit him in my foxhole and cover him with my poncho. Then I returned to my patient.

I said, "Griebe, Munson is going to be dead soon if we don't get that plasma going. Take out all the carbon paper. We've got to have more light."

Griebe stiffened and blurted out, "I can't, Doc. If we show a light, our men will shoot us."

I took possession of the flashlight and removed the rest of the carbon paper. "To hell with it, Griebe. I've got to see what I'm doing. Hold your poncho over us and nobody will get shot."

With the adequate light, it took only a short time to get the life-restoring plasma flowing into Munson's veins. Two hours and two quarts of plasma later, we welcomed daybreak and Munson's return to consciousness. The question was whether he had enough red blood cells left to carry sufficient oxygen to his brain to maintain this present state of consciousness. In order for him to have a chance to survive, he would need all the red cells contained in five or six pints of whole blood. Now that daylight had arrived and traffic was moving, it should be possible to get him aboard a hospital ship.

While Corpsman Smith was corralling a vehicle to take him to the beach, I said, "Munson, you are going to make it. See you later back in Hawaii."

He gave me a wan smile and said weakly, "I got two Purple Hearts now."

While placing Munson on the deck of an amphibian tractor, I instructed Corpsman Smith to stay with him until he left the beach for the hospital ship. Smith was to continue the flow of the plasma and to see that he was sent out to a hospital ship immediately. Due to the confusion and turmoil on the beaches, there was real danger that he might get shunted aside and lost in the shuffle for several hours. In addition, Smith was not to return until he brought back vital resupplies, the most important being potable water.

Smith returned at 1030 with a favorable report on Munson. He was not even unloaded on the beach. The amphibian tractor took him directly out to an LST hospital ship that was lying a short distance offshore.

Smith had also done well in bringing back wool blankets, extra cartons of plasma and dressings, more litters, and six five-gallon cans of precious water. We could now drink freely for the first time in forty-eight hours, and the wool blankets would reduce our shivering time to a minimum on subsequent nights.

The water cans had been filled in Hawaii two months earlier, and the water had a stale, metallic taste acquired from the containers. Under normal conditions, it would have been rejected as being unfit for human consumption, but on Iwo Jima, we were so glad to get it that we drank it without complaint.

The 3rd Battalion was still in the assault, and February 21 was a repetition of the day before. A steady stream of shrapnel-torn men flowed through our hands on the way back to the hospital ships. Apparently the 26th Marines had not yet put their medical act together, for a good third of our treated casualties came from that organization. At 1300 we received orders to move up with our advancing command post, which was located three hundred to four hundred yards closer to the enemy. Again I was given the dubious honor of leading the advance. Hely was left behind with half our medical section to treat and evacuate the fourteen casualties that had yet to be processed.

To look less conspicuous, I again hoisted a folded litter on my shoulder as we left the protection of our sixty-foot embankment in order to follow the remnants of a gravel road that curved off to the northeast. We were at the northern extremity of Airfield 1. Twelve hundred yards ahead we faced the ridge that lay in front of Airfield 2. I knew that this ridge was manned by a well-armed and determined enemy; we were moving directly closer to their gun barrels as we advanced. It gave me a sinking sense of loneliness and abandonment, in spite of my nearby comrades. The tightening and knotting cramps in the pit of my stomach increased with each forward step.

The enemy was apparently too busy dealing with our front-line assault troops to harass us with rifle or machine gun fire. Most of their shellfire was directed at the ammunition dumps located to our rear, but even so, about every ten seconds a shell would burst either in front, to the rear, or on one side of us. Fortunately, none landed in our midst.

As we moved forward along this shell-torn road as fast as the burden of our medical gear would allow, we were given negative encouragement by Marine units who were well dug in along the north side of this roadway. We were drawing shellfire into their area, and they wanted us out of the way quickly.

"Hey you swabbies, get moving. You're not going to a picnic."

"Pull the lead out, you jerks."

"Get going you dumb bastards, or we'll all get blown off the map."

This reception was not appreciated, but we did not waste time or energy hurling insults back.

The new command post of the 3rd Battalion existed in open country in full view of the enemy, who were situated on the ridge a half mile to the northeast. Our men were functioning crouched down in a series of shell holes lying in close proximity to each other. All the senior officers were up with the companies giving them support. Lieutenant Familo, our intelligence officer, was left in charge. He was busy on the field telephone that connected us with regimental headquarters.

On finishing his conversation, he said in his usual amiable fashion, "I'm glad to see you made it up in good shape. We need you closer. The attack has bogged down, but it will be resumed in an hour."

"Where is there a safe place to locate our new aid station?"

He looked at me incredulously and then began to laugh, his oversized dimples appearing on both cheeks.

Then he settled down and said, "There ain't no such place. Just pick a shell hole or two a few yards from our telephone."

A quick survey of the area was not too promising. Corpsman Allen called my attention to a likely possibility located a short distance to the southeast. It was a neatly sandbagged excavation three feet below ground level. There was room for five or six litters at one time. Until it had been recently abandoned by the enemy, the area had served as an emplacement for heavy mortars. We had hardly settled into this location when Colonel Robertson appeared.

"For God's sake, Doc, get your men packed up and out of here right now."

"Why, what's wrong with this spot?"

"Plenty is wrong. The Nips have several artillery pieces zeroed in on these old mortar positions. They'll blast it good when it gets filled with our people. So let's pull the lead out and get going."

"Griebe, you heard what the colonel said. Get the men moving and fast."

Then I asked, "Colonel, where do you want us to go?"

"When your men are organized, come over to the command post, and I'll show you."

About ten minutes later, our medical group reported to Colonel Robertson in the 3rd Battalion command post.

Much to my surprise the colonel marched us about a city block back over the same route we had traversed earlier in the afternoon. We stood beside the same shell-torn road as he pointed at the steeply rising bank to the southeast of us.

He said, "See that sizable cut in the bank? Set up your aid station in the flat area. There is between twenty-five and thirty feet of level ground from the road to the embankment where the casualties can be treated. Your men can dig their foxholes on the side of the bank."

I answered, "Colonel, do you really mean it? We'll get blown to hell and gone if we stay close to that road."

"God damn it to hell, Doc, quit giving me guff. Just do as I say."

This stinging rebuke brought me up short. I had never heard him use a profane word before. My questioning of his judgment, as well as the strain of battle command, must have ignited a short fuse.

In apology I said, "I'm sorry, Colonel. I'm worried about my men. I want to believe you are right."

He seemed to relax, and a flicker of a smile crossed his face as he said, "Take another look, Doc. That cut in the bank puts us in a defiladed position. The Nips on the northeastern ridge can't see us where we are standing. If we step out on that road just ten feet over there, they'll be looking at us along their rifle barrels."

I answered, "Thanks for explaining, and please excuse a dumb doctor for questioning your military judgment. But what happens if some of our tanks or trucks park on the road beside us?"

"The Nips will be sure to throw shells at them, but your men won't get hurt if they duck into their holes until the tanks move off."

With that exchange the colonel moved off in the direction of the battalion command post. While my corpsmen set up our aid station gear on the level ground between the road and the embankment, the litter bearers started receiving calls to pick up casualties on the front lines less than four hundred yards away. Soon we had a surplus of new patients, and shrapnel again was producing the great majority of injuries.

One memorable exception was Dr. Weber of the 1st Battalion, 27th Marines. After the litter bearers had deposited his large-boned, well-muscled body beside me, a careful search uncovered no recognizable wounds. His eyes were rolled upward so only the white sclera were visible. The jaws were so tightly clenched that I could not examine his throat or tongue. Both his arms and legs were held in a rigidly extended position. The elbows could not be bent, and the fingers were so tightly doubled over that the nails were gouging the skin on both palms. His knees were held as stiffly as the elbows, there was no way I could flex them even slightly. In addition, the hips were held rigidly immobile. It was impossible to rotate them in any direction. As he lay there, breathing deeply at a normal rate with the ruddy color of good health on both cheeks, I noted that his bladder was functioning properly. A large area in the crotch of his pants was soaked with urine.

I turned to the corpsman who had accompanied him, "What happened to this guy?"

"Nothing. He just stiffened out like a plank during the night."

"Are you sure a blast from a near shell didn't knock him silly?"

"Naw, nothing like that happened."

"What did Doc Duer say?"

"Get the bastard hauled out."

"Is he working all alone?"

"Naw, Doc French was sent up to take Weber's place."

Could Weber be feigning these unusual symptoms in order to get evacuated? To test this possibility I gave him a jab in the thigh with the sharp points of a mosquito forceps. He uttered a loud grunt, his back arched up off the litter. Soon he settled back on the litter with a sighing groan. The wet spot in his crotch increased in size as the bladder contracted.

I called Kramer over and said, "Fill out a casualty tag on Weber."

"What should I call him?"

"He's got some kind of hysterical reaction."

"Should I write that on his label?"

"No, just call it combat fatigue."

A few moments later he was deposited on the deck of an amphibian tractor that was returning to the beach. As the vehicle moved away to the south, I wondered what had caused Weber's collapse. Physically he was stronger than most of us. But emotionally he was far from strong. For weeks he had been living in a state of anxiety and terror that mounted daily as we neared the shores of Iwo Jima. Perhaps he had become a casualty long before he set foot on the black sands of this bloody island, with this paralysis merely the final stage.

By the middle of the afternoon we had precious few medical supplies left with which to treat our wounded. One of my men was dispatched to bring up Dr. Hely and the rest of our rear echelon.

An hour later Kramer tapped me on the shoulder, saying, "Doc, Hely and our men are on the way up."

About the length of three football fields behind us, I could see a group of men rounding the bend in the road next to the airfield embankment. Some of them were carrying litters, and others were toting sacks of blood plasma. I assumed it was Hely and our men. However, there seemed to be too many to represent our rear echelon group. Maybe some of the corpsmen of the collecting company had joined forces with Hely? Careful scrutiny revealed a taller than average man leading the group. This must be Hely. I wished he would fall back and blend with his men. Tall men leading always made a prime target for snipers.

When the last of the men had rounded the bend, the leading group stopped. Then they all bunched up to hold a roadside consultation. This was a foolhardy move and it distressed me greatly. That section of road had been heavily shelled at intermittent intervals all afternoon. I shouted and gesticulated frantically. My efforts went unnoticed as they continued to discuss their immediate problems.

A few seconds later a frightful enemy barrage completely obliterated them in a blanket of smoke and dust. Two minutes later, when the debris cleared, the road was empty save for abandoned medical equipment and a few broken bodies.

Instinctively I started to run down the road. Realizing the futility of this gesture, I turned back to our aid station after having proceeded only a few feet. Corpsmen Smith and Allen were close behind me.

I called out, "Hold it, men. We are too shorthanded here to go running off. Besides, the regimental aid station is only a few yards from the shelled area. Allen, run up to the battalion command post and call back to the regimental command post to get their help."

I went back to tending the numerous casualties, my senses numbed by emotional shock aggravated by a growing feeling of acute loss. I had developed a definite fondness for Hely, who was about six years my junior. Close bonds had been forged with the other corpsmen—Rhoe,

Radford, Maloney, Murphy, and Gass—since we started our training program nine months ago back in California. It had not penetrated completely that all these men were either dead or disabled. The demands of caring for the wounded kept my mind occupied, but even so, a deep-down feeling of emptiness and loss could not be suppressed.

At this moment, an almost welcome diversion occurred. Pharmacist Mate Willis of H Company sent an urgent message via radio. He needed help immediately because he could no longer evacuate his casualties. Intense shellfire directly behind H Company blocked the medical evacuation route to our aid station.

The three companies of our 3rd Batallion were on the line facing the enemy on the ridge before Airfield 2. H Company was located the farthest to the north; I Company was in the center; and G Company was located to the southeast. I suggested to my litter bearers that we should try a new route to H Company. There would be no problem getting to G Company, as the terrain offered some protection, and then they could slide northwest along the front lines past I Company to H Company if they stayed at the foot of the ridge. The enemy above would not be able to see them, and they could return by the same route with their casualties.

My litter bearers were all eighteen- and nineteen-year-old Marine privates. Many of them had been in uniform only three or four months. Their lack of military training meant they were assigned to litter bearer duty. Since they had to walk upright in order to remove the wounded, their life expectancy was extremely short, and because of this, my new evacuation plan for H Company was met with dull apathy. A couple of the men said dejectedly, "Doc, it won't work."

I answered, "It will work. To prove it, I'll go along with you. I want six volunteers to come with me."

At first no one moved. Ten seconds later, two men picked up their litters as they rose to their feet. In less than a minute, I had my six volunteers.

As the seven of us started our dash up to G Company's command post, which lay a little south but mostly east of us, I was not nearly as confident as I tried to appear. In fact, I was terrified as we worked our way toward the 220-foot ridge immediately in front of us. The enemy was on top of this ridge in force and must have watched our painfully slow progress. We advanced in spurts from one shell hole to another. After we had advanced three fourths of the distance, the enemy fire slackened, probably because they could no longer see us from their positions set back several yards from the crest of the ridge.

The men in G Company's command post were surprised to see us and had helpful suggestions to offer. If we stayed close to the base of the ridge, we would be safe from direct small arms fire; a stray mortar round was all we had to fear. I Company's command post lay at the base of the ridge a bit farther along.

Because of our defiladed location, it took us only a few minutes to reach I Company's command post. I dropped down into a large shell hole that contained Captain Gray, Lieutenant Nelson, and their radio operators. Gray chomped harder on his unlighted cigar as he gave me an incredulous look.

He placed the cigar on his lap as he said, "What in Christ's name are you doing up here? We need live doctors in the aid station."

After listening to the evacuation problems of H Company, Gray pointed out the best route to follow. A few minutes later, and some distance farther to the northwest, we were welcomed by Corpsman Willis and Lieutenant Hewitt, the new commanding officer of H Company.

We wasted no time in loading the three casualties on litters and starting the long, half-mile detour back to the aid station via I and G companies. (Because the attack had bogged down at the foot of this high ridge, we successfully used this evacuation route for the next two days with only four litter bearer casualties.) As I neared our aid station, I heaved a great sigh of relief. We had made it!

On entering our aid station, I found an even greater cause for joy. Hely and his rear echelon men were busily working on the more recent casualties.

"Am I ever glad to see you, Charlie."

"We're happy to be up here, too."

"How many of our men got killed or wounded when you got blasted at the bend in the road back there earlier?"

"We lost nobody."

"Who are you trying to kid?"

"I don't know what you're talking about."

"I saw that artillery barrage scatter medical men and equipment all over the road just two hours ago."

"Jim, those guys were all 26th Marine corpsmen. We lucked out when we came up the same road later."

"You mean nobody even got wounded?"

"Sure do."

"Thank God! Have your men pick spots on the bank alongside of us. Get dug in before dark."

As Hely and his men went to work with their shovels, Captain Knutson came sliding down the sandy bank that loomed high above us.

He said, "Hi, Jim, I've been checking on your defense perimeter for tonight."

"Is everything OK?"

"No."

"What's wrong?"

"There are two things. First, those young litter bearers should be back in boot camp learning how to be Marines. They got a Browning automatic rifle they don't know how to use. Who gave it to them?"

"I relieved it from a wounded Marine. What else is wrong?"

"Second, they know nothing about night defense perimeters. The by-passed Nips in the wrecked planes will slaughter them before morning."

"Can you help us out?"

"Yeah, I'll send some men over from headquarters company to re-organize things up above."

"Thanks, Knute, glad you came by."

A short time later, three battle-tested Marines arrived from the battalion command post and reorganized our night defenses. Short bursts from the Browning automatic rifle could be heard ripping through the disabled planes as our litter bearers were taught the intricacies of the weapon.

As the light was failing rapidly, I climbed up the bank to see how Corpsman Amrosino was making out with our joint foxhole. The work had progressed well, and I was proud of Amrosino. He had dug a very ample pit on the steep hillside that could comfortably hold two prone bodies. It was located twelve feet above the level of the road.

Remus Amrosino was a slim, black-haired, pleasant Italian lad who had had a borderline hearing problem before joining the Navy over a year ago. Now, three days of incessant artillery fire had at least temporarily destroyed his residual hearing. Because his sudden deafness made him very uneasy, I had taken him under my wing several hours before. With gestures, I indicated that I highly approved of our foxhole. Soon we were comfortably asleep under our newly arrived blankets.

A short time later, my sleep was interrupted by a scrambling on the bank below us and a voice shouting "Chicago, Louisville, St. Louis, Boston."

American cities were the password for the night of the twenty-first. Shortly, the voice turned into Sergeant Jusley as he piled into our foxhole. He had been appointed Colonel Robertson's chief aide following Sergeant Tassone's evacuation on the previous day.

Jusley's message was, "The colonel wants you to know that enemy bombers are going to clobber us soon. They will be aiming at the ships and beach installations. The greatest danger comes from our own anti-aircraft weapons as they try to shoot down the planes; spent shrapnel will be dropping all around us. The colonel says to take evasive action by standing up and presenting as small a target as possible. If a fragment does hit anyone, it should bounce off his helmet."

"Thanks, Jusley, I'll pass the word on to my men."

"Amrosino, go and tell everyone to stand up and be prepared to dodge falling antiaircraft shrapnel."

"Amrosino's blank look convinced me that he really was deaf. Without further ado, I routed Rhoe, Maloney, and Murphy from nearby foxholes. Soon the deserted embankment was dotted with small clusters of men silently waiting in the upright position. A few minutes later all hell broke out above us. Every weapon ashore and afloat threw everything they had into the sky. The crisscrossing of the tracers, the exploding flares and bursting shells, produced a spectacular display. Soon chunks of vertically falling steel were thudding into the ground here and there about us.

The air attack lasted only fifteen minutes. Just as relative calm was restored, a wounded Marine was hustled over from the north side of the road in an improvised poncho litter. He had not been awakened during the recent attack. A large chunk of our antiaircraft shrapnel had struck him in the lower leg just above the top of his boondocker Marine-issue shoes.

The tibia, or large bone, was shattered, allowing the booted foot to droop down at an odd angle. The main artery to the foot must have been cut, for bright red oxygenated blood was issuing from the wound at about eighty spurts per minute.

The patient's eyes were squeezed shut, and the teeth were firmly clenched, which further distorted his dust-coated face.

He managed to moan, "Oh God, does it hurt. It was just numb at first."

I said, "Maloney, give him a full Syrette of morphine. Murphy, throw a temporary tourniquet around his thigh; then tighten it enough to check the blood loss."

I rummaged through my surgical bag until I located a large, curved hemostat and a tube of chromic catgut that was attached to a sharp, curved surgical needle. Maloney held the flashlight; Murphy acted as my surgical assistant. Just as I was about to grasp the torn artery with the hemostat, a large mortar round burst across the road about twenty feet away. The shrapnel whistled by close overhead, and we all hit the deck.

I turned to Maloney and asked, "Did they get you?"

"I don't think so."

"Good. Now help me find the hemostat. I dropped it on the ground."

Murphy had retrieved the flashlight and started searching for the missing instrument. We had no luck. When we all fell to the ground we had probably buried it in the loose sand. I said, "We're wasting time," and I fumbled in my surgical bag for another clamp. Although shells were still exploding at frequent intervals, none of them came close enough to disturb our work with the second clamp.

It took only a few more minutes to slip the ligature about the bleeding artery, tie it securely with a second square knot, and remove the tourniquet from the thigh. Then the leg was dressed and immobilized in a plywood splint. We would not have any transportation available till daybreak, so I instructed my men to take turns standing watch with the casualty. They were to run plasma in slowly at four to five drops a minute and use more morphine if the pain got out of control.

Before retiring I handed Murphy the dirty surgical instruments, requesting that he soak them in 95 percent alcohol and then wipe them clean before putting them back in my bag.

After this episode, sleep did not come easily. During lulls in the shelling, enemy activity could be heard coming from the wrecked planes above and behind us. The few stragglers hiding there kept up a singsong chant while banging metal against metal. They undoubtedly were trying to tempt our outposts to fire on them. If our positions could be pinpointed, it would be easy for the Nips to wipe us out with handgrenades. I prayed that my untrained litter bearers would hold their fire until they saw the enemy at point-blank range.

This activity also made Amrosino very nervous. He preferred to sit up with his carbine ready for action. With this added security, I was able to relax and fall asleep.

Chapter Five

D Day Plus 3

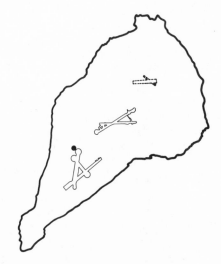

It was 0240 when Sergeant Jusley and Amrosino not too gently shook me into wakefulness. Jusley was bringing additional information from the colonel that was quite unsettling.

"The colonel wants you to know that we are in bad trouble. The enemy has broken through our lines down near the beach. They are circling around to our rear."

To support this alarming information, I could see two of our destroyers probing the northwestern beach areas with all their searchlights. At very short intervals, salvos from their 5-inch guns would rock the area.

I said, "Jusley, if they come down the road from our rear, which way do we head?"

"The colonel wants you to hold your positions and let them run through as they return back to their own lines. Your men are to hold their fire unless the enemy gets within two rifle barrels of your positions."

These new orders spread with rapidity. All my men were alert and wide awake. Some were test firing their carbines into the bottom of their foxholes to be certain they were not clogged with sand or dirt. Others were gazing apprehensively at the road to our rear. Amrosino fired two test rounds into our foxhole. He seemed so pleased with the proper function of his carbine that I thought it would be a good idea to check out my .45-caliber pistol. My chagrin was complete when I found the weapon to be inoperable—the slide was hopelessly jammed. In order not to be totally defenseless, I grabbed my trenching shovel and set the blade in the chopping position.

73

I shouted directly into Amrosino's ear, "If you miss at close range, I'll hack them down with my shovel."

I did not feel nearly as confident as I tried to sound. In fact, I did not feel confident at all. I was just trying to bolster Amrosino's morale as well as my own. As I stood in my foxhole staring back at the road leading to the rear, I cursed myself for my foolhardiness. If only I had listened to my wife, I would never had written that fateful letter to Captain Agnew in Washington to keep me with the Marines, and I would not be standing in this foxhole waiting for the impending banzai charge to overwhelm us.

I tried to say a prayer, but I couldn't find the right words. I felt an urge to break and run, but there was no place to run to; so I stood rooted to the spot and kept my attention focused on the road leading to the rear. At times I was certain that I could see shadowy figures charging down this road toward us. Amrosino must have seen them too, for he was sighting his carbine in that direction. Before he could fire, a newly exploding flare would reveal a deserted roadway. This same tableau was repeated six or seven times. The strain of waiting became so great that I had to put down my trenching shovel and attend to an overdistended bladder. The relief afforded was reinforced by the "all clear" that was sounded up and down the lines. The enemy had been beaten back, and the gap in the lines had been closed.

The cold, gray dawn of February 22 differed from the prior three days. The sky was completely overcast, and a chill wind was blowing from the northwest. Our 3rd Battalion was to continue the assault on the ridge protecting the western approaches of Airfield 2. At 0630, our artillery laid down a thundering barrage on the enemy in the Airfield 2 area. My ears were now battle trained. I could tell which way the shells were traveling. For the first five minutes, 95 percent of the shells passing overhead were friendly. Then the counterbattery fire came from the northern highlands. Soon a good 60 percent of the steel flying above us was definitely hostile. Hearing an enemy shell fly by was something of a comfort, for this shell could never hurt you. The shell that killed would never be heard by the victim. At this moment I was glad to be close to the front lines, for existence in the rear areas was considerably more dangerous.

The aroma of freshly prepared coffee drew my attention away from the ongoing artillery duel. One of my corpsmen had scrounged a one-gallon coffee pot. No inquiries were made as to the identity of the former owner.

As Rhoe stoked the fire under the pot with bits of K ration cartons, he commented, "The coffee will be ready to drink in a few more minutes."

I replied, "It sure smells great. This will be our first coffee since we left the *Sandoval* three days ago."

Hely added, "It sure will help wash down those lousy K ration biscuits."

By this time over half the medical section had gathered around the boiling pot with increasing anticipation. At this point, a loud clanking of machinery, a clashing of gears, and the roar of many motors directed our attention to a column of tanks that ad pulled up and parked on the road beside us. One glance at these iron monsters spelled imminent danger.

I shouted, "Dive for your holes men, we are going to be shelled. Drag your patients in with you."

Seconds later the anticipated barrage of hot steel was landing in the roadway among the tanks. The tankers simply buttoned up their hatches and remained parked for the next fifteen minutes. We took no direct hits, but our area was liberally sprayed with shrapnel. Because everyone was hugging the bottom of his foxhole, we suffered no casualties. One litter bearer had his dungaree jacket set afire by a spent fragment, but quick action by his buddy doused the fire before serious damage occurred.

The shellfire ceased as soon as the tanks moved on. Amrosino and I crawled out of our foxhole together. We were both looking forward to a cup of that hot coffee. About halfway down the bank, we could hear sounds of anger, frustration, and despair coming from the men already huddled about the coffee pot. The large pot had been knocked over on its side. Closer inspection showed it was riddled with shrapnel holes. So once more we were reduced to gnawing on our dry biscuits and washing them down with stale water from our canteens.

We were not allowed much time to mourn the loss of our coffee pot, for we were soon occupied with the endless routine of administering first aid to the wounded.

During this long bloody day, our combined battalion medical sections treated and evacuated 109 living men. We did not trouble ourselves with the dead. They were allowed to lie where they fell and wait for the graves registration detail to collect them later.

A new diversion occurred at 0930 when a young private from the 26th Marines came storming into our aid station. His eyes were rolling about wildly. His facial muscles ran through the gamut of contortions that alternately depicted fear, hate, and rage as he shouted incoherently. He was swinging a large samurai sword about indiscriminately. If anyone tried to approach him, he would make halfhearted lunges with his recently captured weapon. From his disjointed remarks, we learned *we were the enemy and he was surrounded.* Before he died, he planned to kill as many Nips as possible. While several of us drew his hostility in our direction, Pharmacist Mate Meegan slipped up behind him with a trenching shovel. A well-placed blow between the shoulder blades with the flat of the shovel sent the poor demented man sprawling in the sand.

Within seconds he was disarmed and securely lashed to a litter. But his wild activity did not subside in the least. He writhed, thrashed, and tore at his restraints. He finally subsided after I gave him a small dose of sodium Pentothol intravenously. I ordered Kramer to write all the details on his evacuation tag. I did not want him tearing the hospital ward apart when the Pentothol wore off.

One hour later Dr. Joe Duer arrived in our aid station on a litter. A glance at his left leg showed that his career as a combat surgeon was finished. A piece of shrapnel had sliced through several of his hamstring tendons above and behind his knee joint. While the effects of the shot of morphine were taking hold, I immediately went to work on the wound. No large vessels had been cut, so bleeding was reduced to a slight oozing from the shredded muscles. My chief problem was to remove the bits of clothing and particles of sand and gravel that had been driven into the wound.

In order to observe my procedures, Duer had a corpsman remove his helmet and push it behind his head and neck to have it serve as an improvised pillow. His bald spot was completely camouflaged by a thick coating of dried sweat and mud that had been accumulating for the past three days under his helmet. Even so, his true interests were not confined to my surgical activities.

He said, "My men are in bad shape up there. We set up in those mortar pits to the northeast."

"Yah, I know. Our colonel chased us out of there yesterday."

"Worse yet, they have no doctor."

"How come? Didn't French take Weber's place?"

"Yes, but he got hit just at daybreak."

"Does Schultz at regimental headquarters know about it?"

"I'm not sure."

As I fastened the battle dressing in place with a three-inch roll of gauze, I said, "I'll go up to our command post and see what I can do. My men will get you started back to the U.S.A."

We parted with a final handshake as they loaded him onto a passing amphibian tractor.

I found Corporal Tummerly operating the telephone at the battalion command post. After cranking up the machine several times, he finally got Dr. Schultz on the line. I informed him of the urgent situation existing in the 1st Battalion medical section. He stated that he was aware of the problem and was searching for replacements. Somebody would be coming up soon.

Shortly before 1100 a forlorn little figure could be seen trudging up the road from the rear. He was clothed in dungarees several sizes too large. His oversized helmet obscured the upper portion of his face. Only the tip of the nose, mouth, and chin were visible. A fifty-pound backpack was in place. Two handgrenades and a trenching shovel were dangling from his cartridge belt and a .45-caliber pistol was ensconced in his shoulder holster.

Our new arrival was none other than Dr. Link, the assistant regimental surgeon. Although he was a rather timid fellow, he was a competent physician. I was glad that Dr. Schultz had sent him up so promptly.

With quiet resignation, he addressed me, "Jim, I'm supposed to lend a hand with the 1st Battalion medical section. Where can I find them?"

"They are about three hundred yards over to the northeast."

As I pinpointed their position on my situation map, I said, "Link, I think you'll find their location is rather exposed out in no-man's-land. If you agree with me, why don't you bring them back to work in our area? They can dig into the bank to our rear."

To my surprise, he marched out into the open country in search of the orphaned medical section with an unexpected display of courage. A short time later he returned with the remaining corpsmen of the 1st Battalion.

He said, "They were terribly exposed out there. I took your advice and brought them back here."

"OK, Link, get your men dug into the bank behind us."

Link said, "Won't these two dead Japs lying halfway down the hillside be in the way?"

I glanced up at the two bloated bodies sprawled on the bank twenty to thirty feet above the level of the road. A host of flies were hovering about. These bodies had been lying in their present position since our arrival yesterday. The enemy frequently booby-trapped their dead when they had to be abandoned, so I cautioned Link about the dangers as I tossed a sixty-foot length of clothesline to him.

"Don't let your men handle those bodies. They might explode. Tie one end of the line around a foot and drag the corpse across the road, thus keeping at a safe distance."

The bodies were dragged over to a small shell hole on the north side of the road without incident and covered with a few shovelfuls of sand.

A half hour later, while the 1st Battalion men were still busily digging foxholes in the embankment behind us, Link approached me again.

"Well Jim, I guess you won't need me anymore. Everything seems to be under control."

"What do you mean by under control? If you leave, we'll have only two doctors for two separate medical sections."

"Doctor Schultz said I could come back when things settled down."

"Good Lord, man, see all the casualties yet untended? We could easily use a fourth doctor."

"Yes, I know. Doctor Schultz is going to send two permanent replacements up tomorrow to take charge of the 1st Battalion."

"That takes care of tomorrow, but what about today?"

"They need me more back at regimental headquarters. I'll be going now. Goodbye."

I shouted in anger at his back as he started along the road to the rear, "For your sake, I hope God will forgive you."

I never saw Link again. He was transferred out of the division at the conclusion of the operation on Iwo Jima.

Although we were swamped with 1st and 3rd battalion casualties, we continued to be deluged with casualties from the 26th Marines. This burden increased in the early afternoon.

Shortly after 1200, Dr. Trierweiler of the 3rd Battalion, 26th Marines, wandered into our aid station in a state of acute agitation. Between spells of sobbing, choking, and trembling, he managed to blurt out his unbearable problems. His unit had suffered heavy casualties when they had traversed our shell-torn road the afternoon before. Their present aid station was located a few hundred yards to the northwest. They were working in open country without any suggestion of concealment. His men were being picked off at all-too-frequent intervals. His turn was sure to come soon. He just couldn't take it any more. He had felt like running off and hiding many times in the last seventy-two hours, but duty had forced him to stay on with his men. Now he did not care what happened.

It was obvious that he was emotionally unfit to continue to function as a doctor, at least for the time being. His evacuation tag was labeled "combat fatigue." Without further ado, he was loaded on a passing truck with two Marines who had also "cracked up."

About a half hour later, Dr. Root, the assistant battalion surgeon of the 3rd Battalion, 26th Marines, drifted into our aid station with the remnants of his medical section. Until the present, he had been an eager young physician willing to cope with the vagaries of military life. Now he appeared quite discouraged and despondent. Losing nearly half his men in the past twenty-four hours had been a severe blow. The recent collapse of his senior medical officer, Dr. Trierweiler, was more than he could handle. He came to us for both help and companionship.

He said, "Jim, I'm all alone out there. Can I tie in with you until replacements arrive?"

"Sure thing, Root. Do you see the 1st Battalion men digging into the bank behind us? Pick a spot on the bank to their rear. We'll handle your casualties until you and your men get dug in."

Several hours later they were again functioning as a medical military team. We all appreciated their help a great deal. With this latest influx, we had over fifty medical personnel operating in our location.

It had been sprinkling intermittently all morning, but at 1300 it really began to rain in earnest. The temperature had dropped into the low forty's and the strong northwest wind produced a greatly increased chill factor. I tried to work with my poncho draped over my body. The loose flaps kept getting in the way by obstructing my vision or falling into the wound I was trying to treat. In frustration, I finally discarded the poncho and allowed the weather to have its way with me. At least the protection of my steel helmet prevented the water from running down my neck.

In a few cases, the heavy rain actually served a useful purpose. Lt. Russell Hewitt was a prime example. He was a fine, eager young officer who had taken over the command of H Company after Captains Hall and McCahill had been killed on the twentieth. He was thinking of making professional golf his career.

He was carried in late in the afternoon with an ugly wound of the left foot just below the ankle joint. The Achilles tendon was still intact, but the steel fragment had carried away a couple of the tarsal bones in the upper foot, leaving a gaping hole in this area. It was an unusually dirty wound. Bits of boot, sock, sand, and earth particles were embedded in the adjacent tissues. As I pulled out shreds of leather, wool, and small twigs with my thumb forceps, the heavy rain gave the wound a very satisfactory flushing of the smaller pieces of debris. The wound looked much cleaner when the rain and I had finished our work.

During this operation, Hewitt was giving me a modified cross-examination. He wanted to know how long it would take the wound to heal, and would it affect his golfing career? These battlefield interrogations by injured men were not uncommon. I always tried to give a hopeful prognosis.

Just before dusk our jeep ambulance arrived from the *Sandoval,* exactly three days later than planned. It had been buried near the bottom of the hold and had been uncovered just that afternoon. Our jeep was a godsend. It contained many blankets, both canvas and wool. Being water repellent, the canvas blankets were in great demand. Griebe was ordered to distribute them on a fair-share basis.

But best of all, the jeep contained a Coleman gasoline stove and a five-gallon water tin. At last we could have our coffee. As we gathered around the stove waiting for the coffee to boil, a messenger arrived from our command post, "You are to take immediate defensive action. The enemy has broken through from the north, and they are heading this way." To lend weight to this warning, the gunnery sergeant across the road was shouting orders to the men of his 81mm mortar platoon. They were directed to re-aim their pieces from our front to the deep left. After firing several rounds at eight hundred yards, the range was cut to six hundred yards.

Our medical people began scurrying around looking for weapons and then test-firing them. We had all retreated to our respective foxholes, dragging our casualties in with us, where we planned to make our last stand. I thanked Amrosino for cleaning my pistol and making it serviceable as I fired a couple of test rounds. We were ready for the impending attack.

Across the road the gunnery sergeant bawled out, "Elevate your pieces, and fire at five hundred yards."

The 81mm shells, each leaving the mortars with a choking cough, went hurtling off toward the enemy.

Two minutes later the order came through, "Set your pieces for three hundred yards and give them rapid fire."

In the gathering gloom it was easy to imagine that the enemy was closing in. I was proud of my men, for none of them had opened up on imaginary targets. The range was called down to two hundred fifty yards before the "all clear" was sounded. The enemy had been driven back to their own lines.

As Amrosino and I eagerly climbed down the bank to join the crowd gathering about the Coleman burner, we heard mutters of disgust. Our coffee kitchen had been unattended during the recent alert and the finished product was a bit "overboiled." About one third of the coffee had either evaporated or boiled over. The flame of the Coleman stove had been smothered by wet coffee grounds, but the bitter brew remaining in the five-gallon tin was still hot.

No one hesitated to drink his allotment, and we allowed that nothing could have tasted better on this cold, miserable, wet night. Even the dry K rations were almost palatable when swallowed between sips of this hot liquid.

When Amrosino and I returned to our foxhole to bed down for the night, the rain had subsided to a cold mist. The bomber that jutted out above us had not provided any protection, as the moisture tended to condense on the large wing. At irregular intervals, trickles of water would drip upon us and then down on the porous sand to be absorbed into our "bedroom" floor.

We were soaked through and through. Our blankets were a sodden, saturated mess. We improved matters slightly by wringing several cups of water out of them. How could we lie down and try to sleep? Wouldn't we suffer from hypothermia and become permanently disabled? The best solution would be to keep moving. If we were to jog back and forth in our aid station area, we might eventually dry off a little. As we were surrounded by nervous, trigger-happy Marines, this activity had to be ruled out.

Examination of our backpacks produced a pleasant surprise. The contents were dry. Changing into dry dungaree jackets and pants improved our morale considerably. The newly arrived canvas blankets also greatly aided our well-being. We made our bed with one canvas blanket on the ground. Our four wet wool blankets were piled on above. The second canvas blanket served as the top layer. Because it was water repellent, we were insured against renewed soaking during the night.

When the time came to retire, Amrosino and I employed a few delaying tactics. We could not bear the thought of climbing under those cold, wet woolen blankets.

I shouted, "You sack in first, Remus, and I'll see that you get properly tucked in."

Amrosino's answer convinced me that he had received the message, "Thanks for your generous offer, Doc, but enlisted men should look after their officers. I'll make everything shipshape after you get bedded down."

Realizing that we had reached an impasse, I said, "Let's compromise, Amrosino, we'll warm up first by jogging in place for a few minutes, then we'll both jump into our sack at the same time."

Five minutes later we simultaneously crawled beneath the wet, musty blankets. Almost instantly the cold dampness penetrated our recently donned dry clothing and we were both shivering in a lively fashion. In attempting to conserve heat, we snuggled up closely together, allowing no air spaces between our bodies.

It took almost an hour for the energy produced by our shivering muscles to generate enough heat to bring about relative comfort beneath our soggy blankets. This encouraged a general relaxation of our tense and exhausted bodies. The patter of the rain on our outer canvas blanket seemed to ease off just as deep sleep ended another long day of turmoil.

Chapter Six

D Day Plus 4–6

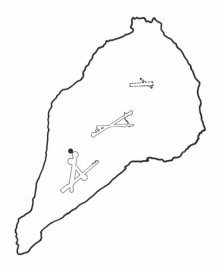

February 23   D Day Plus 4

A column of tanks parked in the road beside us, followed by the inevitable enemy shelling, roused us to the cold, foggy, wet dawn of February 23. The barrage was lifted as soon as the tanks cranked up their motors and moved out. Amrosino was curled up against my body; his deafness made him oblivious to the rising crescendo of the artillery fire crisscrossing above us. He was sleeping so peacefully that I decided not to disturb him. I rolled over on my back and alternately stretched and relaxed trying to loosen up my cramped and aching muscles. I stared up at the gray, overcast sky and tried to identify the shells passing overhead. Their speed made them all invisible, but the rushing sound generated as they split the air above clearly identified which shells came from the north and which were the friendly shells from the south. At this moment two thirds of the shells passing by were coming from the enemy-held highlands to the north.

As I rolled over on my other side I saw Hely settled down at the end of our foxhole. "I got good news."

"From whom, and what is it?"

"Knute said we'll be in reserve for a couple days."

"Where do we pull back to?"

"We don't. We just stay here and keep our heads down."

On hearing this news I decided to get up. But rising to greet the gloomy new day was to prove a formidable task. After lying in a cold, damp foxhole for many hours, all body movements provoked violent, cramping muscle spasms. It took some time just to rise to a sitting position.

Then I became aware of a painful burning and itching sensation on my lower legs and feet. Removing my still wet leather boots and wool socks revealed swollen tissues adorned with an almost confluent red pimply rash. Only willpower prevented me from excoriating the skin with nonproductive scratching. Amrosino, by this time fully awake, thought I had a case of the "jungle rot." Hely and I agreed that we were dealing with acute contact eczema. Lacking any dermatological lotions, we decided on the next best treatment, exposing the affected skin to the fresh, damp air of Iwo Jima.

Barefoot, I gingerly started to make the rounds of the aid station, cautiously sidestepping the abundance of metallic debris scattered about. All the men seemed to have survived the night in good condition, except for one elderly pharmacist mate who had been sent up as a replacement to the 1st Battalion less than twenty-four hours before. In fact, he was an old man of forty-two. The poor fellow was acutely ill. Conrad had a rapid, grunting respiratory rate and an ashen gray color.

I said, "Conrad, you look like death warmed over. When did you start feeling bad?"

He answered, in between short grunting breaths, "Had a chest cold for several days."

After expectorating some blood-tinged sputum, he continued, "Been running a fever for four days, but starting feeling real feverish last night. Ever since midnight, every breath hits my left chest with a grabbing pain."

"Why did they send you up here yesterday if you were feeling so lousy?"

"My commanding officer got sore at me because I nipped at a little of the medicinal brandy. I thought a few sips of the brandy would cure my cold, but all it earned me was a transfer from the ship to the boondocks."

I said, "Conrad, strip down to the waist, I want to examine your chest."

My examination confirmed a diagnosis of lobar pneumonia, complicated by the early formation of pus in the left chest cavity. I put him on the next vehicle headed toward the beach.

After four days on this bloody island, medicinal brandy had served no useful purpose. Not one of our numerous casualties had requested brandy, and not one drop had been dispensed to date. In Conrad's case, brandy had been quite harmful. If it had not been available to our medical personnel, he would not have been banished to the front lines, where the pneumonic process continued undiagnosed and untreated.

Shortly after Conrad left for the beach, Lt. Jim Gass, our quartermaster, pulled into our aid station with a weasel loaded down with 10-in-1 rations. He called out, "Hey, Doc, can you spare a few men to help unload these 10-in-1 goodies?"

While many willing hands were stacking these rations against the embankment, I asked Griebe to take charge of distributing them equally among all the men.

Receiving these 10-in-1 rations was the best thing that had happened to us since we left the SS *Sandoval* four days earlier. Each carton contained cans of beef, pork, bacon, turkey, eggs, potatoes, carrots, peas, beans, butter, powdered milk, and chocolate bars. Each carton was supposed to feed ten men for one day, but individual hoarding of choice items lowered this ratio. It was great to taste bacon, powdered eggs, and freshly buttered wafers for breakfast. Also, it was luxurious to have a choice among hot coffee, tea, or cocoa.

Before breakfast could be completed, it was apparent that these newfound culinary delights were introducing new problems into our closely knit group. An angry delegation of my senior corpsmen presented me with a united complaint. Chief Griebe was not distributing the new rations fairly. In fact, he was hoarding large quantities of the choicer items.

Because I had been listening carefully, the assembled corpsmen soon branched off into numerous grievances both old and recent. In fact, most of the complaints were quite petty; the thing that surprised me was the degree of smoldering animosity and resentment that had been developing over a long period of time. I knew that many Regular Navy chiefs were disliked by their subordinates. Until this moment, I had been unaware that Griebe fell into that category. I resolved to observe the conduct of my chief pharmacist mate more closely during the remainder of this operation.

I said, "Thanks for the information. I'll check into it immediately."

Griebe's foxhole was located a little higher on the bank than mine and about twenty yards to the rear. As I approached this area, I was surprised to see fresh earth flying in all directions. Griebe was busily engaged in enlarging the west end of his foxhole. The eastern section was crammed full of choice 10-in-1 rations like turkey, roast beef, and bacon and eggs mixtures.

His work was interrupted when I shouted over his shoulder, "Griebe, what in hell are you up to?"

He gave me a sickly grin as he turned to see who was addressing him, "Hi, Doc, I'm just making my foxhole larger."

"I can see that, but why have you filled it up with the new rations?"

Griebe replied, "Our men aren't getting their share of Jap souvenirs. We can use these rations in bartering with the front-line companies."

"Griebe, tell me, which of our men are clamoring for souvenirs?"

"Oh, lots of them, Doc, just lots of them."

"It just happens that most of our men don't like what you are doing. They would rather eat the rations. I'll be back to visit with you in one hour. By that time I trust that all these rations will have been passed out on an equal-share basis."

"OK, Doc, we'll do it that way if you say so."

"You damn well had better believe it, Griebe, I do say so. When you distribute that cache of food, I want you to pass on the latest word from our command post. We will not be in the assault today, and everyone should rest up for the next push in a day or two."

Shortly before 0800 about thirty new corpsmen and litter bearers arrived to replace the men killed or wounded the day before. They filled the gaps in the three medical sections now operating in our defiladed area. Doctors Crane and McGeachy were assigned to the 1st Battalion of the 27th Marines. Dr. Red Walton was to take Dr. Trierweiler's place in the 3rd Battalion of 26th Marines. Walton was an eager, enthusiastic physician who immediately boosted the low morale of his medical section.

Dr. Root briefed Walton on his new duties, because they belonged to a different regiment. As both Crane and McGeachy were now 27th Marines, I tried to give them a little helpful advice and emotional support. They had come to this island as staff members of the 5th Division hospital team, which was located in a relatively secure area near Mount Suribachi. They were utterly unprepared to assume their new duties as battalion surgeons on the front lines.

While Crane and McGeachy huddled in the depths of their foxhole, I sat on a five-gallon can of water looking down on them. My back was facing the road to the north. I had just launched into my discourse when I felt a shell hit the road fifteen feet behind me. As the shell exploded, I went sailing through the air, arms outstretched, to land on top of the two new doctors. The palm of my left hand was pierced by a protruding root in the bottom of their foxhole.

While McGeachy was carefully removing debris from the wound, Kramer arrived with the battalion casualty logbook, "Doc, you just won yourself a Purple Heart medal."

I replied, "Don't be foolish, Kramer. A tree root injury is not a battlefield wound."

Kramer answered, "I don't mean your hand. Look at what happened to your left shoulder."

A five-inch rent in my dungaree jacket was oozing a moist, warm, sticky substance that proved to be blood.

I commented, "By God, Kramer, you are right. I have been wounded. McGeachy, check it and see how bad it is."

After a cursory inspection, he replied, "You're lucky, Jim, the shrapnel just creased you. The skin is barely broken, and it should heal quickly without sutures."

Kramer persisted, "Can I log you in the book? That way you'll get the Purple Heart for sure."

"It sounds good, Kramer, but I'd rather not. Some dummy in corps headquarters will note that I'm a casualty and not see that I've been returned to duty. Then the Navy back in San Diego will scare the hell out of my wife when they deliver the news to her."

Shortly after this episode, Colonel Robertson paid us a visit. He was glad to find that my wounds were not serious and that our depleted ranks had been filled with fresh men from the ships.

He then offered some advice: "We are going to be in reserve for the next two or three days. When we go back into action, we'll be hitting the main enemy defense line. It will be tough going all the way. So keep your men out of action and get them well rested. The other two medical sections working with you here are now at full strength. Let them handle their own casualties for a change."

"OK, Colonel. Would there be any objection if Hely or I gave the new doctors some help if they request it?"

"I'll defer to your judgment. Just don't wear yourself out. But under no conditions are the other battalion medical officers to order your enlisted men into action."

"That order won't be hard to carry out. Can I get you another cup of coffee?"

"Thanks, I'll take you up on that offer later. I have to check out our front-line companies. They have a lot of new officers and men that have to be integrated into their units."

A few minutes later, Captain Gray and four of his men from I Company escorted a prisoner into our aid station. They had flushed him out of a cave located in the small grove of trees to our left rear. Gray and his men were elated because the division intelligence section guaranteed twenty samurai swords for each live prisoner. More information about the enemy was badly needed by our high command.

The prisoner was a small, wiry man about five feet four inches tall and weighed close to 125 pounds. He was in very bad shape. A short blast from a flamethrower had caught him in the face. His eyelids were swollen closed. The lips were also cracked and swollen and pouted outward in a grotesque fashion. The upper teeth could just be seen deep in the tunnel of recently cooked flesh. Shreds of skin were peeling from the ears, nose, and cheeks. The man reeked with the pungent odor of burned flesh.

When the two Marines who had been half dragging the prisoner into my presence released him, he collapsed at my feet without uttering a sound. After placing the poor man on a stretcher, we gave him a Syrette of morphine before sending him back to the division hospital. I doubt whether the intelligence section ever obtained much information from this prisoner. I do know that Captain Gray did not survive to collect the samurai swords for his company.

Later that morning we were greatly heartened by the arrival of fresh troops. Just before noon the 9th Marines of the 3rd Division began passing through our lines to take up positions in the center of the island. Due to heavy losses, a gap in the lines had developed between the 4th and 5th divisions, and the 9th Marines were on their way up to man this gap in the center.

We shouted friendly words of encouragement, but these unbloodied troops did not reciprocate in the least. Their comments indicated that they were disappointed in our recent performance. We should have mopped up the island in three days as planned.

Along about 1300, Major Mix wandered in with a rather vacant countenance and an unsteady gait. His speech was a bit slurred as he said, "Doc, give me a Purple Heart."

My initial reaction was, "Fred, where did you get the medicinal brandy?"

"Honest, Doc, I got blasted. I haven't had a drink, but I sure could use one now."

At that point he stepped up close and exhaled within six inches of my nose. Much to my surprise, the odor of recently consumed brandy was not present.

"OK, Fred, tell me what happened."

"An hour ago I was in a shell hole with four of our communications men working on our maps. I was in the middle with two guys on each side. A mortar round landed on us—POW—which knocked me on my ass. When I came to, later on, I found all four of my men dead. In fact two of them were cut to ribbons. Take a look at my wound, will you?"

He pulled up a trouser leg and pointed to his calf. Sure enough, he had a small, superficial splinter nick about one-half inch long.

I said, "Sure enough, Fred, you certainly got yourself wounded. You deserve the Purple Heart. The leg wound needs no treatment, but I'm afraid the blast may have given you a concussion."

"Shucks, that was nothing. I've been hit harder many times in the boxing ring."

"I'm not so sure about that. I'd like to check you out later this afternoon."

I called Kramer over and said, "Log Major Mix in our casualty book and return him to active duty at the end of the day. Also, give him four ounces of medicinal brandy."

"Fred, I want you to take two ounces of the brandy now. Then go up and lie down in my foxhole. I want to check you out later on."

When I woke him up three hours later, he still seemed a trifle confused. However, his speech was no longer slurred.

He sat up and said, "I feel much better. Maybe the blast didn't ruin too much stuff upstairs."

"You've been lucky. You can report back to the colonel at the command post. Use the rest of the brandy when you turn in tonight."

My prior negative feelings toward the medicinal brandy now had to be modified slightly. The small dose given Mix seemed to have had a beneficial effect. However, how could we be certain that he had not suffered some brain damage? If he were to assume command of the battalion via the casualty route, how well could we depend on his judgment under the stress of combat? I planned to discuss this concern with the colonel at some appropriate time in the future.

Late in the afternoon the doctors in the 1st Battalion, 27th Marines, and the 3rd Battalion of the 26th Marines were having trouble processing their wounded. Our combined aid station had become overloaded with untended casualties. Hely and I offered our services, which were gladly accepted.

I felt very sorry for a young second lieutenant who was a platoon leader with the 26th Marines. He had been liberally peppered with hand-grenade fragments on his back, buttocks, and posterior thighs. As I was performing an emergency patching-up job, he was sobbing quite unashamedly.

I asked, "Am I hurting you that bad? I'll try to be more careful."

He answered, "No, I can't feel what you're doing."

"You jerk each time you sob. What in the hell are you bawling about, anyhow?"

"I lost all my men trying to take that damned ridge in front of Airfield 2. The Nips on top kept rolling handgrenades down the hill on us. They came at us in clusters, each exploding at a slightly different level. It was terrible."

I said, "That sounds like a suicidal attack. Why didn't you tell your commanding officer about it?"

"I did, Doc. My commanding officer agreed with me, but the general ordered that ridge taken at all costs. My men have paid the cost, and the Nips still hold the ridge."

I answered, "It's too bad the generals can't get up in the front lines and really see what goes on. At least your wounds are not too bad. You'll probably be returned to duty in about four months."

The lieutenant seemed to be a little more composed as he was loaded onto the jeep ambulance.

Because surplus litters were now available, I assigned Amrosino a special detail early in the afternoon. He was to enlarge our foxhole so that two fully extended litters would rest side by side snugly on the bottom. Because the carrying handles protruded from each end of the litter, the length of the foxhole had to be extended about three feet. The extra digging paid handsome dividends. When I crawled into my foxhole on the night of February 23 and stretched out on my litter, it seemed that I had returned to the lap of luxury. We had our first restful night's sleep since landing on this evil island, oblivious to the battle noises.

February 24   D Day Plus 5

The sun was shining directly in my face when I awoke. I enjoyed the pleasure of rolling over and stretching for the third time. Then a sense of acute itching of my legs and feet brought me back to the realities of our present existence. I pulled the covers off of the offending extremities and exposed them to the sun. With sheer willpower I resisted the overpowering desire to rub and scratch. It was still too soon to put on my boots; I must stay barefoot. Fortunately, we were going to be in the reserve for at least another day or two.

I picked up my mess kit on the way down to the jeep ambulance where some of my men were gathered about a used pineapple juice tin that contained a gallon mixture of steaming eggs, bacon, and corned beef hash. After spooning a liberal portion into my mess kit, I was headed back toward my foxhole when I spotted Hely working on a fresh casualty on the other side of the ambulance, assisted by Corpsmen Murphy and Maloney.

I said, "Charles, why are you guys working on that casualty? He belongs to the 1st Battalion. Crane or McGeachy should be taking care of him. They aren't too busy now and don't need our help."

Hely responded, "I know how the colonel feels. He wants us to rest up until we lead the attack again in a couple of days. But just sitting around is bad for me. I start feeling paranoid and begin wondering if I won't be the next guy to crack up."

"OK, Charlie, if you feel that way. But don't wear yourself out. What's more, it's OK for Murphy and Maloney to help you, but don't let any of the doctors from the other units order our men around."

I was comfortably settled in my foxhole enjoying my breakfast of eggs, bacon, and hash when I heard a high, tenor voice cheerfully singing out, "Mail call, mail call."

The owner of the voice was obscured by a cluster of men surrounding him on all sides. It had to be either Corporal Czecada or Corporal Hoppe, as they were the official mailmen for the battalion. On nudging my way into the circle of men, I soon found myself facing the happy but slightly lopsided grin of Corporal Czecada.

Czecada was more than just the battalion mailman. He was always filled with energy and enthusiasm, even when carrying out his routine duties. His perpetual optimism could not help but brighten the day for even his most dour comrades. Now he was passing out special cheer to the men of our medical section. We were receiving our first mail since weighing anchor in Saipan so long ago.

I received two letters. The largest envelope was an official communique from the Naval Bureau of Medicine and Surgery in Washington, D.C. The San Diego postmark on the second envelope assured me that my dear wife still missed me. I retreated to the privacy of my foxhole in order to savor its contents. The two boys were well. They needed a father, and she needed a husband even more. Not knowing my whereabouts proved to be the greatest strain. They had received no mail from me in over a month. Daily she expected to hear of our combat landing on some remote island.

Our oldest son, Jim, aged four years, had had a wild dream the night before. He talked of it all through breakfast and had harked back to it many times during the day. The disjointed dream consisted mainly of a large group of Japanese tanks that were circling the Marines. His daddy had a big gun that shot at the tanks. They began to burn, and then they would explode into many pieces. His daddy was surrounded on all sides by wrecked and burning tanks. By the time the boy retired for the night, the Japs had lost all of their tanks, and his father had done it all. It would have been nice if things could have been solved in that simple fashion.

After digesting the contents of this letter for a few more minutes, I turned my attention to the message from naval headquarters in Washington. Why would they be writing me at this time? A glance showed it had been mailed on December 7, 1944. The contents left me both shocked and outraged. It was entitled "Correspondence Courses for All Naval Medical Officers, Lack of Compliance."

I was informed, "After twenty-seven months of active duty you have not turned in your first report. If no response is received in thirty days, you will be reassigned to more hazardous duty."

This was the latest of the many lesser warnings I had received from Washington. In the past I had made several honest attempts to complete the first two courses and had spent many late hours working on them. None of the tedious questions had any connection with the practice of medicine. For example, I was never able to determine how many sacks of flour could be stored in the number four hold of a liberty ship or how many bags of flashless powder would fit into the foreward magazine of a destroyer. These unfinished courses were resting with my rear echelon baggage back on Hawaii.

Now I would be transferred to more hazardous duty! Where could that be? What could be worse than the maelstrom engulfing us on Iwo Jima? I hurried over to Hely's foxhole waving the letter.

"Charlie, look what I got."

He took the letter and surveyed it briefly, "Jim, you've lucked out. Where will they send you?"

"Don't know, but any place will be better than this."

Rhoe entered the discussion. "Gosh Doc, we'll miss you. Can I get transferred too?"

Hely said, "No way, Rhoe. Besides, the colonel won't let Doc Vedder go."

A short time later Colonel Robertson dropped by for his daily visit to our aid station. I handed him the recent communication from Washington. Our medical group waited expectantly.

Suddenly he folded the letter, and as he handed it to me, he burst into peals of uproarious laughter. This was the first time I'd head Robertson laugh since we hit the beach.

"Don't worry about those armchair admirals in Washington. That's the only way they can contribute to the war effort. Now how about a cup of coffee?"

"How much longer will we be in reserve?"

"At least two more days; we're scheduled to lead the attack on the twenty-seventh."

"By the way, Colonel, how long will it take to wind up this business on Iwo?"

"It will last a lot longer if we have many more rocket attacks like the one staged yesterday."

"What went wrong, Colonel?"

"About half the rockets landed on the 9th Marines in the center of the island. My younger brother, who is a junior officer in that outfit, got racked up pretty bad."

"I'm sorry to hear that. It must be tough to get wounded by your friends. How badly was he hurt?"

"I don't know."

"Would you like to have me make a trip to the hospital to check on his progress?"

"I wish you could, Doc, but he's already been flown out to Guam."

"To change the subject, Colonel, what did you think of Fred Mix after his injuries yesterday?"

"He seemed a little more sluggish and slower on the uptake than usual."

"He suffered a severe jolt when that shell wiped out the four men with him. When I first saw him, I thought he was drunk, but he must have suffered a concussion in that blast."

I continued, "I like Fred a lot, but what happens if you get clobbered? Do you think he is capable of taking over command of the battalion?"

"Doc, I'm not sure what should be done. Colonel Warnham and I talked it over at regimental headquarters this morning. What do you think?"

"For what it's worth, you can tell Colonel Warnham that I cast my vote for Kennedy, unless Fred recovers completely in the next few days."

"Maybe my luck will hold out and no replacement will be needed. I'll have to pass up that extra cup of coffee. I'm due for a briefing at division headquarters in twenty minutes."

February 25   D Day Plus 6

The next day also dawned bright and clear. Of greatest immediate importance, the skin of my legs and feet was no longer itching, and the inflammation and swelling had completely subsided. The outer layers of skin were being shed as large, white, flaky scales.

I decided that it was time to don my footgear. It was a real pleasure to be able to walk about our aid station without fear of cutting my feet on the littered debris left from seven days of intense fighting.

After paying my respects to the medical personnel working behind us, I wandered back up to our jeep ambulance to see what my corpsmen were preparing for breakfast. The two-gallon tin was filled with various items from our cache of 10-in-1 rations. The mixture stewed over our Coleman stove, giving off a delightful aroma. I hurried back to retrieve my mess kit from my foxhole. When I returned to our improvised field kitchen, I found Major Mix in the center of a disturbed and incredulous group of corpsmen.

I heard Allen say, "You can't mean it, Major!"

Corpsmen Rhoe quickly added, "Are you really telling us to dump this stew out and bury it?"

Mix held up a sheet of paper in his right hand and said, "Orders are orders, and this makes it official."

I entered the conversation by asking, "What in hell is going on? Fred, let me see that piece of paper."

Mix gave me a wink and a sly grin as he handed it over to me. He said "Sure thing, Doc. Take a good look at it and then pass it around for your men to see."

It was a direct order written on official stationery from regimental headquarters. The words had been written by Dr. Schultz, our regimental surgeon, and had been countersigned by Colonel Warnham.

A summary of these orders stated that cooking food attracts flies, and flies carry dysentery. From this moment all cooking will cease. All food will be consumed without prior heating.

I asked, "Fred, are you really serious? What do you think about this silly business?"

Mix answered, "I don't think about it. Colonel Robertson told me to pass the word among all the units in our battalion."

As he turned to leave, his grin turned into a throaty chuckle as he said, "Don't forget, Doc, an order is an order."

I shouted back angrily, "OK, Fred, we'll take this matter under advisement."

The fly population had increased during the past few days, but their numbers had not reached alarming proportions. I couldn't see how heating the food would increase the danger of bacterial contamination; these obnoxious insects seemed just as eager to eat our *un*heated food.

Corpsman Rhoe, who was tending the stove, looked at me rather uncertainly as he said, "Do I really have to turn the fire off and dump out our breakfast stew?"

"Hell no! Douse the flame only if Dr. Schultz or Colonel Warnham walk into the aid station. We haven't seen either one of them up here yet, and I doubt they'll pay us a visit in the future."

Hely heaved a sigh of relief and said, "I sure hoped you would say that, Jim."

Later in the morning Lieutenant Pope from headquarters company came in to see me. Pope usually was a taciturn young man. Now he seemed visibly shaken and eager to talk.

"Pope, you look real shook up. What happened?"

"Earlier this morning Czecada, Hoppe, and I were carrying some wire up to G Company. The Nips caught us out in the open and dropped shells on all sides of our shallow shell hole. A larger hole lay ten yards ahead. We decided to head for it. My foot slipped in the sand and I fell back. Czecada, Hoppe, and a large mortar round arrived in the shell hole at the same time. They were all torn apart! Killed!"

"You mean one damned shell wiped out both Czecada and Hoppe?"

"I sure do."

Just twenty-four hours earlier Czecada had been delivering our mail with such enthusiasm. Now he was dead. Our battalion was lying in reserve for rest and recuperation; we shouldn't be losing men like this when we were not leading the attack. Every one of us in the 3rd Battalion was subject to a similar fate. There was no place to hide from a mortar round, which could snuff out my life at any time with equal ease. It was a sobering thought to live with, and here at the rear echelon there was more time to dwell on this somber fact.

I asked, "Who will deliver our next batch of mail?"

"I don't know. Knute will pick somebody later today."

"Yah, I suppose so. How are you going to make out, Pope?"

Pope and the dead men had been foxhole buddies since the initial landing, and I was concerned about him.

"Don't worry Doc, I won't crack up. God must be saving me for some other purpose; otherwise my foot wouldn't have slipped."

At 1200 I proceeded the fifty yards forward to our battalion command post to learn the latest battle plans. I was surprised to find Major Mix huddled over a can of beef stew being heated by a brightly burning quarter-pound block of TNT. Mix presented me with a guilty smirk as he turned his back toward me in an attempt to ignore my presence.

I addressed the colonel, "The major is violating regimental orders. Besides, he is wasting ammunition. That TNT will never blow up any Nips."

The colonel smiled and said, "Some orders are more important than others. I have to pass them all along. Let me know when we start getting some dysentery cases. Then I'll apologize to the regimental staff for being a little lax in carrying out this frivolous order."

"That sounds like a good deal. How much longer will we be held in reserve?"

"I don't know. We have tomorrow off for sure. By the way, warn your men to stay under cover when the 5th Division tanks assemble beside your aid station a little before 1300. At 1300 the combined tank forces of the 3rd, 4th, and 5th divisions will begin a drive from the south end of Airfield 2 in the center of the island. They plan to push straight up the runway and break the enemy's main line of resistance."

I had no sooner passed the word along to our combined medical sections when 5th Division tanks could be seen clanking up from the rear. As usual, they parked in a long column beside our aid station. Again the enemy artillery fire came pouring down about us. At the same time we were introduced to the enemy's huge spigot mortars, which hurled rocketlike projectiles sixteen feet long and two feet in diameter. Once they came screaming over the ridge, their high-trajectory course could be followed visually. On impact they exploded with a roar that drowned out the ordinary bursting shellfire. Steel rods eight feet long could be seen flying off laterally in all directions. Later on we treated some of the victims mutilated by these lethal missiles.

After our tanks moved off to join the others at the foot of Airfield 2, we climbed the bank to peer over the top and observe the action due to take place a half mile away. The number of tanks involved made an impressive sight. With our field glasses we could observe the action of the individual tanks.

There was a slight delay. Forward movement began at 1315. After proceeding only a few yards, one of the tanks began to exude an oily, black smoke that soon changed to bright, dancing flames. Soon a second, then a third, and finally a fourth tank were either smoking or burning. Within fifteen minutes I was able to count twelve of our tanks burning at one time. Some of them flared up like newly activated volcanoes as the ammunition in the tanks started exploding.

My thoughts drifted back to the contents of the letter I had received the day before. Maybe my young son did possess extrasensory perception. At least his dream had told him that his father would be on hand during the destruction of many tanks. It was too bad they could not have belonged to the enemy.

I turned away and slid partway down the bank as a severe wave of depression swept over me. There was not going to be a quick breakthrough and mopping up of the enemy. This campaign might go on for weeks and weeks.

2d Battalion, 27th Marines land on Iwo Jima. The 3d Battalion, including the medical section, crawled over this same terrain one hour later.
Official USMC photo

A wounded Marine going back with plasma still entering his veins.
Official USMC photo

Wounded occasionally straggled into the aid station on their own power.
Official USMC photo

Coming in from the front lines. Four-man litter teams frequently returned with only two or three men. Official USMC photo

2d Battalion Aid Station of the 27th Marines. Dr. Brown (with surgical instrument) was one of author's best friends. Official USMC photo

3d Battalion's aid station site from 2/21/45 to 2/26/45, dug into the bank on left foreground. 1st Battalion operating in the center of the photo, and 3rd Battalion, 26th Marines are in the rear. Official USMC photo

Casualties being loaded on vehicles parked on the road. Regular ambulances were still in the holds of the ships. Official USMC photo

Chapter Seven

D Day Plus 7 and 8

February 26   D Day Plus 7

Shortly after daybreak on February 26 my waking reveries were abruptly ended when a hand reached down and began roughly shaking my shoulder. A deep steady voice said, "Hit the deck, Doc. I've got news for you."

Sitting up, I found myself staring into the placid, grime-stained face of Captain Knutson, whose stubble of wispy blond beard made him momentarily difficult to recognize.

I said, "Hi, Knute. It's nice to see you are still alive, but why are you pestering me at such an ungodly hour? Besides, where have you been the past few days?"

"I've been up on the lines breaking in new company commanders for G and H companies. So far we haven't had to use any second lieutenants."

"What kind of hot scoop do you have for me?"

"The colonel sent me over to fill you in on the latest battle plans."

"Don't tell me we've got to get back into action today?"

Knutson answered, "The news isn't good, but it isn't that bad. We've been ordered to break the enemy's main line of resistance. We get into position before dawn tomorrow at the south end of Airfield 2 and drive straight north along the west side of this airfield. We keep going straight ahead until we capture Hill 362A, which is almost a mile off to the north."

"Does 'Hill 362' mean 362 feet above sea level?"

101

Knutson replied, "Yeah. There happen to be three hills of the same elevation; 362A is on the west, 362B is in the center, and 362C is on the east side of the island."

"How long will it take us to reach Hill 362A?"

"The colonel hopes to get there in one day, but it might take longer."

"What do we do to get ready?"

"Make a list of all the surgical supplies that need to be replenished. Then turn your request over to Jim Gass or Wentworth in the quartermasters section and see that he gets this information before 1000."

"Anything else I should know, Knute?"

"Yah, report to the command post at 1300. The colonel wants to give all the senior officers a final briefing at that time."

After Knutson left, I proceeded down to the jeep ambulance, where our Coleman stove was brewing coffee and heating the rations. I found Griebe eating by himself and told him to round up everyone in our medical section.

Ten minutes later the men of the 3rd Battalion were gathered around me. I said, "Tomorrow our unit resumes the assault. We'll be leading the attack for the next several days until the main line of the enemy resistance is broken. Medical supplies will be difficult to come by during this offensive, so be sure to stock your medical kits with extra supplies right now. I want Maloney and Allen to check out the jeep ambulance and get it fully resupplied. Everyone turn requests over to Griebe."

At 1300 I reported in at the command post as requested. Mix, Kennedy, Knutson, Familo, Pope, Gray, and the two new company commanders were gathered around the colonel discussing the battle plans for the next day.

The colonel stated, "Yesterday's massed tank attack was not a complete fiasco. Although many of our tanks have been lost, they enabled the 3rd Division troops to make sizable gains in the center. The enemy's main line of resistance has been cracked but not breached. If all goes well, we should make a clean breakthrough."

Colonel Robertson then laid out the battle plan for the next day. "Tomorrow reveille will be sounded one hour before daybreak. There will be no time for a heated breakfast. We want to replace the 26th Marines and be in position while it is still dark. This will give the Nips no chance to shoot at us until we are ready to attack. Our attack will start at the south end of Airfield 2 and will proceed parallel to and along the ridge that we have been facing for the past five days. Our objective will be Hill 362A, which lies about a mile to the northeast. This is the highest outcrop of rock on the west side of the island. Any questions?"

After thirty minutes of tactical discussion with the Marine officers, the colonel turned to me, saying, "Major Mix will take you up to the jump-off area later this afternoon to find an aid station site. We want your men set and ready for business before daylight."

"Can we expect heavier casualties than we've had on our past drives?"

"I hope not. As we get in closer contact with the enemy, you can expect to treat more wounds due to small arms fire."

At 1600 Major Mix appeared in our aid station and said, "How about a cup of coffee, Doc? Then we'll go up and locate your new aid station site."

As we drank our coffee Fred pulled out his situation map and pointed out the route. I would have preferred taking a more circuitous route to the southeast that was defiladed most of the way. But Mix said no. "It won't work, Doc. Your way increases the distance from one half to one mile. Besides, it is such a roundabout way that your medics are sure to get lost when you come up there in the dark tomorrow morning."

A short time later Mix and I started picking our way over the exposed battleground on the short, half-mile route to the south end of Airfield 2. It took us only a few seconds to leave the protection of our sheltering bank and to start across the tortured battlefield. Less than a half mile ahead lay the escarpment that rose three hundred feet above the surrounding sea. Only two thirds of this looming high ground still remained in enemy hands; the southern third of the ridge had been captured by our 3rd Division Marines during the prior three days. However, many hostile eyes off to the northeast were watching our tortoiselike progress.

The countless shell holes in the flat, black field we were traversing made direct, point-to-point navigation a physical impossibility. If the shell holes were less than three feet deep, we marched directly through them but the majority of the shell holes ranged from four to twenty feet deep. A great many of these man-made excavations overlapped each other, necessitating long, circuitous detours. What should have been an easy seven-minute trip became a long twenty-minute journey.

During our painfully slow progress the unseen enemy eyes were overstimulating my nervous system in several disagreeable ways. The sweatband of my steel helmet could no longer contain the droplets trickling down both sides of my face. My heart was pounding, and occasionally it would skip a beat or two. Worst of all were the gripping abdominal cramps set off by an overstimulated intestinal tract. Mix, noting my rising state of apprehension, attempted to allay my fears.

"Don't worry, the Nips ain't going to blast us."

"How can you be so sure?"

"It would take fifteen or twenty shells to wipe us out. The Nips need to conserve ammo."

"Hope you're right, Fred."

My anxiety was not alleviated by Mix's simple explanation, but it was relieved somewhat when we arrived on the lee side of the hill leading up to Airfield 2. As we plodded up the steep hillside, we knew that the enemy no longer was able to observe our progress. When we completed our climb, we were 300 feet above sea level. We found ourselves among a cluster of deserted plane revetments at the south end of Airfield 2. However, we were not entirely alone. All eight of these revetments sheltered the bodies of our fallen comrades of the 3rd Division.

Some of the bodies were sprawled out in grotesque positions, but over half of them were crouched against the sides of the revetments as if they were waiting for the order to charge. I wondered how many of these men had been killed by the enemy and how many wiped out by the wild rocket attack three days ago. This very likely was near the spot where Colonel Robertson's brother was wounded by our rockets.

Mix brought me back to our present situation. "We are going to set our command post up yonder near that burned-out tank. That revetment a short distance to the rear will make a good aid station site."

We went back to check it out.

The revetment possessed a flat area the size of a regulation basketball court. Three sides enclosed the space with steeply sloping, sandy banks rising fourteen to eighteen feet. The western end of the enclosure was wide open and faced a trail that led up to Airfield 2 just north of us.

As we entered this chamber, we encountered no debris of smashed planes but a wreckage of a different sort. The space was occupied by fourteen Marines. Insignia on their uniforms identified them as members of the 3rd Division.

One of the men was obviously dead, as he lay sprawled on his back in the center of the revetment with most of his face blown away. The other thirteen men were crouched aginst the north and east slopes in very lifelike positions. The leading Marine was a first lieutenant huddled against the north bank with the hand of his extended right arm resting just inches from the top. The position of this arm seemed to say, "Follow me men, let's charge."

The other men lay scattered in similar natural positions lower down on the banks. It seemed that they would soon heed the lieutenant's silent call to battle, and all would rise up and disappear over the top.

As Mix and I stood in this ghostly chamber, the sounds of battle were only slightly muted, for the screeching, roaring shells still passed by overhead traveling both from north to south and from south to north. The thought of working with all these dead men watching was abhorrent.

"This is a damn poor place for an aid station."

"What the hell is wrong?"

"One mortar round in the revetment will wipe out our whole crew."

"If you stay in the open, snipers will nail you one by one."

"Perhaps so. All these bodies will be bad for morale."

"Christ, Doc, get your men to lug them out in the morning."

"I guess you are right, but if the Nips drop another shell in that hole, there will be a lot of dead Navy corpsmen and doctors."

On returning to our old aid station, I called Hely and all my corpsmen together for briefing.

"Tomorrow reveille sounds at 0430 and we move out at 0500. We have to travel a half mile to get to our new aid station. It will be located in a revetment just behind the new command post. It happens to be full of dead Marines. We'll stack them in a shell hole that lies slightly to the rear. Griebe, you will supervise this detail."

I continued, "We move out quietly as one body at 0500. There will be no yakking or grab-assing. The smoking lamp will be out until after our new aid station is set up."

I continued, "As we move along in the dark, the Nips on the ridge can't see us, but we might encounter a stray infiltrator or two. So as I lead the way, I want two men up with me. Their carbines should be ready to fire. Also, I want six guards posted on each flank as we proceed. Are there any questions?"

Allen asked, "When do we eat?"

"Not until after the new aid station is set up."

Rhoe then asked, "How does the jeep ambulance make the trip?"

"That's a good question. Corporal Wyatt will wait until full daylight. Then he will take the trail southeastward back to Airfield 1. From there he will come up to our position from the south."

Before turning in for the night we were visited by our friends in the 1st Battalion, 27th Marines, and the 3rd Battalion, 26th Marines. They wished us success on our new mission. As they were being held in reserve, both of these battalions would occupy our old position. They all seemed quite satisfied with this arrangement.

February 27   D Day Plus 8

At 0455 our medical section was lined up in a long double column. I was in the lead with Amrosino and Brautigen, one of the litter bearers on each side of me, their carbines ready for action. Maloney and Murphy plus four litter bearers served as the six flank guards; Hely and Griebe brought up the rear.

Before starting I passed the word back to the rear, "Remember, keep close together. Use body contact if necessary. No talking or smoking. When a flare goes off, everyone stops. If there is no motion the Nips won't notice us. OK, men, let's go."

We trudged fully loaded in total blackness over the same uneven shell-pocked terrain that Mix and I had covered the afternoon before. It was impossible to stay clear of all the pitfalls of the tortured terrain. We led our stumbling column through many small and medium-sized shell holes that Mix and I had been able to avoid. On one occasion Brautigen and I stepped off into space and rolled down to the bottom of a twelve-foot hole. The column promptly stopped, avoiding a general pileup as they waited patiently for us to scramble back to the surface and resume our plodding pace.

Our progress was further delayed by the flares that illuminated the battlefield at three- to five-minute intervals. Each time a flare exploded above us, I would stop dead in my tracks and halt the column. Each time a lump would catch in my throat and I would pray that the enemy would not see us during the few seconds that the ghostly light of the flare illuminated our advance.

Although these flares slowed our pace, they had a very beneficial side effect, for they outlined the ridge. At times the light of a flare would show that we were starting to wander off in a circular path. I would then correct our course.

At this snail-like pace, it took us fifty minutes to reach the protection of the embankment leading up to Airfield 2. In no time we scrambled up the bank, and found we had missed our mark by a full city block. We found elements of our command post team that were supposed to be to the north of us, so it did not take long to correct our error, and soon I was able to identify the revetment containing the fourteen dead Americans.

It took only a few minutes to remove the dead Marines and stack them up like cordwood in the nearby shell hole, where we covered them with three ponchos. We had our aid station set up and ready for business at 0615. Just a few minutes later the first radio call came to send a litter bearer team to the front lines to extricate a casualty.

Before 0800 we had about twenty new casualties on our hands. Most of the injuries were caused by .25- and .30-caliber bullets. Corporal Wyatt was working overtime with our jeep ambulance, but he could not keep up with the demand. The jeep ambulance could only hold two litters. At our new location, it was now a four-mile round trip to the hospital. Wyatt could only make four to five trips in an hour. In addition, our new aid station was off the beaten path. There were no amphibian tractors, weasels, or ducks passing by that we could commandeer for emergency evacuation. On a hurried trip to the new command post, I found Major Kennedy in charge.

"Bill, we need more vehicles to get our wounded back to the hospital. How about getting a few weasels attached to our unit?"

"OK, I'll give regiment a call. How many do you want?"

"At least three."

Kennedy's request was granted. The weasels would first have to be released from the division motor pool, and it would be at least noon before they would arrive at the battalion level. As I returned to our aid station grumbling about the efficiencies of the military system, I spotted the crew of a 6 by 6 graves registration truck a few yards away, busily collecting bodies. A hurried consultation with the corporal in command of the truck brought a mutually satisfactory arrangement. My men would help them load bodies, and our wounded would ride back to the hospital as the top layer.

The dead were soon loaded in head-to-toe positions aboard the truck in layers three bodies deep. Then they were covered by a heavy canvas tarpaulin. We then found room for fifteen of our wounded on top. I sent a corpsman along to see that the plasma infusions on three of the patients were not discontinued on the trip back to the hospital.

The truck pulled out, and I went to work on a sucking chest wound. Just after I had tied my last suture, Corpsman Rhoe grabbed me by the arm, saying, "Doc, look what happened to our casualties."

Rhoe was pointing to the southwest in an agitated manner. Off to our rear, near our old aid station, the truck full of dead and wounded was lying on its side with smoke pouring out of its undercarriage. It had obviously run over a large land mine. Rhoe wanted to lead a detail back to give them a hand.

I vetoed that, "No way, Rhoe, we need everyone up here. That truck's only a few yards from our old aid station, where Root's or McGeachy's men are still located. They'll pick up the survivors."

Root later told me that six men were still alive when they sorted out the wreckage.

A short time later Corpsman Allen said, "Look at Griebe; I wonder what he's up to."

Indeed, Griebe's behavior was a bit strange. He was up and out of his foxhole. Usually he crouched down in his hole and shouted orders at the men. Now he was carrying a restored bottle of plasma with attached tubing to the next revetment behind our aid station. Why would he be going back there? Its only inhabitants were two Marines who had just died within the last half hour.

Curiosity dictated that I follow my chief pharmacist mate. By the time I reached the revetment, I was greeted by an interesting tableau. Griebe was kneeling beside one of the corpses. The needle had been jabbed into the dead man's arm, and Griebe was holding the plasma bottle aloft while grinning vacuously at two men, each holding large official cameras. They were reporters for *Yank* magazine, and they needed some action pictures for the March issue.

After the press had departed, I led Griebe deeper into the revetment for a quiet conference.

Griebe asked defensively, "What's wrong with getting my picture taken?"

"It's not necessarily wrong, but you sure as hell are making a mockery of our aid station. Rhoe and Allen are already back there telling the other men of your latest antics."

"Shucks, one of the reporters is an old friend from pre-Pearl Harbor days."

"You're missing the point, Griebe. A majority of our men hated your guts before we ever landed on this miserable island, and since then your popularity had decreased to subzero."

"I can't believe it, Doc. What have I done that has been so bad?"

"The biggest gripe was your hoarding of the 10-in-1 rations a few days back. Besides that, the men expected you to show leadership qualities as a chief pharmacist mate. You are never around when needed. When you *are* available, you shout contradictory orders from the depths of your foxhole. You have been especially hard on the litter bearers, and all the corpsmen resent your arbitrary handling of our inexperienced Marine recruits."

"I'm sorry about grabbing those rations, but I don't think I've done that bad otherwise."

"Griebe, I don't want you to get the same lethal treatment First Sergeant Califano got back in Hawaii. It would be a lot simpler for one of our men to put a bullet through your chest out here. A lot of people feel that our medical section would function better without our chief pharmacist mate."

Griebe seemed momentarily disconcerted, but he soon recovered his composure.

He said, "Thanks for the warning, Doc. I won't turn my back on the bastards like Califano did."

At that point I gave up and returned to the forward revetments to attend the backlog of casualties.

At 1200 we received orders to join our new command post, which had moved over a half mile to the northwest. We followed along the ridge just below its crest. One of the runways of Airfield 2 ran parallel to our course. By taking this route, we were safe from small arms fire and the hostile artillery shells safely passed over our heads, landing well to our rear and left flank.

We set up the new aid station a few yards south of the command post, which was located just below the crest of the ridge. I found Major Kennedy and Lieutenant Familo in charge of the battalion. Major Mix and Colonel Robertson were up with the front-line troops.

The news was good. We had broken the main line of resistance and had overrun a number of enemy artillery positions. In a few more days we would be back aboard ship. From now on we would also have a telephone in our foxhole.

The ability to communicate directly with the front-line troops would be a big improvement over radio contact. In the past we often had received radio calls for five or six litter teams at one time. When these teams arrived at a company headquarters, often only one man needed removal by litter. Two of the wounded would be able to walk, and the other three would be dead. On several occasions, litter bearers were picked off while making needless trips to the front lines. With the help of the telephone, I would be able to sort out the dead from the living and send only the necessary litter teams to the trouble spot.

On returning to the aid station, I found the men gathered about two partly dug foxholes from which small jets of steam were issuing. They had opened up one of the vents in the active volcano, and the sand about these vents was very hot.

Hely suggested that we heat up our C ration cans.

I suggested, "Bury a couple of bean cans first and see what happens."

A few minutes later, while helping Amrosino enlarge our foxhole, I heard a dull "pow" behind me, followed by another "pow" a short time later. Both cans of beans had exploded. We soon learned that our C ration cans would stand no more than five minutes of heating.

Our delight at being able to use our volcano for cooking was interrupted by big Lt. Red Nagel, who came limping in with a .25-caliber muscle wound in the thigh.

He was grinning as he said, "G Company just had a hell of a good firefight up in the next gully. We knocked the Nips over like tenpins, only we used handgrenades instead of bowling balls."

Then he sobered up. "They got a lot of my pals. Lieutenant Walsch got plugged through the heart. We had planned a big celebration on our return to Hawaii. I sure as hell am going to miss not having Walsch with me."

Chapter Eight

D Day Plus 9–12

February 28   D Day Plus 9

At 1300 on this day the forward echelon of our battalion command post moved up to keep in touch with the front-line troops who were preparing to make the final assault on Hill 362A. Being the highest elevation on this side of the island, this eminence dominated all activities on the western and southern approaches. The enemy had been defending this position with great determination for many days. Now our 3rd Battalion was positioned on the lower western slopes of the hill.

Our advance soon took us into eerie, broken-up country. We had to thread our way carefully, close to the side of the cliffs that lay to the west of Hill 362A. Sharp rock outcroppings, jagged rock pillars, and occasional deep gullies forced us to take many strenuous detours. As the land was too rugged for our tanks to operate in, we had no tank support for our attacking Marines.

For the first time since the landing on Iwo Jima, the comforting sight of our fleet lying offshore was completely hidden from our view. My corpsmen carried their carbines at the "ready" position with the safeties off. We expected to see the enemy pop up in every nook, crevasse, and cave entrance. Instead, we only encountered their dead strewn about, along with bloating dead horses and broken-up artillery. As we picked our way over and around these bodies, it seemed odd that so many of these sightless faces should possess such luxuriant black beards. I had always thought that hirsuteness was not a Japanese racial characteristic. My ruminating

111

ended quickly when I observed some of my men rifling the pockets and removing the split-toed, rubber-soled shoes of these dead.

I shouted, "Knock it off, you dumb bastards. Keep alert, there may be live ones waiting to let us have it."

A short time later we arrived in a bowl-shaped area that could have served as a natural amphitheater for several thousand spectators. To the east, the jagged, broken lower slopes of Hill 362A loomed high above us. Pinnacles of rock partly obscured the summit of the hill. To the north we faced a sheer, rock-walled cliff that tapered down as it extended to the west. There was a sharply inclined, narrow trail that had been cut out of this rock face as it led eastward up the lower reaches of Hill 362A. At the 150-foot level, this path disappeared behind a jumble of rocks as it made a sharp bend to the north.

We set up our new aid station at the foot of this hill where the rock-hewn trail descended to our level. Twenty-five yards to our west a fifteen-foot gap in the rock wall gave us an unobstructed view of the tortured terrain lying to the north. Machine gun bullets whistling through this opening told us that the enemy was still energetically contesting our presence. Several yards to the west of this opening the remnants of a road led off to the western beaches over a mile away. There was no way to avoid exposing our casualties to small arms fire as they passed this fifteen-foot gap on their evacuation from the aid station to the ambulances waiting on the road farther to the west, but our luck held throughout the day, and we suffered no increase in casualties when our men ran this gauntlet.

Before we were quite ready to function, calls came for litter teams. Four-man teams were requested to get the wounded transported from the battlefield above. They all had to be carried down the one narrow, rocky path cut in the face of the cliff. The attrition rate among our litter bearers soon became painfully apparent. Returning four-man teams were often reduced to two or three men. Additional corpsmen from the collecting company would have to be sent up the cliffside trail to lend a hand in bringing the casualties down to the aid station.

The morale of the surviving litter bearers plummeted progressively as their numbers dwindled. While busily working on the seriously wounded, I could hear Griebe above the roar of the battle shouting imprecations as he drove these men up the stony path to collect new casualties. Although his manner was quite abrasive, he was showing more energy than usual.

An hour later, just after Hely and the rear echelon joined our group, Griebe tapped me on the shoulder, saying, "Doc, I would like to show you something over by that gap in the north cliff wall."

Our abdomens hugged the ground as we crawled up the last few feet to the opening in the wall. The rush of rifle and machine gun bullets cracked by close overhead. Griebe pointed to a cache of several hundred pounds of high explosives packed into a small cave located just to our right. Two wires led from these explosives toward the enemy territory in the north.

Shouting into Griebe's ear, I said, "My God, Griebe, that looks like a land mine. Cut those wires."

Without hesitation, he crawled out a little farther into the open and severed both wires. On our way back to the aid station, I complimented him for spotting and defusing this giant booby trap.

In fact, I was quite proud of him for taking this action on his own initiative. Perhaps my intermittent fatherly talks during the past few days were beginning to pay dividends. At any rate his conduct today was worthy of a good Marine.

At this moment I thought it was timely to discuss his rough handling of his subordinates. He had to learn that gentle firmness would eventually produce greater compliance.

I said, "Griebe, I wish you would be a little gentler in handling our litter bearers. This has been their roughest day yet. Use firmness and patience, but keep them moving."

He answered a little sullenly, "OK, Doc, I'll try."

That bloody afternoon was a nightmare.

At one point Lieutenant Fischer of I Company came stumbling down the narrow, cliffside trail without his helmet. He was a handsome, rawboned man in his early twenties. His eyes had a wild, dazed look and the muscles of his grime-stained face were twitching rhythmically. His hands were jerking at the same rate as his facial muscles. His speech was slurred and almost incoherent because of an inability to swallow and salivate properly. With difficulty, the following story was pieced together.

I Company had pushed ahead of the rest of the battalion and had advanced almost to the top of Hill 362A. Then the enemy counterattacked in force. I Company was sure to get wiped out up there. They just had to get help right now.

As he talked, Fischer continued to hyperventilate, until he collapsed at my feet.

As his consciousness returned, I said, "Fischer, Colonel Robertson will take care of the problem. I'm going to send you back to the hospital for a couple days of rest."

He did not object. As he rode away beside the ambulance driver, he looked through me with a vacant, faraway stare.

Fischer was the only Marine officer to "crack up" in our battalion under prolonged severe combat conditions. Much to my surprise, his combat fatigue status lasted only forty-eight hours. He returned to full duty and served with distinction as the leader of his platoon until he was killed late in the operation. The esprit de corps of the Marine Corps certainly had a remarkable hold on these young officers. I never could understand why more of these men were not pushed beyond the breaking point.

At 1500 just after controlling the bleeding from a shoulder wound, I glanced up at the cliffside trail to the north. Four husky Marines approached carefully, inching a litter heavily burdened with a larger than average man. The helmetless head of the casualty was being cradled by a fifth Marine who brought up the rear of the procession.

When they reached the level land at the bottom of the cliff, I could identify the litter bearers as combat veterans from I Company. Combat Marines as litter bearers? They belonged on the front lines facing the enemy. What could have happened? The handsome masklike face on the litter with a ten-day stubble of straw-colored beard became Captain Gray, the commanding officer of I Company.

A pinkish blood-stained mucus was extruding from both nostrils, and a frothy foam was drooling down his chin. I ripped his shirt open but could detect no external wounds. Listening to his chest revealed a strong, steady heart action, but the bronchial tubes rattled with loud, bubbly rales. His muscle tone was completely limp. His pupils were widely dilated, as in a state of deep coma.

During this examination Thronson, the corpsman who had supported his head all the way to the aid station, hovered over me weeping unashamedly, occasionally clutching my arm while pleading, "Can you save him? You've got to save him. You can't let him die. We need him, we need him."

Meanwhile the four Marines who had brought Gray down the hill were milling around the casualty expressing similar thoughts.

I turned on them, "Knock it off, you jugheads. Clear out and head back up to I Company."

They turned to climb the cliffside to Hill 362A, and Thronson tried to tell me what had happened.

"We got to the top of the hill just as the Nips charged out of their caves. Gray called in close naval gunfire support. One large round landed too close. Wham! Gray and the three men with him got knocked flat on their asses. When I got over to them, the captain was the only one still breathing, but he was already unconscious."

Gray was mortally wounded, and there was very little that could be done about it. The concussion of that naval shell blast had caused severe cerebral damage. Many small vessels inside the brain had been disrupted, and the oozing serum would cause gradually increasing pressure on the swollen brain tissue. The only hope was that the brain damage was less severe than we feared, and the excess fluid would gradually be absorbed.

I ordered Allen to start a unit of plasma but to give him only one half of it. This small amount would replace the amount of serum lost from the blood stream, whereas too much would pass into the brain to increase the swelling.

At this point Hely arrived with the rear echelon of our aid station. Like all the rest of us he was quite dismayed when he saw Gray lying helplessly on the litter. Gray had always seemed impervious to death or injury. He was the last of our original company commanders and one of the most respected officers. No one could take his place in the eyes of his men. His loss would affect everyone's morale.

However, a new crisis quickly put an end to our despondent mood. Griebe, Rhoe, and litter bearer Brock presented me with an urgent problem.

Tears were streaming down Private Brock's face as he choked out his story, "Brautigen, Blauch, and myself went up the hill to get a guy from H Company. Just as we picked up the litter, a machine gun opened up. Everybody got shot dead except me."

Corpsman Rhoe interjected, "That's not the worst of it. The collecting company corpsmen are close to mutiny. They won't go out again unless armed bodyguards go with them."

I answered, "I'll see what I can do. Griebe, keep Brock busy in the aid station, don't send him out anymore today."

I then hurried over to the command post, which was located a few yards to the east. Lieutenant Familo was the only officer present. I demanded to see the colonel right away.

"If you really mean it," Familo said, "take that rocky trail up the cliffside. Keep your head down after the path veers off to the north."

I jogged up the trail, the roar of the battle reverberating louder and louder with each stride. At the 150-foot level where the path turned north, I paused momentarily to evaluate my further upward progress. Bullets were cracking by at very close range. Forty yards ahead, I could see Colonel Robertson and a small cluster of men huddled behind an outcropping of rocks. On closer observation I could also identify Major Mix, Captain Knutson, and several enlisted men as they helped direct the course of the battle.

Without waiting to be immobilized by caution, I dashed out at full speed to reach the shelter of a small boulder lying fifteen yards up the trail. From there I finally reached the advance command post by crawling up a slightly defiladed depression. Momentarily winded, I lay there unnoticed by my comrades. Small arms missiles were whipping by in several directions. As the bullets ricocheted off the rocks, small chunks of the hillside were intermittently showered down upon us.

When my strength returned, I slid up beside the colonel and clutched his arm. He turned in my direction, giving me a startled look as he shouted above the battle din.

"What the hell, Doc!"

He then leaned over me as he yelled directly into the ear of his radio operator, "Send this message in the clear to Kennedy in I Company: 'Bill, bring the men down on the double. We're pulling back.'"

I grabbed the colonel's arm again in another attempt to gain his attention. He tapped Knutson on the shoulder while pointing the other hand at me.

"Help Doc out if you can." Then he handed another message to his radio operator.

Knute crawled over beside me, asking, "What's the problem?"

I quickly outlined the difficulties of our litter bearers. We desperately needed combat Marines to protect our litter teams.

"Doc, we have nobody to spare."

"We've got to get help in getting new casualties out."

"There won't be any fresh casualties."

"How can you be so sure?"

"As soon as Kennedy brings I Company back down the hill, we pull back and shorten our lines."

"Will our aid station stay where it is?"

"No, get the dope from Familo. Now get the hell out of here."

It took me less than half the time to get down off that lethal hill. Familo pointed out our assembly area, which was three hundred yards to the south. Then I broke the news to our medical section. I would take the forward echelon with the bulk of the men. Hely's group would finish caring for the latest casualties and then would join us. I didn't mind this arrangement too much. It is much easier to advance to the rear than to go forward into unknown territory under hostile fire.

Fifteen minutes later, while we were frantically packing our gear, Knutson approached me, saying, "Hurry up, Jim, get your men moving. Our front-line troops will be digging in right here."

To lend force to this statement, G Company men had started scooping out makeshift foxholes on all sides of us. Also, reserve troops of the 26th Marines could be seen retiring southward on the lower slopes of Hill 362A at a slow, jogging pace.

Our new location proved to be on familiar terrain. We were to bed down among the enemy dead that we had passed earlier in the day, along with their bloated horses and broken artillery. A fresh sea breeze obliterated any offensive odors, but we were not too happy with this location. The reserve battalion of the 26th Marines was dug in just south of us. We would be in the direct line of fire if any of the enemy broke through our front-line troops from the north.

Doctor Hely brought the rear echelon back a good hour after darkness had settled in. Fortunately, the reserve battalion of the 26th Marines to our south did not fire any random shots in our direction. Hely's rear echelon had brought out all the remaining casualties and supplies except for a crate of plasma and a bundle of blankets that were abandoned on the newly established front lines.

My slightly built, redheaded Corpsman Prince reported in at about this time. Tears were running freely down his freckled cheeks as he sobbed out H Company's trials on Hill 362A earlier that afternoon. Corpsman Willis had been killed trying to protect two wounded Marines. The enemy persisted in lobbing handgrenades into the shell hole where he was working on these wounded men. Willis had tossed eight grenades back at the enemy successfully, but his luck ran out on grenade number nine. As Willis was Prince's best friend, he felt duty bound to inform the newly made widow of these tragic events.

Prince continued, "How can I tell his wife about his death? He could have saved himself after the first grenade landed by pulling back and abandoning his patients. As it turns out, all three of them are dead anyway."

I answered, "You know Willis could not have done that. He could never have lived with himself afterwards."

"Maybe not, but his wife and unborn child could have managed."

"No matter what, Prince, Willis is one of the real heroes of this day's bloody business. I'm going to recommend him for a posthumous Congressional Medal of Honor."

This suggestion seemed to appease Prince somewhat. To help him through a rough night, I asked Amrosino to bunk in with him. I would share with Corporal Wyatt, our jeep ambulance driver, a shell hole five feet deep and eight feet in diameter made by one of our battleships.

At 2100, two fresh casualties had to be evacuated to the hospital without delay. As Wyatt started back with them, I gave him strict orders not to return until daybreak. It was definitely too dangerous for a jeep ambulance to be traveling around at this late hour.

It would be a long, lonely night in the bottom of my shell hole. I was somewhat comforted by the proximity of my .45-caliber pistol. I

successfully test-fired the weapon twice. Amrosino had done a good job
of cleaning it out; the automatic slide worked perfectly. Sleep came soon
as the traumas of the day were lost in complete exhaustion.

At 2340 I was roughly wakened to a nightmare situation. The concussion from a nearby shell burst had sent half a cubic yard of sand cas-
cading down upon me. My right arm and shoulder were completely buried
and sand was infiltrating down my neck and up under my helmet into
my right ear. A few moments later, after extricating my arm and dusting
the sand from my hair, ears, and underclothes, I took time to consider
my dilemma. If I stayed where I was, a closer shell burst might bury me
alive. If I crawled out of my crumbling shell hole, I stood a good chance
of picking up some of that hot shrapnel.

After a brief debate, entombment lost out to the dangers of spending
the rest of the night in the open. I crawled up to the south border of the
shell hole and scooped out a shallow depression that partially concealed
my body. I kept a careful watch toward the north for signs of the infiltrating enemy. At the burst of each flare, I would strain my eyes looking
for some sign of hostile movement. My pistol was "at the ready" with
the safety catch released. With the aid of each flare, I also checked the
time, which seemed to drag by interminably. My determination to stay
alert and awake began to wane after 0200. My last recollection of that
dismal night came when a flare told me it was 0308.

March 1   D Day Plus 10

When next aware of my surroundings, I saw it was full daylight, and
friendly troops of the 26th Marines were wandering about the area.

I had not eaten in twenty-four hours; a search of my pack sack produced only dried biscuits and cheese. In past days consumption of these
concentrated K ration items had caused considerable heartburn and flatu-
lence. Only the ingestion of copious amounts of water made this diet
tolerable at all.

While washing down the last of the biscuits, I watched Pharmacist
Mates Radford and Rhoe poking around in some rubble about fifty yards
to the southwest. "What are you guys looking for?"

Radford answered, "Souvenirs. We must be in a smashed-up bar-
racks."

"What have you found so far?"

"Not too much, just some old dishes."

They showed me some cracked and chipped Japanese Army china

embossed with the regulation blue star. These finds stimulated me to rummage through the wreckage. I discovered one intact porcelain cup that served me well through the rest of the campaign. It was far better than drinking from my old tin cup.

On turning over a couple of planks I discovered a three-by-four-foot hole leading down at a sixty-degree angle. About two feet down into this cave I discovered a U.S.-made Columbia portable phonograph. As I fished the machine out, I found that it had been resting on the split-toed, rubber-soled shoes of an enemy soldier. The owner of the shoes was sprawled out face down farther into the cave, and from the pungent aroma that greeted my nostrils, he must have died some time ago.

I was delighted with my find. Although shrapnel had punctured the carrying case in several places and had bent the turntable, the machine was basically intact.

My delight with this new acquisition was diverted by a very disturbing sound. A paroxysm of coughing came echoing up from deeper in the cave. This coughing spasm had a hollow, unworldly ring as it bounced back and forth traveling up from the subterranean depths. It was a chilling thought that there were Nips inhabiting the apartments below us. If several of them were to suddenly pop out of that hole, we would be in trouble.

I called Rhoe over and said, "There are some live ones down in that hole. I heard one cough. Stand guard while I get reinforcements."

I enlisted the aid of the nearby 26th Marines. They were eager to help us get a few more Nips. A smoke grenade was dropped into the hole. Within minutes, white phosphorus smoke was pouring out of five other partly concealed openings, the farthest vent being fifty feet away.

The Marine corporal in charge said, "It's no use, Doc. They've honeycombed the whole north end of the island with caves and tunnels. Anybody that goes in after them will just get killed."

While we were discussing our problem, Captain Knutson arrived to give us the latest scoop. "Don't worry about those underground Nips," he said. "We just got new orders from division headquarters. Our troops are to be pulled out of the lines. March 1 will be used to regroup and reorganize."

"Where do we go to regroup?"

Knutson pulled out his situation map and pointed to a spot one third of a mile to the southwest as he said, "The whole battalion will bivouac in this area. Tie your medical section in with the command post."

While we were preparing to move, I bound up the wounds of my portable phonograph with three-inch gauze and placed the machine on the floorboards of the jeep ambulance, where it safely rode out the final three weeks of the campaign.

On the way back to our rest area, we passed through the 1st Battalion of the 28th Marines, who were on their way up to take our place in the front lines. These men were very unhappy. They felt badly put-upon, having captured Mount Suribachi. Helping to secure the north end of the island had not been part of the bargain.

I was appalled when we arrived at our so-called rest area. It was located on the open plain about halfway between the sea and the enemy-held high country to the north and east. We again were under the direct observation of the enemy gunners. Our only safety rested on the fact that many more lucrative targets were available.

The carnage of war littered the landscape with broken vehicles, abandoned weapons of all types, and the putrefying corpses of our stubborn enemy. These decaying bodies scattered over the uneven ground were attended by hosts of swarming and buzzing flies. I advised the colonel that elementary public health measures were urgently needed, and soon work details were busy.

When the dead were buried, the flies turned their attention to the living. Some of the more aggressive tried to crawl into our ears, mouth, and nostrils. Worst of all, their persistence was rewarded with the first helping of any of the food we tried to eat. A desperate call to division headquarters produced the epidemiologist and his special jeep. A liberal spraying of the area with DDT soon brought the fly population down to a tolerable level.

While fighting the battle with the flies, we were being harassed by our human enemies and their spigot mortars. We could hear these huge rockets take off from their launching pads in the hills to the northeast with a screeching roar. Within seconds the giant projectiles could be seen heading skyward as they appeared above the crest of the ridge. Each rocket continued straight up for several hundred yards. At the height of the journey, the size of the missile would appear to be reduced in size by 75 percent, then, for a brief moment, this lethal projectile would seem to hang suspended in space. While I huddled in a shell hole far below, I was certain that this engine of destruction was to land directly upon me. I closed my eyes, tensed my muscles, and waited for the end. When the earth-trembling explosion came, I was glad that the rocket had landed two hundred yards off to the south. None that were to follow came any closer, but each subsequent rocket at the height of its trajectory seemed to pause and then to descend directly at us as we waited helplessly below.

Several merchant ships had gathered some distance off the western beaches in hopes of discharging their cargoes. They must have hoped that the enemy's retaliatory powers had been reduced during the past ten days of combat, and to test this theory, one small steamer with one stack was sent in first. When the little ship got within three hundred yards of the sandy beach, two geysers of water straddled her bow, momentarily obscuring the vessel. As more rockets and shells landed about the ship, black smoke poured out of the single funnel as full power was applied to the twin screws to make a hasty withdrawal.

My corpsmen were delighted that they were no longer objects of the harassing fire, even though they wished the merchant vessel no bad luck. Soon wagers were being taken on the chances for the ship's survival. The odds were running four to one against her. However, Lady Luck sailed with her and she returned to the anchorage beyond shellfire range without taking a direct hit. When she was safe from further shelling, a fair amount of money exchanged hands among our corpsmen.

It was 0900 when I asked Griebe to call in all the medical personnel for a conference. When they were assembled, I began outlining the plans for the immediate future. "It looks now as if our planned three-day campaign is going to last several more weeks. I suggest that we start rotating all our men through the different 'duty' areas. In other words, I'd like to have the company corpsmen change places with the men now working in the aid station. I would like to know what you think of this idea?"

The first reaction came from our aid station corpsmen. I was very pleased with their response. In rapid succession, each man volunteered to trade places with a company corpsmen and accept the more dangerous duty. The only holdout was my reliable friend, Kramer. He felt that he was performing an essential job in tagging and logging the casualties. Kramer chose to ignore the looks of disdain being hurled in his direction as he pretended to study the battalion casualty book.

The corpsmen with G and H companies were also glad to trade places with our aid station corpsmen. Aid station duty was much less hazardous, and their chances for survival were greatly improved. I was quite baffled when the corpsmen of I Company took an opposite stand.

Thronson, acting as their spokesman, said, "We started with I Company and want to finish with them."

"Why do you say that?"

"We don't want to desert our Marine buddies." ·

"Do you really mean that?"

"Yeah, if we have a choice we'll stay where we are."

"You guys sure surprise me. OK, stay up there, but let me know if things get too tough later on."

At 1215 we were honored by a visit from Comdr. Chauncey Alcott, the division surgeon, and Lieutenant Dewgaw, the chief medical supply officer. Alcott was a handsome, fit man in his early forties. Dewgaw, being a warrant officer in the Regular Navy, was a bit older, with a moderate-sized paunch. My relations with these men had been excellent in the past. I liked them both and had been glad they represented our medical people at the division level; I was not prepared for their attack when they started talking with me.

Dewgaw presented the opening questions, "Vedder, why in the hell are you flouting naval regulations?"

"What regulations? Who told you that?"

Dewgaw continued, "Dr. Schultz, your regimental surgeon, gave us the word. He says you have been using the collecting company corpsmen improperly."

"How would Schultz know what is going on? We haven't seen him for the past ten days. Which regulations did I break?"

"Schultz says you were using these corpsmen for litter bearers. Is that true?"

"Yeah, I had to yesterday. All but five of my Marine litter bearers were killed or wounded. We needed ten litter bearing teams to remove the wounded from the front lines."

Dewgaw persisted, "So you admit to breaking naval regulations. Only Marines may carry litters."

"No, I admit to nothing. I only had to improvise. There were no Marines available. The collecting company corpsmen were not busy. They saved lives by getting casualties off the battlefield."

Dewgaw continued, "Vedder, you have broken naval regulations by using those corpsmen improperly. I am going to file an adverse report with General Rocky."

I turned my attention to Dr. Alcott, who had been uncomfortably shifting his gaze from one boot to the other during Dewgaw's interrogation.

I said, "Chauncey, how would you have handled the situation if we could have changed places?"

While looking over my left shoulder, he said, "I would have evacuated the wounded but would not have used corpsmen."

"How would you have done that?" I asked incredulously.

He answered, "That was your problem to solve. I wasn't there."

I had nothing further to say as they climbed into their jeep to head south toward division headquarters. At first I was very angry with Dr. Schultz for blowing the whistle on me. Then I had to admit that these men were right. Naval regulations clearly stated that *Navy corpsmen* were only to be used for their medical or surgical expertise. Naval regulations assigned the transportation of the wounded strictly within the province of the *Marine Corps* personnel. The drivers of the ambulances and other wheeled vehicles were all Marines. Where vehicles could not travel, Marines were required to carry the wounded out by hand. So by directing Navy corpsmen to function as litter bearers, I had flagrantly violated the Navy code.

However, it still was unthinkable to leave all those wounded Marines unattended out on the battlefield just to protect a Navy regulation. I did not feel guilty about using these Navy corpsmen illegally. I decided to consult with Colonel Robertson, and perhaps he would present my side of the story to General Rocky.

Five minutes later I plopped down beside the colonel on the edge of his foxhole and poured forth the details of my recent encounter. At first he appeared quite incredulous but soon broke into a hearty chuckle.

"Did they really hand you all that crap?"

"They sure did. What's more they are going to fix me up with a bad fitness report."

"That's just a lot of baloney."

"How can you say that? I did violate Navy regulations."

"Because I'm the only guy that can put a bad report on your record."

"Yeah, but what about those regulations?"

"Don't worry Doc, extenuating circumstances can temporarily void most Navy regs. Besides, I'll tell our side of the story when I see General Rocky this afternoon."

"Thanks, Colonel, I'll sleep better tonight."

A short time later while heating up some C rations hash on our Coleman stove, Griebe approached me, "I would like to borrow our jeep ambulance for a few minutes."

"What for?" I asked.

"I want to deliver the casualty report to regimental headquarters in person. In addition, I would like to visit with my old friend, Chief Pepper."

My first inclination was to say no. Then I recalled that Griebe's conduct had improved since our frank talk on February 27. In addition, he had performed well yesterday at the foot of bloody Hill 362A.

So reluctantly I said, "OK, Griebe, but be damn sure to be back with the jeep by 1430. We will need it to transfer medical supplies this afternoon."

While consuming my lunch of lukewarm hash and dry biscuits, I made a quick survey of our bivouac area: the enemy bodies were interred; fewer flies remained; but the wrecked equipment of war was still strewn helter-skelter over the landscape.

At 1600 Dr. Hely came over to see me. His scowling countenance told me he was bringing a problem with him.

He said, "That worthless Griebe has run off with the jeep ambulance. H Company has been ordered up on the high ground to serve as a reserve for the new front-line troops. They need the vehicle to haul up extra litters, splints, and plasma."

"I gave him permission to use the jeep to deliver the casualty reports to regimental headquarters, providing he returned by 1430."

Hely replied, "That makes him one and a half hours overdue. He and his buddy, Pepper, are probably getting drunk on the regimental brandy supply."

"I hope you're wrong, Charlie. I don't want to be forced to keep that promise I made aboard ship unless he comes back plastered. I want to see him as soon as he gets back."

At 1815 Griebe and the jeep ambulance returned in the half darkness. Ten of my corpsmen surrounded the vehicle and greeted the one occupant with enthusiasm. Within seconds three of the men detached themselves and hastened over to my foxhole, where I was greeted by a chorus of gleeful anticipation.

"Griebe is drunk, drunker than a skunk. Griebe is drunker than a low-bellied skunk."

As I approached the jeep, I was alarmed by the hostile comments.

"Now's our chance to get rid of the sonofabitch. We can stuff him down one of those cave holes and let the Nips down below slice the bastard up."

When Griebe saw me, he ventured a silly, slack-mouthed grin. "Everyone keep your hands off Griebe until I get back from seeing the colonel," I said. I did not want Griebe or anyone else pushed down one of those tunnels.

A few minutes later, I was seated beside Colonel Robertson telling the story. I started from way back on shipboard when I had warned the men of the dire things that could happen to any of the medical personnel who got drunk while on combat duty. Then I mentioned the hostility Griebe had engendered among the men under him by his negative attitude and lack of leadership qualities. Most of all I feared for his personal safety if he were to be restored to active duty with our battalion when he sobered up.

The colonel then said, "I would like to see how bad off he is. Bring him over here."

When I returned to the jeep, Griebe was still seated in the driver's seat. The entire medical section was standing by with eager anticipation. "Griebe, get out and come with me. The colonel wants to see you."

Compliance with this order was attempted unsuccessfully. As soon as his second foot hit the ground, he stumbled and fell flat on his face. No one helped him stagger to his feet.

I said, "Come on Griebe, the colonel is waiting for you."

As he started weaving and wobbling forward, I grasped his left arm to lend a steadying hand. While hurriedly negotiating the rough, uneven land in the darkness, Griebe stumbled into a small shell hole and I was jerked off balance; as he fell, I landed on top of him with considerable force. When he sat up, he began to vomit into his lap. Between retching episodes he sobbed and babbled incoherently.

A few moments later I presented him to the colonel, who was seated before his Coleman stove brewing coffee. All his staff officers were present. The odor of brandy-laced vomitus that emanated from Griebe's clothing was overwhelming. When I released my grip on his arm, he collapsed in a heap at the colonel's feet. The colonel demanded, "What have you got to say for yourself, Griebe?"

The only answer was uncontrolled weeping interrupted by spasms of retching as he continued to eject the contents of his stomach.

The colonel then glanced at his assembled officers and asked, "Is there any question about what we have to do with this man?"

The opinion was unanimous. We had to get rid of Griebe.

The colonel then pulled out a note pad and began writing. When he finished, he called for his orderly.

He said, "Deliver this man to the provost marshal at the prisoner of war stockade and give him this written order."

Griebe was carted off to be locked up with the Jap prisoners—too bad, but at least we could be certain that he would return stateside in one piece, and there was no longer any danger of his being pushed down one of those cave entrances or killed by an "accidental" discharge.

March 2   D Day Plus 11

Church services were to be held today at 1000. The Protestants would worship in the nearby spigot mortar crater, and the Catholics would assemble among the wrecked enemy antiaircraft guns. Both locations were incongruous settings for Christian gatherings.

I drifted over to the site of the Protestant service, which the Japanese had recently excavated with one of their huge, rocketlike mortars. The pit was slightly larger than those made by our 16-inch naval shells. About forty men had preceded me: some were sprawled out on the steeply sloping banks of the great hole; others were clustered in small groups on the surface nearby holding subdued conversations; and four men playing cards sat on the edge with a small pile of American currency between them. The game was five card draw poker, jacks or better.

Promptly at 1000 the chaplain's jeep appeared. After unloading Reverend Valbrecht, the portable organ, and the organist, the driver then took Father Calkins to the designated site for the Catholic services. Valbrecht announced that his pulpit would be the bottom of the spigot mortar hole. Volunteers helped the organist haul his instrument down level with his pastor sixteen feet below ground level.

By the time Valbrecht was ready to start the service almost a hundred parishioners had joined him in and around this man-made amphitheater. Garbed in the vestments of the Lutheran church, Valbrecht presented an imposing picture, despite the dirty dungarees that lay under his religious trappings. When he removed his helmet and his wavy blond hair floated about, he appeared even taller than his six feet two inches.

He called out in his deep, sonorous bass voice for all men to bare their heads and join him in prayer.

As we put our helmets back on, Valbrecht asked his organist to play "The Battle Hymn of the Republic," which was sung by all in a lusty fashion. Then our pastor read briefly from the Scriptures, which included the Twenty-third Psalm. After another hymn, he launched into a brief sermon with the message that the Lord was our shepherd and He would look after us. After singing a few more hymns, we were dismissed, to be greeted by our Catholic comrades returning from their mass nearby. After the services the men seemed rejuvenated. They appeared much more relaxed, they walked straighter, and some were even able to break into subdued laughter for the first time in days. I thanked both Father Calkins and Reverend Valbrecht. I hoped they would return to us after our next tour of front-line duty was completed. This request was honored several times during the next three weeks.

Before leaving for regimental headquarters, Father Calkins, still garbed in the vestments of the priesthood, solemnly approached me and said, "Vedder, I'm glad to see that you are still with us. Do you recall that traumatic artillery shelling we suffered through on the afternoon of D day?"

"How could I forget it? I've never been so scared before or since."

"I'm going to let you in on a little secret."

I answered, "Good, let's have it."

"Never before have I prayed harder for the salvation of a non-Catholic. I want you to know that my prayers will still be going with you."

"Thanks much, Father. I will need all the help I can get."

The rest of the day was spent receiving and integrating replacements into our battalion. Corpsman Meegan, who had a first class rating, was selected to replace Griebe. We were especially happy to get a full complement of Marine litter bearers. These new men were only eighteen or nineteen years old but did their best to adjust to our alien environment; some had a great deal of trouble, and a few died trying.

One of them, Corpsman Dewolfe, had been drafted out of a New England high school shortly before his nineteenth birthday. He had graduated with his class in absentia. He looked like a cherub—curly brown hair, wide-spaced eyes, and an upturned nose. Although he tried to conform to the rigors of military life in the front lines, he managed to muddle even the simplest orders. I advised Meegan that we should break him in gradually and not send him out to one of the front-line companies for a few days. I would keep him in my foxhole with me; for the time being, Amrosino would bunk in with Prince, who was still quite depressed over the untimely death of Willis. To date, he had been unsuccessful in composing his promised letter to Willis's widow.

March 3   D Day Plus 12

At 1400 on March 3 the dreaded order came. We were to move back up to the high ground and function as the backup battalion for the 28th Marines. Late that afternoon we began trudging up toward the front lines loaded down with all our combat gear. While passing through I Company, I was called over by Corpsman Bacan to see a recent leg wound inflicted by a stray bullet. The casualty was doing an improvised jig on his good right leg, while blood flowed from a superficial muscle wound in his left calf. His joy at receiving a minor wound was so great that it took a bit of persuasion to get him to lie down for an examination. While we dressed the injured leg, he babbled ecstatically about all his old girlfriends back in San Diego. Soon he would call on them one by one and make up for a lot of lost time. Meanwhile his buddies looked down on him with scarcely concealed envy.

Our bivouac area for the night was a small sugar cane field on the southern slopes of Hill 362A. The 28th Marines had secured the entire hill during the past two days of fighting. I assigned Dewolfe the task of digging our foxhole as I proceeded forward with Colonel Robertson and

Captain Knutson. During the past two days, the 28th Marines had pushed our lines a third of a mile northward. Our combined command post and aid station was to be located on the summit of Hill 362A the following day.

When we arrived near the crest of the hill, we found a desolate lunar landscape. All vegetation had been blown into limbo. A rudimentary road skirted the northwestern flank of the summit, then wandered down toward the enemy-held north. To the east of this road lay a relatively flat area about a half acre in size. Our new aid station was to be located on this site the next morning. To the east of this level area, the terrain degenerated upward about twenty feet into a tangled mass of large rocks and medium-sized boulders, where a number of partly closed cave openings were scattered. Farther on, a sheer drop of twenty-five feet formed a cliff down into a small ravine below the eastern boundary of our boulder-strewn field. On the face of this rock wall a huge gaping cave stared back at us. The opening measured ten feet wide and fourteen feet high. The tunnel of this huge cave led back to the west directly under the ground we were going to inhabit.

The colonel and Knutson were not satisfied with our location, as the enemy could infiltrate the position with relative ease. However, there were no better locations to choose. The entire north end of the island was honeycombed with interconnecting tunnels and passages. The colonel recommended that Knute bring up a demolition team in the morning to close the giant cliffside cave. Knute also commented that night sentries would have to be posted around the command post perimeter. In addition, a second perimeter of defense would have to be established inside the outer ring. This plan would require that half our medical personnel take turns guarding the other half while they slept. I returned to our temporary camp in the sugar cane field.

On retiring to my foxhole, I encountered a strange situation. Dewolfe was curled up in the bottom, which lay four and a half feet below ground level. Even though the soil was a soft, sandy loam, it was incredible that he could have dug such a deep pit in such a short time. Lying on my abdomen, I reached down and gently shook him awake.

"Dewolfe, get up and climb out of that hole! You've dug it too deep. If that sand caves in or if a shell lands nearby, we can both get buried alive."

Without protest he helped me push sand back in until our foxhole was only two feet deep.

After stretching out on my canvas litter preparing for a restful night's sleep, I noted that Dewolfe was huddled up against the eastern margin of our foxhole with his back toward me. Only after I heard the audible sobs did I note the spasmodic heaving of his chest muscles.

I placed my arm over his jerking shoulder and applied gentle, reassuring pressure.

I said, "I'm sorry I got a little rough with you while we were filling in our foxhole. You just did too good a job by digging it too deep."

As he calmed down and gained control of his emotions, he said, "That had nothing to do with it. I just got to worrying about things back home. My mother is not too well. Maybe she needs me right now. I am her youngest son and have never been away from home before. Oh God, how I would like to be home for just a short time."

At this point my homesick boy broke out unashamedly in alternate bouts of shuddering and sobbing. My attempts to alleviate his suffering were totally unsuccessful. In fact, my efforts to console the lad only called forth renewed outbursts of uncontrolled weeping. An hour later, just before I drifted off into troubled sleep, I could still hear an occasional choking sob.

Sending him back to his mother would have quickly cured his illness. However, that favor was not in my power to grant.

Chapter Nine

D Day Plus 13–15

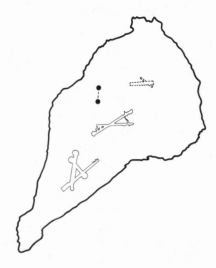

March 4   D Day Plus 13

As we struggled up to the summit of Hill 362A, on March 4, encumbered with our full battle gear, we encountered elements of the 1st Battalion of the 28th Marines heading the other way. Soon I was face to face with their surgeon, Dr. Jim Bond.

He said, "Glad to see you, Vedder. Tell your boys to get on the stick and clean up the rest of the island. We don't want to come back up here again."

"What happened? Was the north end rougher than Suribachi?"

"Hell, yes! It was many times worse! They were banging away at us from every nook and cranny."

"I'll pass your request on to our 27th Marines. By the way, do you have any supplies left over that can be left with us?"

Bond answered, "Sure thing, Jim. You can have all our leftover blankets, plasma, and splints." Before parting we set an indeterminate rendezvous date at the Camp Catlin Officers' Club in Hawaii.

As we moved into our new combined aid station and command post on the top of Hill 362A, it looked even less inviting than it had appeared to the colonel and Knutson last evening. The boulder-strewn field rising to the east with the partly closed cave openings staring back at us made our new bivouac area seem positively unhealthy. After hopping over the boulders to check out the far eastern border of our command post, I found myself staring down at the huge cave cut in the cliff wall twenty-five feet

131

below me. Six men abreast could readily come charging out of this opening. I could visualize a battalion of the enemy pouring out to overwhelm us during the long hours of darkness. I would feel much better when Knutson's demolition team arrived and closed this gaping cavern.

A quick scouting trip around the edge of our new command post convinced me that the colonel's judgment had been sound. There were no better sites available in the immediate vicinity. The enemy had burrowed into the north end of the island better than an army of gophers. We would have to maintain great vigilance during the night if we were to avoid being cut to pieces.

On returning to our new aid station, I marked out a spot about twenty feet east of the road and requested that Dewolfe start digging our foxhole while I attended to the immediate needs of our medical section. A short time later he stood dejectedly before me.

He said, "I can't dig nothing. That mud is hard like a rock."

"Really," I said with disbelief as I took the trenching shovel from his hands. I was certain that we were dealing with another facet of this young man's ineptitude, but a few moments of effort convinced me that Dewolfe's assessment had been correct. The hard-packed volcanic soil was totally unyielding.

At that point Corpsman Allen offered a helpful suggestion.

"Why don't you use the jeep ambulance's pickax? It worked real good on our foxhole."

By midafternoon Dewolfe had planted our two canvas litters the required two feet below ground level.

Although our men of the 27th Marines were now occupying the front lines five hundred yards north of us, we had no casualties to treat. They had been ordered to hold their positions for the time being and maintain a low profile. The enemy in turn made no attempt to dislodge them.

By late afternoon in the battalion command post area we had made our final preparations for defense. Then, after a hasty snack of C rations, everyone bedded down in his respective foxhole before complete darkness settled in. A raw northwest March wind made the 40 degrees Fahrenheit seem even colder. However, no one suffered from the cold; our volcanic island home furnished us adequate heat in this location. The earth temperature in the bottom of our foxholes was slightly over 100 degrees, so we were quite comfortable with only one blanket covering us.

I dozed off with pleasant thoughts of home and family on my mind. Dewolfe's fingers digging into my shoulder quickly brought me back to reality. In a loud whisper he said, "The Nips are after us. Hear them digging? They're coming up to get us."

During the past few days the nights had become much quieter because the enemy's counterbattery artillery fire had fallen way off. Perhaps the Nips had fewer pieces to fire at us, but more probably our stubborn adversary was compelled to conserve his remaining ammunition for more productive targets. On this dark, cloudy night the loudest sounds came from the frequent popping of our own exploding flares.

I said, "Keep your voice down, Dewolfe. Your whispered voice carries out a good fifty feet. If there are any Nips out there, your whispered shouts will draw them right to us."

"I'm sorry, Doc. I'll keep my voice way down."

In the meantime I placed my ear flat on the ground between our litters. Dewolfe was right. There were sounds of human activity coming up from below. Most of the noise beneath us was like metal striking against rock. These sounds could have been produced by metal picks striking against unyielding lava.

I placed my ear, my cheek, and the palms of my hands firmly against the floor of our foxhole. With each metallic clang coming up from below, I could feel no concomitant vibration against my hands and face. This discovery convinced me that any new tunneling under us was proceeding either laterally or deeper into the heart of the volcano. So I said, "Relax, Dewolfe, and go to sleep. The Nips down below are digging down deeper to get away from us. Don't wake me up again unless something new happens."

Dewolfe did not appear to be too convinced; he was still wild-eyed and jumpy. He said, "I'm not a bit sleepy, Doc. I'll stay awake and keep watch."

"OK, Dewolfe, but don't bother me again until you see a Nip crawling about on top of the ground; he's the only one that can hurt us."

Within minutes after this comment, I was again sound asleep.

March 5   D Day Plus 14

A few hours later a forceful blast accompanied by handgrenade fragments whistling close overhead jolted me into full consciousness.

I asked Dewolfe, "What's happening?"

He answered, "I'm not sure, Doc. Right after a flare popped off, a rifle shot came from the direction of the naval gunfire section across the road. Then the grenade exploded right near us."

I carefully peered over the rim of our foxhole with the safety catch released on my pistol. In the darkness I could barely discern the outlines of our jeep ambulance, which was parked only ten feet away. When the next flare gave us light, I thought I could see a prone figure huddled behind the rear wheels of the jeep. If it was a man, it certainly did not move. After twelve more flares, still no movement could be detected. By this time I felt that daylight would turn my imaginary enemy into a small heap of medical equipment. I congratulated Dewolfe for using restraint and not firing his carbine at this imaginary enemy.

In the half dawn Dewolfe again aroused me by digging his fingers into my shoulder. "Doc, there is a Nip lying out behind the jeep ambulance."

Dewolfe was right. A human form was sprawled out behind our jeep. As the light improved, patient observation showed that the man was very dead. The top of his head had been blown open. His uniform identified him as a member of the enemy garrison. Next to the body lay a sack containing a dozen handgrenades. Fortunately for us, the wounded victim had chosen immediate suicide rather than lobbing his reserve supply of grenades in our direction before dying for his emperor.

His billfold contained ninety-five yen and several photographs. One poignant photo showed our recent adversary dressed in a white uniform of the Imperial Navy. He appeared as a handsome young man seated in a small formal Japanese garden. Two small boys, each in the three- to five-year range, balanced happily on either knee as they fixed their adoring attention in their father's direction. Behind them stood a smiling young woman dressed in a gay, flower-patterned kimono. It was hard to believe that the mutilated corpse at my feet was the same individual, though not so hard for me to identify with his family. The husband would never return to his wife, and the children would never get to know their father. My thoughts then turned to my wife and two boys waiting for me back in San Diego. If fate had so ordained, our roles could have easily been reversed. I gave silent thanks to God that my children were not yet orphaned or my wife widowed. The body was disposed of in a nearby shell hole and covered with the rubble that had been excavated from our foxholes yesterday. A plasma box propped up at the end of a broken bayonet bore this epitaph, "Here lies one good Jap." Although the grave site lay in the center of our medical working area, my men avoided trampling on or desecrating his last resting place in any way.

Welcome news came down from headquarters while we were finishing breakfast on March 5. Although our troops now occupied the frontline positions, no orders to resume the attack were issued. The day was to be spent in reorganization and integration of the many replacements with their combat units. Therefore, we could expect few—possibly no—casualties.

While making the rounds visiting with my corpsmen, I ventured the wistful thought that it would be great to take a shower and remove the accumulated dirt and grime of fifteen days in the field.

Corpsman Bukowski, who had overheard this casual remark, said, "I know where you can take a rainwater bath."

I answered, "You've got to be kidding."

Even as I made this statement, I knew that I could take Bukowski's offer seriously. During the past seven months I had never known him to fabricate, tell tall stories, or engage in practical jokes. Until his recent reassignment to the aid station, he had served with distinction as the senior corpsman with G Company. As was his custom, he looked me straight in the eye with a deadly serious countenance without the trace of a grin or a smile.

"You know me better than that, Doc. I would never fool you on an important matter like this."

"OK, Bukowski, tell me; how do I go about taking my bath?"

He answered, "Just follow me a few yards off to the northwest. Many barrels of fresh water are half buried in a big circular pit about one hundred yards across."

I asked, "Is it safe to go wandering out over there?"

He replied, "There's no danger at all. The 28th Marines captured the place three days ago and there are no cave openings there."

Radford, from Tennessee, one of my bright-eyed younger corpsmen, chimed in, "There's lots of water left. I took a bath earlier this morning. Don't forget to take the ax from the jeep. The lids have to be chopped off."

A short while later, the three of us were cautiously picking our way over the rocky, uneven terrain in a northwest direction. Bukowski and Radford had their carbines ready for action. I carried the battalion's ax, a towel, and a clean pair of skivvies. On reaching the crest of a small ridge, we found ourselves looking down into a small inactive crater of the dormant volcano, which measured about one hundred yards in diameter. Inside the crater we could see the tops of thirty-two barrels that were two-thirds buried in an arching row twenty feet from the crest. The lids had recently been torn off four of the barrels.

Bukowski said, "Hand me the ax and stand guard with my carbine. I'll knock the top off a fresh barrel."

While he was so engaged, I carefully surveyed our circular amphitheater. It seemed deserted except for one rectangular opening below one of the barrels.

I said, "Radford, there is someone in that cave over there."

I fired one shot in the general direction while Radford placed four carefully aimed rounds into the opening. Then he rushed over to inspect his handiwork. A short time later he returned with some tattered remnants of clothing.

With a happy grin Radford said, "That was no cave, it was just a small storage chamber."

The water from the newly opened barrel was very clear and soft. It converted my GI soap into a slippery, foamy lather. With my steel helmet held high overhead to serve as an improvised showerhead, the lukewarm water streaming down over my body was the most delightful sensation I'd enjoyed since leaving the *Sandoval*. It was especially nice to get all the food and grit washed from my inch-long beard and to shampoo my shaggy, sweaty, matted hair. The only disagreeable moment came when my grimy old dungarees had to be pulled over the brand new skivvies.

When we returned to the command post, Lieutenant MacCumbie, the third and most recent commanding officer of H Company, was waiting to see me. He had only recently graduated from Officers' Candidate School. He took command of his company like a "gung ho" Marine officer even though he knew his two predecessors had died violently in the line of duty.

"Hello, Doc, H Company is short one corpsman. Meegan suggested a guy named Dewolfe might fill the bill."

I called Meegan over and asked, "Don't we have anyone else to send up with Lieutenant MacCumbie to H Company?"

Meegan answered, "I'm afraid not, Doc. Except for Kramer and Amrosino, all the rest of the corpsmen have been on the front lines for several days. Amrosino is deaf, and Kramer is our indispensable keeper of casualty records."

I turned to MacCumbie and said, "Dewolfe came to us three days ago. He was so jumpy that I was sure he'd blow a gasket if we sent him up to the lines. Since then I've kept him with me in my foxhole."

MacCumbie asked, "What kind of a job will he do if he goes to H Company?"

"He seems to have settled down. Last night he kept quiet and held his fire when we were infiltrated by the Nips. If Rhoe, your new senior corpsman, takes charge and lends him a hand, he might make the grade."

MacCumbie said, "If that's the best you can do, we'll take him up with us. I'll be back to get him after I discuss some other matters with the colonel."

A few moments later, after last-minute counseling, I watched Dewolfe slog off at MacCumbie's heels as they threaded their way toward the front lines with all their combat gear on their backs.

The day passed quickly and not too unpleasantly. Brunner and Aarant, recycled corpsmen from I Company, led the group in singing the latest country and western music.

Upon returning to my foxhole at 1730, who do I find curled up and asleep? Dewolfe! I jabbed him in the ribs and asked, "Dewolfe, what are you doing back here?"

He answered, "I don't know, I got real scared. I had to get back before dark."

"What did you do with your gear?"

"I left it in the H Company's command post."

"Did you get permission to come back?"

"No sir. I just took off. I just couldn't stand it."

"Do you know what they do with deserters under combat conditions?"

"No sir."

I was about to quote Navy regulations when Dewolfe broke down in tears and begged, "Please give me another chance."

He presented such a pathetic picture that I wanted to send him home to his mother. Instead, I cranked up the field telephone and asked the operator to get Lieutenant MacCumbie on the H Company line.

"Hello, Mac, this is Doc Vedder. Did you lose a corpsman this evening?"

He answered, "Yeah, Corpsman Rhoe can't find that new guy, Dewolfe."

"He's back here with me. It's too late to send him up alone. He'll come back in the morning. I wish you would give him a second chance."

"OK, Doc, if you say so."

After dark things were a lot quieter than the night before. The sounds of enemy activity beneath us were greatly diminished. We were still apprehensive about the large cave opening just to the east of us, for two double charges of TNT had failed to seal it off completely. The enemy under us could readily emerge to infiltrate our positions at any time during the night.

March 6   D Day Plus 15

Trouble broke out at 0040 on our eastern perimeter where the 81mm mortar section was camped. First came the roar of bursting handgrenades, which was soon augmented by a loud clatter of small arms fire. I did not peer over the edge of the foxhole to investigate, as large chunks of shrapnel were whistling by close overhead. Dewolfe slid over onto my litter and did his best to crawl beneath me as he clutched my arm tightly. I grabbed the telephone and desperately attempted to contact the operator. The instrument was dead, probably a victim of the shrapnel barrage.

In less than two minutes silence again returned to our bivouac area. The only disturbance came from the more frequent popping of the overhead illuminating flares. Suddenly a figure appeared from the vicinity of the naval gunfire section to the southwest of us.

This individual came running in our direction shouting, "Doctor, Doctor, where are you? Doctor, why don't you answer me? Doctor, we need your help."

Recalling stories of past Japanese trickery, I remained concealed as I pulled back the slide to arm my pistol for instant firing. He could be one of the enemy masquerading as a Marine. As he came closer, it seemed that he was too small to be an American. Although he was less than twenty feet away, I still held my fire. If I were to miss him with the first shot, Dewolfe and I were sure to get blasted by handgrenades.

A quick glance in Dewolfe's direction showed that our total defense revolved around my inaccurate .45-caliber pistol. He was prepared to make no move to help in our joint defense; while he clutched my side tightly, his carbine was resting unattended on his litter.

When the unidentified man came within ten feet of our position, I began to squeeze on the trigger with a slow, steady pressure.

Fortunately, the man cried out again, "Oh, Dr. Vedder, why don't you answer me? We need your help."

Quick reasoning told me this man had to be one of our own, as none of the enemy could possibly call me by name. As I returned my disarmed weapon back to its shoulder holster, I gave thanks to God that I had been spared from firing at one of my own men.

I stood up and beckoned our visitor to hurry over. He jumped into our foxhole, identifying himself as a seaman in the naval gunfire section. Major Mix had sent him over to get help for some brand-new casualties. At this point I was glad that Dewolfe's terror had frozen him into immobility, otherwise he would have had his carbine zeroed in on this lad, and there was a good chance he would have fired that lethal shot. As it was, I came within a fraction of a second of doing the same thing with my pistol.

By the time I reached the aid station working area, my corpsmen had just brought in the last three men on stretchers, and Dr. Hely was examining them. Captain Knutson and several other Marines were observing the activities.

Hely said, "These guys are all dead. Looks like they got blasted from the front by .30-caliber rounds. They have small, clean entry holes over their breasts with large, ragged exit wounds on their backs."

Knutson said, "These men were all battalion cooks standing guard in the outer perimeter near that large cave."

He then turned to the enlisted man standing next to him and said, "Scottini, you were standing watch with these men. Tell us what happened."

Private Scottini, having just lost three of his fellow cooks, was visibly shaken. He blurted out a rather incoherent story.

"Everything was quiet. Suddenly the Nips started tossing handgrenades our way. My buddies jumped up. I stayed low. Many shots came from the 81mm mortar section. My buddies dropped dead all around me."

As he concluded, his agitation increased. His eyes rolled vacantly in all directions. The grip on his carbine increased as the weapon began jerking spasmodically. At this moment Lt. Joe Stees, the commanding officer of the naval gunfire section, crossed the road to be briefed on the recent happenings.

Without warning Scottini flipped up his carbine, taking quick aim at Stees as he called out, "Look out, there's a Nip coming."

Fortunately the weapon misfired as it was clogged with sand.

It took Knutson and Corpsman Thronson almost a minute to disarm our struggling, irrational cook.

After Scottini was escorted to a safe haven, Knutson shouted, "Head for your holes, you medics. Take cover."

"Why the rush, Knute?"

"If we keep milling around, the Nips may just walk in and wipe us out like they did one time on Bougainville last year."

"OK, you birds, do what the captain says. Get out of sight. Meegan, see everyone gets the word."

Seconds later I slid down into my foxhole as Dewolfe moved over to his own litter.

"Jesus, Doc, am I glad you're back. It's scary in here all alone."

"Keep alert! Wake me if you see any prowlers."

The enemy infiltrators did not trouble us again that night. We were allowed five hours of uninterrupted sleep.

When I approached the command post on that dull, overcast morning of March 6, I found Knutson already working on organizing our security measures for the coming night. He dispatched a detail to regimental headquarters for enough accordian barbed wire to encircle our entire bivouac area. A hurried call went through to division headquarters to send up another demolition team. We would have no peace until that huge cliff-side cave was permanently closed. The stacked bodies from last night's fracas were being loaded on a passing truck. They were to be dropped off at the 5th Division cemetery.

When these arrangements had been completed, Knute said, "Jim, how would you like to go with me and check out the infiltration route used by the Nips last night?"

I answered, "Sure. Lead the way."

He took us on a circuitous southeasterly course, hopping from boulder to boulder, that led toward the cliff marking the eastern border of our encampment. After leaping over two of the dead enemy, we veered due east toward the cliff. Within ten yards of the drop-off, I noted a dead Marine, neatly covered with a poncho, lying directly below the boulder I was then resting on. A few feet ahead, two more of the enemy lay sprawled where death had overtaken them.

I was just about to step over the dead American when Knutson turned back and shouted, "Hold your position. Don't move."

While giving this order, he raised his carbine and fired one shot into the body of our fellow countryman. The corpse uttered an animal-like cry and the feet jerked convulsively. Within seconds Knutson had pumped six more shots into this animated dead man before he again lay still.

Before I could utter a questioning word, Knutson jumped down from his boulder and jerked the poncho away. His carbine was ready to fire again should it prove necessary. At our feet lay a very dead Nip. Beside the body lay the inevitable sack of handgrenades. The corpse lying at our feet obviously planned to reside under a Marine poncho until nightfall, when he would try to eliminate as many Marines as possible.

Having recovered my voice by this time, I asked, "How did you know there was a live Nip hiding under that poncho?"

Knutson answered, "It was quite simple. The morning casualty report was just sent to regiment. All our dead and wounded were accounted for. As the body under the poncho could not be an American, it had to be one of the enemy. If the body were a dead Nip, who would have covered it so neatly with a poncho? Not the Marines! The answer was quite obvious. The body had to be very much alive and had covered himself with the poncho!"

This sound deductive reasoning could not be faulted. Knutson, by his clear thinking and quick actions, had saved a good many lives!

When I returned to my foxhole, I found Dewolfe still huddled up on his litter nervously gnawing on a K ration biscuit. He presented a sad picture of total dejection. It seemed unlikely that he would ever become an asset to our medical section. My impulse at that moment was to sign him out as a combat fatigue casualty and send him to the rear.

But second thoughts ruled out this simple solution. The morale of the whole group had to be considered. After all, Dewolfe had yet to serve any front-line duty. Many of his comrades, who were just as frightened as he, were functioning well under adverse conditions. If Dewolfe were sent back now, how many others would elect to follow the same course? So Dewolfe had to go back to H Company.

I said, "Dewolfe, get out of that hole and come with me over to the command post. Lieutenant MacCumbie wants you back."

He complied in a painstaking fashion, but without protest. I turned him over to Lieutenant Pope in the communications section. He was to accompany the first detail making the next trip up to H Company.

While the coffee was brewing on our Coleman stove, Colonel Robertson dropped in for one of his routine visits. As he settled slowly to the ground to accept a cup of hot coffee, he appeared both weary and worried. His usual calm self-assurance seemed shaken for the first time.

"What's gone wrong, Colonel?"

"Plenty, the Nips bagged Butler's jeep at a road junction southwest of here."

"How bad was he hurt?"

"Killed instantly."

"Who'll take over the 1st Battalion?"

"Warnham is sending up Colonel Duryea from regimental headquarters."

"I hope he can fill Butler's shoes."

"He'll do all right, but that's only part of the problem. Kennedy will move over as his executive officer."

"That's not fair—not Kennedy!"

"I agree, Doc, but all the field grade officers in the 1st Battalion have been wiped out."

"Why can't they send up a major from the regimental pool?"

"They don't have many left. Besides, Warnham thinks Mix and I can run the show here."

"Yeah, but what happens if you get clobbered?"

Robertson gave me a relaxed smile, "My luck isn't going to run out."

"But what if it does?"

"Warnham will find someone to come up to give Mix support."

Colonel Robertson then placed his empty cup beside our stove. As he rose to continue his rounds, he said, "By the way, Doc, you will now have to look to Familo for any help needed around the command post. I will be needing Knutson and Mix up forward at all times to coordinate the movements of the front-line companies. They will be required to carry out the duties formerly performed by Kennedy."

I answered, "Good luck, Colonel. I still wish Kennedy could finish the operation with us."

Late in the day, while I watched our evening stew simmer, Corpsman Radford greeted me with an amused grin, saying, "I'll bet you can't guess what I saw in your foxhole just now."

"It couldn't be Dewolfe, could it?"

"Yup, he's all rolled up in his poncho asleep on his stretcher."

"Thanks for telling me, Radford. Let him stay there until I get around to the problem." A little later I sought out Chief Meegan and said, "Dewolfe has funked out for the second time. He's over there bedded down in my foxhole."

"What would you like to have me do, Doc?"

"Call up MacCumbie in H Company and tell him what's happened. Get his permission to send Rhoe back here just for tonight. We'll send both Dewolfe and Rhoe back to him well before sunup."

When Rhoe arrived, I said, "Gil, I need some help for my present foxhole buddy. I wish you would take charge of him right now and take him up with you to H Company very early tomorrow morning. Maybe your steadying influence will encourage him to follow your example."

Rhoe said, "I'll do my best. Can Amrosino bunk in with you tonight? Dewolfe and I can use his foxhole."

"That sounds like a good idea, Rhoe. Amrosino is getting so deaf that he'll be better off staying with me from now on."

The night of March 6 passed uneventfully. The encircling coils of accordian barbed wire and the final closure of the large cave had effectively eliminated all hostile enemy activity. The movements of the enemy beneath us were also greatly reduced. Even so, I looked forward to the coming day with a feeling of dread. Our battalion had been ordered to drive straight ahead and seize Hill 215, which lay a half mile due north of our present location on Hill 362A. To attain this goal, our front-line troops would have to advance only half that distance, but through cut-up, ugly terrain. Only time would tell us how many maimed and mangled men would pass through our hands before the new day was done.

Chapter Ten

D Day Plus 16 and 17

March 7   D Day Plus 16

March 7 was a dull, overcast day. A brisk northeast wind produced a chill far below the 50-degree Fahrenheit temperature. The assault had been launched a half hour before sunrise. Now, some three hours later, we had no calls for litter bearers.

This was unprecedented. In the past, calls to come and remove casualties would be pouring in only minutes after a renewed assault got under way. Now, three hours later, not one call for help had come from even one of our three attacking companies. This was strange, not at all reassuring. Something terribly wrong had to be going on. Maybe the attack had bogged down, or had been called off at the last moment. With feelings of foreboding, I proceeded over to the command post for the latest information.

"What is going on, Familo? Did the attack get called off?"

"No such thing. The unbelievable has happened. Our men have moved downhill a hundred and fifty yards toward Hill 215 without opposition."

"If there is no contest, why did it take three hours to travel such a short distance?"

"There are two reasons. First, they do not want to walk into a trap. Second, the land they are traversing is fit only for mountain goats. The land goes up and down with no level spaces."

"Familo, I don't know why, but I'm getting bad vibrations concerning today's operation, as though something terrible is going to happen."

Familo said, "Doc, quit worrying yourself about tactics. Go back to your aid station and get your medical section ready to move up when the need arises."

On returning to the aid station, I found my men gathered around the coffee pot singing hillbilly songs with Corpsman Aarant serving as director. Aarant certainly had a melodious tenor voice; with some formal training, he would very likely rise to the top in the world of music.

My men were delighted to learn that the Nips were giving ground without a fight. Maybe we would be embarking aboard ship in the next few days.

I called Meegan aside and said, "I don't like what's going on up forward. The Nips have got to be planning something bad for our people. Get our medics ready to move on instant notice. Our Marines may be walking into a trap."

We finished lunch at 1200, and still no calls came for litter bearers. Returning to headquarters after lunch I asked Familo for the latest report.

"The troops are still moving cautiously forward without contest. They have covered over three hundred yards since they jumped off this morning. I'm glad you came over. The colonel just called in. He wants us to move the command post up closer. So get your medical people packed up now."

"We're two jumps ahead of you, Familo. We are all packed up and ready to move as soon as we get the word."

At 1500 a messenger asked me to report to headquarters. Familo greeted me with the latest developments, "Our troops occupied Hill 215 without firing a shot, but as soon as they started working down the north slope toward the sea, all hell broke loose. The Nips were waiting for them, and now all our companies are pinned down by intense knee mortar and small arms fire. They are reporting heavy casualties, so get your medical section on the move."

"Where do you want us to locate our aid station?"

Familo circled a spot on my situation map about six hundred yards north of our present location. It was located just southwest of Hill 215.

I asked, "Can we get our jeep ambulances through to this point?"

Familo answered, "Our bulldozers have just worked it over. I think the jeeps can make it if they use their four-wheel drives."

Before 1600 we were digging in on a flat patch of coarse black sand, the only level piece of land visible in this corner of the island.

To the east the boulders on top of Hill 215 looked down on us. Although the crest of the hill was only one hundred yards away, we were separated by two deep ravines and a sheer precipice of forty feet on the hillside itself. Fortunately the entire hill belonged to our Marines, so we would not have to evacuate any casualties from these intimidating structures.

To the west the sea was blocked out by a low, north-to-south, irregular ridge that rose only ten to twenty feet above us. To the north the land fell away one hundred fifty feet from our present location to the sea a half mile away. However, this distance to the sea was obstructed by a series of eight blocking ridges with sharp serrated tops resembling long rows of oversized sharks' teeth. As they approached the sea each ridge was about ten feet lower than the one closer to us. Through the gaps between these sharks' teeth, we could catch occasional glimpses of the sea below.

It was in this lacerated territory that our men were now fighting, and each casualty would have to be brought up over these ragged ridges to our aid station. This giant washboard terrain would be much more difficult to traverse than similar areas in the badlands of South Dakota. Six-man litter teams would be needed to rescue our casualties. To the south a well-worn footpath led back up toward Hill 362A, now several hundred yards behind us. The new road promised by our bulldozers ended one hundred yards to our rear. Our treated casualties would have to be hand-carried back up the footpath to our ambulances waiting at the end of the bulldozed road. A hasty call to Familo extracted a promise that the dozers would return soon to complete the road.

Just as the first casualty arrived from the front, I happened to glance up the footpath to our rear. A man on a bicycle was coming down the hill hooting and hollering while waving his right arm in the air. Our mad rider slid to stop and Corpsman Allen materialized. While hopping off the bike, he flashed a smile, saying, "Doc, look what I found in the gully."

"Don't be stupid, Allen. Just leave it there."

"Why?"

"Some bypassed Nip will pop you off as you sit high and noisy on that bike."

"Aw, Doc."

"We already have some casualties in the aid station. Get over there and give our replacement corpsmen a hand taking care of them."

Soon our aid station was filled with mutilated and wounded men. Our jeep ambulances were able to remove the casualties fast enough so that we experienced no congestion in our working area. All of the wounded were arriving from either I or G companies. However, we were receiving desperate pleas for help from H Company. They had been leading the advance and were trapped the farthest forward. None of our litter teams were getting through to remove their accumulating casualties.

About this time, young Corpsman Kendo came straggling in with his left arm dangling uselessly at his side. After a .30-caliber bullet had shattered both bones of his lower forearm, Kendo had worked his way back from H Company. A slightly built teenager, Kendo had always been a cheerful, spunky fellow. Between grimaces of pain that gradually lessened as the Syrette of morphine took effect, he gave us valuable information concerning H Company's predicament. H Company was caught in a pocket below and to the north of Hill 215. To get out, one had to scale a series of five- to eight-foot jagged rock steps. Kendo gave Corpsman Fox a careful description of the only feasible route down to H Company.

While Kendo was giving directions to Fox, I wondered how Rhoe and Dewolfe were making out in that cauldron of death where H Company was trapped. I hoped that Dewolfe would be able to function as a useful corpsman. Rhoe would be far too busy with casualties of his own to be of much help to Dewolfe.

Following Kendo's directions, Fox successfully led three litter teams of six men each to H Company, and before darkness fell they were able to evacuate all the wounded. On the last trip, Fox was rewarded with a flesh wound in the left calf.

As I dressed his wound, I complimented him on his gutsy performance. Before this day I had always seen him as a rather immature, freckle-faced teenager who belonged at home with his family. How wrong I had been! He had completed a man's job this day, over and above the call of duty. He certainly deserved his trip to the naval hospital. His only response to my praise was a weak smile as he took a deep drag on his cigarette.

Good news filtered down from headquarters. The 28th Marines were going to relieve us early the next morning.

March 8   D Day Plus 17

The first casualty arrived very early on March 8—a small-boned, frail-looking figure, garbed in oversized Marine dungarees with a wide bandage covering both eyes.

Dr. Hely checked his dog tags and said, "My God, it's Morrison."

Corpsman Morrison was a shy lad of eighteen, who appeared much younger. He had joined us as a replacement a few days before and had been readily integrated into our combat unit. In the early morning hours, while he helped his buddies repel an enemy counterattack, a grenade had exploded on the edge of his foxhole, blowing sand and dirt into both his eyeballs.

Although Morrison had received a Syrette of morphine only three hours earlier, he was again grimacing and clenching his jaws in an effort to control the pain. A half hour after giving him a second shot of morphine, we were able to cleanse the eyes with a saline solution. After rinsing out much debris to better assess the damage, we could see that the injuries to the cornea were quite formidable. Both corneal surfaces were pitted with multiple embedded foreign bodies. Each one would need painstaking removal. The job could be done only in a well-equipped hospital.

As we loaded him aboard the first ambulance returning to the rear, I shook his hand and thanked him for a job well done. At the same time I said, "When you get back to Guam, the eye surgeons will fix up your eyes as good as new."

His only response was, "I hope so."

Soon calls came to evacuate other men who had been wounded during the long night. Most of them had relatively minor wounds from mortar or grenade fragments. One young Marine private was at the other extreme. He had received multiple grenade wounds several hours before. Although he was no longer actively bleeding, he must have lost a lot of blood, as he was in deep surgical shock. His color was ashen white, no pulse was palpable, and the respiratory effort was shallow and irregular. It looked as though he had passed the point of no return and that death was inevitable.

If his life were to be saved, the volume of fluid in his circulatory system had to be restored immediately with blood plasma. Because of shock, the veins remained collapsed even after tourniquets were applied to the arms and legs. The corpus cavernosum of the penis was the only avenue left open to receive the life-restoring plasma; however, I doubted whether that approach would prove successful.

After thrusting the needle into the shaft of his penis, I was gratified to note the free flow of the plasma from the bottle. By the time the first unit was near completion, the circulation had been improved sufficiently to permit the use of an arm vein for additional plasma administration. By the time he was loaded on the ambulance, the man was fully conscious and asking about the whereabouts of his buddies.

Although the 28th Marines were busy relieving our troops from their front-line duties, the enemy was very uncooperative. Our 27th Marines had pushed a salient out into enemy territory the day before and were surrounded on three sides by the hostile Japanese. The division commanders had ordered our fighting men not to give up any of this hard-won territory. As a result, the retiring 27th Marines and the advancing 28th Marines both acquired unavoidable casualties from the encircling enemy.

Sergeant Jacobson of the 28th Marines was the most remarkable of these casualties. Separate mortar bursts had produced gruesome injuries. One blast had shattered his upper right arm, and the second round had landed between his thighs, producing massive areas of shredded muscle. In addition, his scrotum had been sliced open, leaving both testicles fully exposed to an alien environment.

Maj. Fred Mix, who had accompanied Jacobson back with the litter bearers said, "Take good care of him. He is one of my old buddies from South Pacific days."

"Sure thing, Fred, I'll do my best."

At this point, Jacobson interrupted our conversation by asking, "How about sewing my nuts back in first thing?"

After closely checking his multiple wounds and noting from his evacuation tag that morphine had been given less than an hour ago, I said, "That sounds like a reasonable request."

After tucking the testicles back into the scrotal sack, I began the painstaking task of closing the gaping scrotal wound with interrupted silk sutures. At the same time, Hely was removing foreign matter and tying off bleeders in the shattered arm. Corpsmen Allen and Thronson were busy administering plasma and dressing the thigh wounds.

While the above procedures were being performed, a not unusual dialogue began between Mix and Jacobson. Morphine injections frequently inspired many of our hard-bitten combat Marines to discussion.

Jacobson opened the conversation by making the following observation, "Looks like we are going to let our top brass down today."

Mix: "How are we going to do that?"

Jacobson: "Our orders are to secure the rest of the island and mop up the remnants."

Mix: "That's a dumb order. Our troops are looking at a gorge two hundred yards across that extends seven hundred yards back up from the beach. Looks like the Nips will be making their last stand in this pocket."

Jacobson: "I guess the 28th won't be making much headway today."

Mix: "I'm afraid not."

During this conversation, the two men chain-smoked the same cigarette. Mix would take the first puff. Then he would hold it to Jacobson's lips for the second drag. This process would then be repeated until the exhausted cigarette was discarded for a fresh one. This smoking did not hinder their rapid-fire conversation, which soon shifted to the early war years.

Mix said, "Wish I could offer you a nice cold beer like we used to have on Guadalcanal."

Jacobson: "Yeah, it sure would taste good right now."

Mix: "This is a lousy island. We have no beer and no one that could take it upstairs for cooling."

Jacobson: "Ramsey was a great fly-boy. He was always willing to take a case of beer up to twenty thousand feet for an hour, and he never charged us more than three bottles."

Mix: "Wish we could get back to Nouméa again and sample some of that French cognac."

Jacobson: "Remember that crummy bar down on the waterfront, where those three frog-faced boys jumped me?"

Mix: "That sure was a good fight."

Jacobson: "It was great to have the Navy's champion welterweight on my side, or the Frenchies would have cleaned my clock. Thanks again, Fred."

While they worked on cigarette number six, the emergency repair job was completed. Jacobson was loaded into the ambulance. The two old friends said an almost tearful goodbye.

Our last troops from H Company were not extricated until 1400. Corpsman Rhoe came over to see me a short while later. His careworn face was streaked with grime and dust. Thirty hours without sleep had made him appear much older and quite withdrawn. He was no longer the same amiable farm boy from Minnesota that had left us less than two days ago.

I said, "Looks like you had a rough time up there with H Company."

"It was worse than that. I'm lucky to be alive."

"What happened?"

"Late yesterday they blitzed us with knee mortars. One round glanced off my helmet and landed on its side without exploding. If the detonator had been activated, I wouldn't be here now."

"It looks like the man up above was looking after you. By the way, how did Dewolfe make out?"

"He did real good. He got over his fright and treated casualties along with the best of us."

"I'm sure glad to hear that. Tell him I want to talk to him later on."
"I'm sorry, I can't do that. A mortar round exploded on top of his helmet and it killed him instantly."

Although I had known Dewolfe for less than a week, his sudden departure brought feelings of both loss and shock. Until that moment, I had been unaware how close my attachment to this young man had become. Together we had faced death several times during those long nights on Hill 362A. There was some comfort in knowing that he had died honorably, while performing his duty serving his fellow combatants. Still, a vague sense of failure could not be completely eradicated from my consciousness.

While we were working on our last casualties and making preparations to move back to a reserve position to the southeast, two Marine privates stopped by for directions. Each man was equipped with a flamethrower and a carbine. They were attached to division headquarters and were bored by the inactivity of the rear areas. They had been given the day off.

They asked, "Where can we find some live Nips? We would like to fry a few of them."

I said, "There are lots of stray Nips in the ravines due north. Be careful or they may nail you first."

Twenty-five minutes later, the two men approached us slowly from the north as they struggled up over the jagged, broken landscape. One man had lost his carbine but still had his flamethrower strapped to his back. He had extensive first- and second-degree burns of both hands. The other man was minus both his flamethrower and his carbine. Both of his hands were clutching his left flank just below the rib cage. Closer inspection showed that he was holding several loops of intestine in his cupped hands.

Our two action seekers had not caught any of the enemy but had been ambushed in their own turn. One rifle bullet had broken the flamethrower and set it afire. The same bullet then passed through his left abdominal wall in a tangential direction, slicing it open as neatly as a surgical incision. One loop of small intestine had been torn open and three other loops of bowel protruded around this ruptured segment of intestine. The other Marine had burned his hands while tearing the burning flamethrower from his buddy's back.

After rinsing off our hands with 95 percent alcohol, Dr. Hely and I both went to work on the bowel injury. Attempts to push the uninjured loops of intestine back into the abdominal cavity proved futile. As soon as one loop would be pushed in, the patient would grunt with pain and another loop would pop out elsewhere. It soon became obvious that it would be impossible to replace the intestines without the help of a general anesthetic.

Because the man would need extensive surgery and repair of the damaged loop of bowel at the hospital, a foolproof mode of transport would have to be devised. If he were bounced back to the rear in the ambulance in his present condition, the hospital personnel would find most of his intestines dangling out onto the floor of the vehicle by the time he arrived.

To prevent this, delicate Alyce forceps were attached to the edges of the torn intestine. Small strips of saline-soaked gauze were then tucked between these forceps. Then a row of towel clamps were fastened to the skin margins on both sides of the wound. Many strips of moist gauze were placed between the Alyce forceps and the skin clamps. In this way the normal loops of bowel were covered. Then Corpsman Smith was seated beside the patient in the ambulance with all ten fingers holding the moist dressings firmly in place. By this technique the man was successfully evacuated without experiencing any further evisceration of the intestines.

As they left, I said, "Smith, don't come back until you bring all of our instruments with you. We can't get any replacements."

In obeying this order, Smith was not able to return until the following afternoon, because our medical bureaucracy moved slowly in the rear areas.

Our aid station finally pulled back and rejoined the rest of the battalion at 1600. Being in reserve, the 3rd Battalion had set up camp high above the sea a short distance south and east of recently captured Hill 215. Our battalion area was strewn with wrecked enemy searchlights, antiaircraft guns, and ancillary equipment. Except for the irregularities produced by numerous shell and bomb detonations, this bivouac area was the smoothest terrain of any place we had camped since leaving the protection beside Airfield 1 on February 27. We could readily walk from one point to another without making long detours.

We tied in with headquarters company serving as the northern part of the perimeter of defense. I lent Amrosino a hand in digging our foxhole for the rapidly approaching night. The soft soil in this location enabled us to complete this task in short order.

I had just opened a can of C rations when exciting news spread through the encampment with electrifying speed. A truck had just arrived from division headquarters bringing fresh-baked bread and several pots of hot pork and beans. This was our first real cooked food since landing on the island eighteen days ago. I have never enjoyed hot food more than I did then. After a long drought, small favors are often very much appreciated.

The morale of the men was boosted only temporarily. While we feasted on this rare treat, the rumor mills again began to operate. One ominous report stated that we would have to move over to the east side of the island and capture territory in the 4th Division area. To support this conjecture, we knew that the 1st Battalion of the 27th Marines was already fighting to the northeast of Airfield 3. The general consensus was that we had had enough and should be evacuated forthwith.

War dogs were most effective in detecting enemy infiltrators trying to penetrate front lines at night. Official USMC photo

Author is lying beside photographer peering over the screening bank of sand, watching our rocket trucks fire. Official USMC photo

A typical shell-hole aid station. Official USMC photo

Corpsmen giving aid to some less serious cases. Official USMC photo

Medical Ward tent. After the third day casualties could be evacuated here. Official USMC photo

A land mine injury on the rocky north end of the island. Official USMC photo

A Navy Chaplain kneels beside a wounded Marine—a casualty from an artillery regiment. Official USMC photo

Communion at Mass atop Mt. Suribachi. Official USMC photo

5th Division Cemetery. Cross in foreground marking grave of John Harland Willis.

Close-up of the Willis Gate at Naval Air Station, Memphis, Tennessee. Willis was awarded Medal of Honor posthumously.

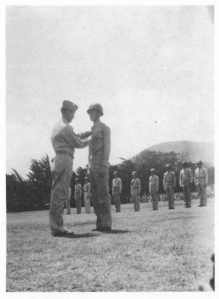

General Hermle pinning Silver
Star on author, Tarawa, April
1945.

March 24, 1945, en route back to Hawaii. Left to right: Vedder, Gass,
Familo, McMullen.

Chapter Eleven

D Day Plus 18–21

March 9   D Day Plus 18

March 9 proved to be a quiet day in the regimental reserve. In the early morning, trucks arrived and started taking relays of men to the rear for shower baths. The Seabees had built a series of shower stalls on the west beaches not far from the foot of Suribachi. Although I had enjoyed my recent shower with Bokowski and Radford, this one was far more satisfactory. The water flowed more freely, and there was no danger of being ambushed by the enemy.

On the way back I stopped off at the 5th Division hospital to visit Pvt. Tuffy Gilbert, who was the brother of my sister-in-law. He had been wounded in early March while serving with the 28th Marines.

The hospital was housed under canvas, and it appeared to be the scene of utter confusion. Persistent inquiry finally determined that young Gilbert had been flown out to Guam two days earlier. During my search, I encountered two of my old corpsmen from the Field Medical School in San Diego. When they saw the tattered and filthy condition of my dungarees, they gave me two complete changes from the supply tent of the hospital.

I said, "Gentlemen, my uniform is in prime condition compared with the dungarees worn by some of my corpsmen. How about tossing a few more pants into the back of the ambulance?"

These newfound treasures were accepted with great enthusiasm when I returned to our battalion headquarters in the northern highlands. I assigned Acting Chief Meegan the task of doling out these garments to the corpsmen in greatest need.

The ugly rumors that had been circulating yesterday afternoon were now confirmed. The 4th Division was to be withdrawn from combat and removed from the island on March 10. Our 3rd Battalion was to be shifted over to the east side of the island, and we were to capture territory previously assigned to the 4th Division. It just did not seem fair that we had to keep fighting while they made a clean escape from this hellhole. After all, both divisions had landed at the same time on D day, and they had suffered equal punishment ever since. We had captured all the territory assigned to the 5th Division. In all fairness, we were the troops that should be sent aboard ship the next day.

Some of our more disgruntled troops claimed that all the Marines should be evacuated forthwith. We had destroyed the enemy's unified command structure. Their resistance had been broken up into isolated centers of last-stand defense. This situation would afford the newly arrived Army garrison troops a fine opportunity to demonstrate their prowess. These unbloodied Army troops could liquidate the remaining pockets of the enemy at their leisure. After all, the first two airfields had been secured and they were both operational. Crippled B–29 bombers had been making emergency landings on these airfields on their return from Japan every day for the past week. We had been told ever since leaving Hawaii that our main mission was to secure these two airfields.

On approaching the command post in headquarters company, I noticed several company officers clustered about Robertson's foxhole while he worked at tying his bootlaces.

The ongoing part of the conversation I overheard came from Lieutenant Nelson of I Company.

"But why are we being shafted?"

The colonel looked up at the men after tying the last bootlace, "Who says we're being shafted?"

Lieutenant MacCumbie burst out, "I do, and the whole caboodle of us!"

"What should be done?"

The assembled lieutenants sang out in unison, "We took all our assigned territory. We should get pulled out tomorrow instead of the 4th Division."

Robertson slowly rose to his full height and, looking down on his junior officers, said, "You men are dead wrong."

Some of the men began to back off, but MacCumbie was not ready to give up.

"Why the hell *us*?"

"Their casualties were much worse. The 5th Division's fighting efficiency is still fifty percent better than theirs."

Lieutenant Brennan interjected, "Fifty percent of nothing isn't much. Why can't the dogface troops finish the job? Then we could leave with the 4th Division."

"I'm all for that, but these garrison troops are under Army control. Our Corps command can't order them around."

Nelson spit out his wad of tobacco, "So we get shit on again."

The colonel fixed his gaze directly at his officers, "Does anyone have anything more to offer?"

MacCumbie swallowed once, seemed about to speak, but remained silent. The colonel then suggested they return to their units and start looking after the welfare of their enlisted men.

By early afternoon the morale of our idle men had reached a new low. Perhaps none of us would leave this infernal island alive. If our casualties continued at the present rate for another two weeks, no one would be left to walk up the gangplank.

I said to the colonel, "Our men have pretty well hit bottom. Could we get Valbrecht and Calkins up to hold church services again? It did a lot of good last week."

A few hours later our chaplains were holding separate Protestant and Catholic church services in our bivouac area. The restorative powers of prayer and devotion again proved to be a remarkable tonic.

Later in the day a few of our men began to taunt, hurl threats, and throw clods of dirt at a score of enemy prisoners that were working on the nearby road. In no uncertain terms, Knutson told them to "knock it off." These men were all Koreans who had changed sides and were now our allies. From now on they were to be treated with respect.

A short while later a somewhat dispirited Meegan approached me, "I've got a problem that I can't solve alone."

"What is it?"

"Thronson and his buddies from I Company are sitting on some 10-in-1 rations, and they won't share them with the rest of the medical section."

"Why not?"

"He won't give me any reasons. He's resented me ever since I was made acting chief. He's ugly and surly whenever you or Dr. Hely are not around."

"OK, Meegan, I'd better talk to them alone. Where can I find them?"

"They're behind that wrecked truck over yonder." Meegan pointed to a partially demolished enemy sound detection truck that had been flipped over on its side.

I approached this rendezvous area with certain misgivings. I knew that a confrontation between these two men was a very likely possibility, but I just hoped that it would not happen. I found Thronson, Aarant, and two other I Company corpsmen settled down in a medium-sized shell hole immediately behind the truck. They were sampling an opened case of 10-in-1 rations. Three unopened cases were stacked beside them.

When Thronson noted my presence he greeted me with a sullen, defiant stare and a determined, out-thrust chin. He was a handsome son of a gun with crew-cut black hair and a thick stubble of jet black beard—Humphrey Bogart in one of his angry moods.

Thronson had the charismatic ability to attract other men. He could be very charming and ingratiating when necessary. It was obvious that the three junior corpsmen with Thronson were sympathetic to his cause, and the 10-in-1 rations would not be surrendered without a struggle.

I said, "Hi, men. It looks like you guys are stocked up with some good chow. How did it come your way?"

Thronson said, "We traded with some division quartermaster troops."

"How much did it cost you?"

Thronson answered, "One Nip saber, one rifle, two belt buckles, and a dozen uniform buttons."

"They sure made you guys pay a lot."

Thronson added, "I guess so. We were just real hungry."

"Now that you birds are members of the aid station section, how would you like to share with the rest of our corpsmen?"

Thronson scowled as he said sullenly, "We got our souvenirs on the front lines with I Company. These 10-in-1 rations should be ours to eat."

I could sympathize with his viewpoint, but after Griebe had sequestered all those 10-in-1 rations early in the operation, we had all agreed to share and share alike while working in the aid station. Besides, I could not undercut Meegan.

I said, "Thronson, ever since Griebe swiped all the 10-in-1 rations, we have followed an equal shares policy. You men have been aid station corpsmen since March 3. When you get back to I Company, you can make separate arrangements with your company commander. In the meantime, all four of you lend a hand and bring those rations over to the jeep ambulance for division."

While complying with my request Aarant's fine tenor voice said, in a quiet undertone, "Simmer down, Thronson, I think Doc is right."

Before settling down for the night, I made the rounds of our inner defense perimeter. I reminded the men to be fully squared away for a move at 0530. We would eat breakfast after we set up in our new location north of Airfield 3. The 1st Battalion of the 27th Marines would be on our right, and the 21st Marines would support our left flank.

March 10   D Day Plus 19

By 0800 on March 10, we were settled in our new position a short distance north of Airfield 3, which ran from east to west. Only three thousand feet in length, it was much shorter than the other two airfields. The rough stones and small rocks on its surface attested to the fact that our invasion had interrupted its completion.

With the help of field glasses, from our high-ground observation point we could look beyond Airfield 3 to observe the construction crews at work on the two southern airstrips. Many bulldozers were scurrying about pushing up high mounds of earth large enough to form revetments able to contain and protect our B–29 bombers.

The airstrips themselves were dotted with crawling roadgraders busily smoothing rough spots on the fields. Each roadgrader was followed by a ponderous, slow-moving steamroller carefully packing the loose earth into a hard, flat runway.

There were many small fighters and light bombers scattered about the edges of both fields, but the most impressive sight was three B–29 bombers, and a fourth just landing on its return trip from Japan. It gave us a warm feeling to see that these airfields were operational.

The terrain presented new problems in the handling of casualties. Our bivouac area was tied in with the southern rim of the defense perimeter of headquarters company. We were camped on the northern end of a V-shaped draw. The point of the V was considerably lower and it lay a three-minute walk to the east. The lower arm of the V headed back southwest an equal distance, where it gradually rose to meet the only road in our area. As our casualties were being brought in and evacuated by ambulance, we would have to operate our aid station beside this road. Even though our 81mm mortar platoon was set up just south of our new aid station, infiltration dangers would not permit us to spend the night there. It was imperative that we rejoin our comrades in headquarters company for defense each night.

The path from our foxholes in the headquarters bivouac area to our aid station working area presented a problem. The shortest distance lay over the high ground between the two arms of the V. However, the volume of small arms fire made this a very risky route. Bypassed enemy on the highlands to our east could readily identify human targets through their telescopic rifle sites on this short, elevated route. The safer path led down the ravine to the point of the V and then back up the southern end of the draw to the road and our jeep ambulances. Later that day, Colonel Robertson assured me that it was extremely dangerous to take the short route to the aid station. He put out an order to all personnel. All traffic from the campsite to the aid station would use the long detour down the draw and back up the southern arm of the V.

As our 3rd Battalion Marines were not in the assault that day, we had only occasional casualties that drifted in from other units to treat and evacuate. We were hearing a lot of bullets passing above us most of the day. The colonel assured us those bullets were passing high overhead, but they sure sounded close!

Two men from the engineer battalion demonstrated the dangers of souvenir hunting. They had been poking about in the ruins of Motoyama village, just south of Airfield 3, when a bypassed resident tossed a grenade at them before withdrawing into his cave and tunnel system. They were lucky to receive only multiple superficial wounds for their efforts. I advised my men to stop all souvenir hunting in this dangerous area.

Later that afternoon I received a call from Dr. Hely, who was manning the aid station at that time.

"Jim, I got some good news."

I answered, "Great, what happened?"

"Wentworth came by and dropped off sixteen one-gallon cans of pineapple juice. Could you send a detail to tote them back to the headquarters area?"

Because of their value as an item of barter for other foods, I took charge of the entire supply in order to manage an equitable distribution. I stacked the cans two tiers high along the north rim of our foxhole. I instructed Amrosino to keep a careful eye on them during my periodic absences when called to the aid station.

A few minutes later Lieutenant Familo called me over to the command post.

He said, "Here's some dope you should pass on to your men. This scoop is hot out of division headquarters. General Kuribayashi, the top Nip commander, and the bulk of his remaining men are holed up in one square mile just to the north of us. The center of the resistance is that deep gorge that the 28th Marines ran into a few days ago. As you know, it stopped them cold. The gorge is two hundred yards wide on the sea coast and extends back inland one half mile. Its depth varies from a hundred to two hundred fifty feet. We are to advance into that canyon and wipe them out tomorrow."

"That sounds like a big order. What are our chances of succeeding?"

Familo answered, "Not too good, even though the top brass at division headquarters say it will be a breeze."

At 1800 we had our first contact with our "dogs of war." Without warning, our command post was invaded by ten ugly-looking dogs, each weighing between 75 and 125 pounds and held on a short, tight leash by his Marine master.

The animals appeared docile enough as they sat quietly, but when a stranger approached within the length of the leash, they would snarl, growl, and crouch down in preparation for a leaping attack. A verbal command from a master would instantly turn off this belligerent attitude.

These dogs had been trained to attack man-sized dummies dressed in secondhand Japanese uniforms retrieved from battlefield corpses. The animals could identify a night infiltrator by his Japanese odor.

The dogs' handlers requested guides to lead them up to our front-line companies where they were to stand guard duty during the night. The animals had been trained to kill, and they would attack any enemy infiltrator without hesitation.

I asked the sergeant in charge of this group if one or two of the dogs could bed down with our medical section. He was sorry, but all of his canine squad had been assigned to the front-line troops.

During the subsequent days the war dogs became a part of our daily routine. They would arrive shortly before dusk to take up their positions in the front lines. Then a few moments after sunrise they would again make their appearance as they retraced their path back to the rear areas for a day of rest and relaxation with their masters—all but those who had been killed on night patrol.

March 11   D Day Plus 20

At 0305 on March 11, I was roughly jolted awake by several large shells that exploded in our vicinity in rapid succession. One burst was so close that dirt and sand was showered down on us. I didn't realize it at first, but those shells came from the Nips. In spite of his deafness, Amrosino was finally roused by all the commotion.

Two minutes later he leaned over and whispered hoarsely, "It doesn't hurt yet, but I think I've been wounded. My right shoulder is all wet and sticky. I must be bleeding pretty bad."

After reaching over and touching him, I had to agree. His dungaree jacket and sleeve were saturated with a wet, sticky substance. How could he have been hit by shrapnel while lying in the bottom of our foxhole! My flashlight soon solved the mystery. Three of the large pineapple cans had been wounded, and the juice was still freely flowing down onto Amrosino's back and shoulder. From the damaged cans we managed to salvage two canteen cups of the precious nectar. If that one shell had traveled just twelve feet farther, it would have wiped us out, along with all sixteen cans of the pineapple juice.

At first light on that cold, windy dawn, the final attack on the last pocket of organized enemy resistance got under way with a minimum of preliminary air, sea, and land bombardment. A few minutes later our war dogs began passing through our positions. A quick count showed ten handlers but only eight dogs. The enemy infiltrators had been very active during the long night, and two of our dogs in their zeal to attack had died heroes' deaths. In turn, the Marines had taken a heavy toll of the attacking enemy.

By the time our aid station personnel finished our breakfast stew washed down with pineapple juice, it was apparent that something had gone wrong. We had received no calls for litter teams. If the attack had been progressing, we should have been swamped with casualties. I felt the need of a quick consultation with Familo.

On approaching the command post I asked, "What's gone wrong?"

Familo answered, "Plenty. Things are going to hell, but they could be worse."

"Tell me about it."

"First the attack bogged down in all sectors when the men ran into a withering fire. Then while holding a conference as they walked down a lateral trail, all three of our battalion commanders got blown up by the same land mine. Colonel Duryea of the 1st Battalion stepped on the antipersonnel land mine, losing an arm and a leg, Colonel Antonelli of the 2nd Battalion got blinded by crap blown into his eyes, and our Colonel Robertson was knocked on his ass but was only shook up."

My first spontaneous comment was, "Thank God we still have Robertson."

After making this statement, I felt a bit guilty. After all, both Duryea and Antonelli were capable young officers and I wished them no bad luck. However, Robertson stood out as an exceptional commanding officer. I felt that no one in our regiment, including Colonel Warnham, could measure up to this exceedingly capable man. He was well versed in military tactics and strategy and possessed the intelligence to use this knowledge wisely. Even more important, he was a born leader of men. The men trusted his judgment and would follow him willingly into situations that led to almost certain death.

Because he spent so much of his time on the front lines with his men, it was a continuing worry that he might not survive this operation. Now it looked like divine providence was working in his favor.

Then I asked Familo, "Will Bill Kennedy take over the 1st Battalion?"

"Yes, he's already in charge and should do a good job."

"Who is going to take over Antonelli's place in the 2nd Battalion?"

"I don't know. Colonel Warnham is about out of new commanding officer material. They may send up some staff officer from division headquarters."

"When will we resume the assault?"

Familo answered, "Not today. Our regiment has to have a little time to digest two new battalion commanding officers. I think we'll be ordered to start all over again tomorrow."

On returning to the bivouac area, I passed the recent unpleasant developments on to my corpsmen.

Amrosino said, "We sure are lucky that our colonel didn't get clobbered too bad. Dr. Hely just called in. He has a big problem over in the aid station and would like to have you come over right away."

I was tempted to take the short cut over the high ground, but caution overruled this action. As I trudged down one side of the V-shaped detour and then up the other side, I wondered about the wisdom of this choice. Those bullets whipping by overhead sounded so close, and the direct, over-the-hump short trip would involve less exposure time than this long, back-and-forth detour. However, now was not the time to ignore the colonel's orders.

Hely said, "Thanks for coming, Jim. We've collected some bad land mine casualties. Could you give Corpsmen Smith and Thronson a hand with the lad over yonder?"

A young private had been horribly mutilated. A land mine had blown off both his legs.

My first question was, "Are you sure the patient is still alive?"

At that moment the casualty opened his eyes and asked for a cigarette. As he took his first drag, I checked his battle tag. It stated that he had received his half grain of morphine over two hours earlier. I could not understand why he was not experiencing unbearable pain. Even though I had observed similar reactions in other badly shattered men over the past three weeks, I could never explain their lack of pain perception. Perhaps the multiple centers of pain stimulation overwhelmed the brain's awareness, causing the pain signals to bypass the conscious mind. At any rate, with the exposed tissues finally covered with sterile dressings, the large arteries tied off, and the second unit of plasma completed, the patient left our aid station in a fairly stable condition. As with so many previous badly injured casualties, we never found out whether this man survived.

As the ambulance pulled out with its disabled cargo, Meegan approached me saying, "I have a continuing problem. Could I talk to you alone?"

"OK, but let me take a cup of coffee with me."

When well out of earshot of Thronson and the other men, Meegan said, "Ever since we divided those 10-in-1 rations among the medical group two days ago, Thronson and his I Company buddies have been even more unhappy and uncooperative. They want to be sent back to the front lines with I Company right now."

"Has Aarant been giving you trouble too?"

"No, he is the one exception. He seems to bear no grudges and would probably like to stay on in the aid station for a few more days."

I said, "Keep Aarant back in the aid station, but send the rest of the unhappy I Company crew to the front lines right now. There isn't too much daylight left, and they will need a little extra time to settle in with their company before dark. Our troops will resume the assault early tomorrow morning."

A visible look of relief crossed Meegan's face as he said, "Thanks much, Doc. I'll take care of it right away."

All efforts at forward movement by our front-line troops ceased in the early afternoon, and so did the influx of new casualties. On returning to our bivouac area in the north end of the V-shaped draw, I noted that the 81mm mortar platoon was digging in on the high ground just to the west of us. I could not understand why they had abandoned their snug position just to the south of our aid station site on the southern arm of the V.

I put this question to their senior officer, Gunnery Sergeant Honneywell, and he answered, "Nip stragglers got in with us last night and raised lots of hell. We wiped them out, but they killed three of our men. Tonight we are going to tie in with the command post defense perimeter."

While observing their preparations, I noted a constant stream of mortar men who were taking the high-ground shortcut while carrying pieces of dismantled mortars and ammunition north to their new positions.

I said, "Honneywell, aren't you afraid some of your men will get plugged while crossing over the hump? The colonel told us to take the long road down and up the draw."

He said, "Naw, that's just random high overhead fire. It ain't going to hurt nobody."

At that very moment Corporal Holton was approaching us from the south, toting several 81mm shells in a balanced sling draped over his shoulders. When fairly close, he gave us a friendly wave with his right hand. Following this gesture, he took two or three more steps and crumpled up in a heap.

Seconds later as I reached his side, he greeted me with a puzzled look on his face saying, "They got me."

In less than a minute he was dead. Examination showed a bullet wound through the left chest at the level of his heart. As I was crawling back to the lower ground occupied by the mortar platoon, Honneywell was shouting frantic orders at his men.

"The colonel's orders are to be obeyed. There will be no more shortcuts over the hump. The remainder of the transfer to the new area will be conducted via the detour through the draw."

Later on, while waiting for Meegan and Murphy to finish cooking the mulligan stew in a pineapple juice can, I was idly watching the 81mm mortar men, who were now located twelve feet above and several yards to the west of us, complete their defense preparations for the coming night. My curiosity turned to alarm when I noted they were stringing accordian barbed wire just below the plateau on which they were encamped. This left us out in no-man's-land on the lower ground to the east.

Closer inspection in the center of their redoubt proved even more disquieting. The men were tense and jittery. This was quite understandable. They had lost three men to infiltrators the night before. Corporal Holton's sudden death two hours earlier had augmented these apprehensions.

Each foxhole contained a sack of handgrenades. Seven of these foxholes faced in our direction and overlooked our positions. If any Nips should break through into our medical area, it would be quite simple for these nervous men to roll grenades down the twelve-foot bank into our laps. To make matters worse, the American grenades had twice the killing power of the Japanese variety.

After I pointed these facts out to Sergeant Honneywell, he said, "Gee whiz, Doc, I guess you're right, but I don't have any more wire."

I said, "Come over to the battalion command post with me and let's see what we can work out."

Fortunately, Captain Knutson had just come in from the front lines. He agreed that changes would have to be made. By judicious arrangement of the wire, we were included in the defense perimeter of headquarters company. All the grenades were removed from the seven foxholes that overlooked our medical section. In addition, the mortar men facing us were ordered to withhold their rifle fire. If any of the enemy should climb up that twelve-foot embankment, bayonets would be used to eliminate them.

With these preparations completed, the night proved quite restful. We were subjected to only a minimal amount of harassing fire from the remaining enemy to the north of us.

March 12   D Day Plus 21

March 12 was essentially a repetition of the day before. Although our 27th Marines were ordered to attack, very little forward progress was made. However, that did not stop us from harvesting a crop of casualties.

One of our volunteer night perimeter guards from an amphibian tractor battalion presented an unusual problem. He had been standing guard all night on our eastern flank. At daybreak he rolled over on his back with his boondocker shoes removed and feet crossed to take a well-earned nap. He had stretched out on a flat patch of sand in order to be warmed by the early morning sun.

Suddenly at 1015 he let out a howl of pain and rage as he began thrashing around with his feet firmly fixed in the crossed position. When I reached his side, he was still shouting, "Help! Help! My feet are nailed together."

After cutting away his socks, I could see an obvious point of entry for a .30-caliber bullet on the dorsum of his right foot, but there was no point of exit on either foot. Because both feet were glued firmly together, the bullet must have stopped halfway between the two feet. For this to happen, it must have been a half-spent missile, otherwise it would have blasted through both feet with ease. At any rate, his feet were effectively nailed together.

I told the unhappy private, "Just relax and take it easy. You and our Lord Jesus now have experienced something in common. Both of you have had your feet nailed. Two thousand years ago they used a large spike. In your case a .30-caliber bullet has done an equally good job."

I then asked Murphy to give the patient 30 mg of morphine hypodermically.

I turned to my patient, "As soon as this shot starts working, we'll go to work and yank your feet apart. In the meantime, help yourself to another nap."

The patient asked, "Will the operation hurt real bad?"

I answered, "It will hurt some all right, but it will be over in a few seconds."

Forty minutes later, Corpsman Murphy held his left foot and leg firmly on the ground while I grasped his right foot with both hands. After warning the patient to grit his teeth, I gave the right foot a sudden upward jerk. The feet came unstuck with a howl of pain from the patient as blood gushed from a second wound on the plantar surface of the right foot. This bleeding was readily controlled with sterile compresses.

The butt end of the bullet could be seen protruding one-half inch above the level skin surface on the dorsal surface of the left foot. The point of this bullet was tightly wedged between two of the metatarsal bones. I could not budge it with my thumb forceps. After firmly grasping the base of the bullet with my largest Kelly forceps, I was finally able to rock it loose and remove it. This maneuver caused very little additional pain.

I quietly slipped the bullet into a dungaree pocket with the intention of keeping it for a postwar memento. My casualty observed this action, and he immediately protested, "Doc, give me back the bullet. I earned it."

"Do you really want it that bad?"

"I sure do."

Murphy tied the trophy up in one end of a strip of three-inch gauze and secured the other end to the patient's wrist. A happy Marine and his souvenir were soon bouncing back to the hospital in a jeep ambulance.

Later in the morning I had to deal with another unique surgical problem. A young private edged into our aid station with a slow, straddle-legged gait. His trouser fly was unbuttoned and both hands were cupped over his genitalia.

His initial comment was, "For God's sake, help me! They shot my balls off."

Inspection showed that the damage was not that great. A bullet had passed cleanly between his upper thighs as it tore off a segment of skin from his lower scrotum. The testicles lying above the wound had not been damaged. It was a simple matter to close the wound in a few minutes with a running silk suture.

The patient was so delighted at retaining his manhood that he insisted on riding the jump seat back so there would be room for two stretcher cases.

After a noon siesta, while proceeding in a leisurely manner from the bivouac area to the aid station site to relieve Dr. Hely, I had another close call with death. The random overhead bullets were cracking by as usual. Trusting in the colonel's judgment, I chose to ignore them completely.

When a short distance from my goal, I was shocked by the complete absence of human activity in the aid station. Suddenly Hely and Allen popped up from behind nearby rocks and began making frantic arm and hand signals. Their message indicated that I was to take cover immediately.

As I took a few more steps before diving into a nearby shell hole, I saw two bullets kick up dirt under the jeep ambulance and heard a third bullet ricochet off the vehicle itself.

It was obvious that we were dealing with more than just aimless overhead fire. One or more of the enemy garrison must have crawled out of a cave in the vicinity and let us have it at point-blank range. Thanks to their poor aim, I was lucky enough to be alive and uninjured.

After a decent interval, I cautiously peered over the rim of my temporary shelter. It did not take me long to identify most of my men, as they in turn began peering over protecting boulders and from nearby shell holes.

Because there was no evidence of frantic first aid endeavors anywhere in the aid station, I was hopeful that we had acquired no additional casualties.

A few minutes later helmets suspended on carbines or rifles began appearing above the various places of concealment. These disembodied helmets began to move slowly up and down. Others rotated in a circular fashion as they were moved from side to side. This activity of the helmets continued for the next twenty minutes without provoking further attacks from the enemy.

A half hour after the original attack, Hely and Meegan dashed over from their hiding places and plopped down beside me for a quick briefing.

Meegan said, "It looks like the Nips have crawled back into their tunnel system."

Hely added, "I agree with Meegan. I think it's safe to get back to work."

"How many casualties were here when the attack started?"

Hely turned to Meegan, "Was it five or six?"

"Six, but no one got hit a second time. We dragged them into shell holes right at the start."

"Good."

Meegan looked at me, "Since we've been holed up, H Company has called for one litter team and G Company has two casualties that need removal."

I agreed, "Sound the all clear and let's get back to work."

Meegan then said, "If it's OK with you, Doc, I will assign three men to guard duty. They'll let us know right away if any firing resumes."

Hely and I both nodded in agreement to Meegan's recommendations.

After activities resumed in the aid station, it appeared that our tormentors had moved on to another area. Only the high overhead fire continued as it had for the past two days. With all the bullets that had been sprayed about our area during this attack, it was incredible that none of my corpsmen or our battle casualties had been killed or suffered further wounds.

Late that afternoon I checked with Familo in the command post concerning the progress of the battle. Our casualties had been moderate in number, but our progress had to be measured in feet rather than yards. If we continued to lose one man for every two feet gained as we had this day, we would be completely wiped out before we reached Kitano Point at the most northern tip of the island.

Chapter Twelve

D Day Plus 22–24

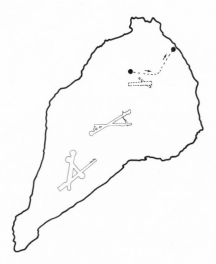

March 13   D Day Plus 22

Zero hour on March 13 started at 0515 with essentially negative results as far as ground gained. However, the harvest of war continued unabated. We soon had many maimed and wounded men in the aid station. The real blow came at 0850 when I Company called in requesting a corpsman replacement. Aarant was dead. He had been shot through the head while treating a wounded Marine.

Hely and some of the other men broke down and openly wept. How we'd miss him and those musical jam sessions with his melodious voice! A mantle of gloom settled over all the men. Would any one of us live long enough to escape from this inferno?

At the news of Aarant's death, I had been stunned. How could a young man with so much musical talent be suddenly wiped out? Bob Crosby had planned to arrange a scholarship for him at The Juilliard School of music in New York after the war. With this additional voice training, his future advancement in the musical world would have known no limits. Now this great voice was gone. War was such a horrible waste.

Then a new thought crossed my mind. What had Aarant been doing up in the front lines with I Company anyway? When I had discussed the problems of the I Company corpsman with Meegan two days before, it had been agreed that all of them would return to the front lines except Aarant. Aarant cooperated well with the other men and had shown no desire to join Thronson and his clique in the front lines with I Company.

175

I immediately sought out Meegan and asked, "Brainard, what in the hell was Aarant doing up on the front lines? Didn't we agree to let him work in the aid station a while longer?"

"That is true, Dr. Vedder. I did my best to talk him into staying in the aid station."

"Well, why didn't he stay with us?"

Meegan answered, "Thronson and his buddies twisted his arm real hard. They made him feel so guilty that he just went along with them."

All I could say was, "Damn, damn, damn it all!"

A little later that morning the word was passed out via our field telephone that an official celebration would be held the next day at 1100 on March 14. At this moment the admirals and the generals would meet at the south end of the island. They would raise the American flag and declare to the world that Iwo Jima was secured. No mention would be made of the fighting and dying still going on in the north.

At 1300 we were honored by our second and last visit from Commander Alcott and Lieutenant Dewgaw from division headquarters. Their jeep sputtered to a stop in almost the same place where our jeep ambulance had been ambushed by small arms fire the day before. They seemed so smug and happy that I almost wished the enemy would fire a few rounds to churn up the earth around their vehicle.

Because they both seemed to be in such a genuinely relaxed and friendly mood, my antisocial thoughts quickly evaporated. I really didn't want any traumatic experiences to befall these men.

Dewgaw smiled amiably and said, "How have things been going since we last saw you?"

"We have been getting along fine since you have been feeding us with a continuing resupply of new litter bearers."

Alcott broke into the conversation as he said, "Since we last saw you, we realized that we caused part of the problem with the collecting company corpsmen. We have decided not to fill out a bad fitness report for you on that issue. I'm sure you won't abuse the collecting company corpsmen again."

I said, "Thanks for your generosity. As long as you men keep me supplied with Marine litter bearers, these collecting company corpsmen will only be asked to function as Navy regulations stipulate."

Dewgaw then asked, "How is your new acting chief making out?"

I said, "Meegan is doing a great job. Will you fellows help me get him a permanent chief's appointment after this operation is over?"

Dewgaw said, "We'll work on that. There shouldn't be any real problem."

Then I asked, "What happened to Griebe?"

Alcott glanced uneasily at Dewgaw and said, "I had him evacuated as a war neurosis. After all, he was not the only one on this island to sip a little brandy. If every brandy drinker got locked up, we'd lose a lot of important people."

I answered, "I guess you're right, Chauncey. What won't work on the front lines probably does little harm in the rear areas. Besides, Griebe tried to do his job most of the time. On February 28 at the battle for Hill 362A, he saved us from getting blown up by a giant land mine. I was afraid that if Griebe stayed up here longer, he just might get bushwhacked by one of his own men. I'm glad he's off the island."

Then Dewgaw asked, "How is your supply of corpsmen holding up?"

"Not too well. We lose a few every day. Mule Aarant got shot through the head a few hours ago. He was one of our best men."

Dewgaw said, "Take good care of the rest. We have about reached the bottom of the barrel for replacements."

"What about those flag-raising ceremonies? Does that mean we head for the beaches and home at high tide tomorrow?"

Dewgaw answered, "Hell, no. That's just a public relations show put on by the top brass."

"Why do they have to play games with us?"

Alcott interjected, "They are not worried about you fellows up here. They have to placate the folks back stateside. The total casualties of our three divisions as of last night added up to nearly twenty thousand men. There is sure to be a big stink when the final tally is scored."

I walked over to their jeep with them, and we parted with friendly handshakes.

At 1500 the casualties stopped coming in, because a halt had been called on attempts to advance into the gorge that lay to the north. No new ground had been taken the entire day.

While finishing up with the last casualty, I heard a jeep pull up beside our aid station. A lone figure in the vehicle said, "Hi, Vedder, how would you like to ride up to Kita village with me? I know where a cache of choice Japanese signal equipment is located."

It took me a few seconds to place the owner of the three-week luxuriant growth of black beard. Yes, it had to be Lieutenant Smith of our regimental intelligence section.

I said, "Don't talk so loud, Smith. I told my men that it was too dangerous to go souvenir hunting. Is it safe to go up there?"

"Sure thing. Climb in, Jim. The Nips were all wiped out four days ago."

"That may be so, but they tend to come back. One almost plugged me right here yesterday."

Smith answered, "This is different. Four of my men are already up there sorting the stuff out."

The quarter-mile trip to the northwest over an almost nonexistent trail was precariously completed only by the help of our four-wheel drive vehicle. The flattened remains of Kita village lay a short distance to the north. Kita was only a spot on the map, for it no longer existed. The village had once occupied a fairly level patch of ground an acre or two in size. The wooden buildings had been reduced to a few broken planks and shredded splinters of wood scattered in all directions. Traces of foundations could be identified in a few places. Pottery shards and a few punctured cooking utensils were the only real evidence that humans had once inhabited this area.

The booty lay in a small chamber that had been hewn in the north-facing side of a twenty-foot precipice. I was offered numerous and sundry signal flags of both the Imperial Army and Navy. Because of transportation problems, I selected only one item. It was a handsome three-by-five-foot rising sun flag of the Japanese Empire. Later I carefully tucked it underneath my Columbia portable phonograph, which had been successfully riding in the bottom of the jeep ambulance since March 1.

Meegan, who had been waiting for my return, greeted me with an unhappy countenance.

He said, "Thronson and three of his I Company buddies want to be relieved."

I answered, "What the hell for? They have been up there less than forty-eight hours."

Meegan said, "I know that, Dr. Vedder. You know how it is. There would be no problem if Aarant had not been killed this morning."

"That's true, but if they hadn't pulled the 'old buddy act' on Aarant, he would still be alive working here in the aid station."

"That's part of the problem. If he were alive things would be different. So, what would you like to have me do with these men?"

I shot back, "What would you like to do with them, Meegan?"

Meegan thought a while and answered, "I'd like to bring them back and give them another chance."

"OK, Meegan, you can bring them back on one condition. If any of them start hassling or handing out any more crap to our aid station personnel, I want you to send them back up to I Company and tell me about it after the deed has been accomplished."

"Thanks, Doc, I'll have a long talk with them before they get reassigned to the aid station tomorrow morning."

The field telephone rang at 2100. Lieutenant Familo was on the line.

He said, "I have some hot scoop. One hour before sunrise, our battalion will prepare to move over to the east side of the island. The distance is about one mile. Then we will attack the enemy pocket from the east and drive to the west. When your men get packed up, tie in with the rear echelon of the command post. They will guide you over to your new working area. Any questions?"

"What's the deadline for getting on the move?"

"By 0800 at the latest."

"Thanks for nothing, Familo, and good night for now."

March 14 D Day Plus 23

For the first time in this location we were not disturbed by sporadic enemy shellfire during the night. The enemy's retaliatory powers were definitely ebbing. By first light on March 14, everyone was up either preparing breakfast or packing for the impending trip into new territory.

After getting a final briefing in the command post shortly before 0800, I called my men together to give them final instructions.

"Here is the latest word from headquarters. We are to set up shop on the east side of the island. Our men are going to attack from east to the northwest. The colonel wants us to stay off recognized roads and trails. They are all well seeded with antipersonnel land mines. We are to proceed cross-country for the entire mile-long trip. Our route will roughly parallel Airfield 3, but we will stay on the high ground well to the north. Our vehicles will meet us later after they take the southern detour via Road Junction 336."

While scrambling over the uneven ground burdened down with our full combat gear, we caught intermittent glimpses of the feverish activity on the two southern airstrips, which had shown daily increases for the past week. On Airfield 2 alone we could count eight B–29 bombers parked in recently constructed revetments. Many bulldozers were scurrying about moving earth in several directions. Large roadgraders were busily leveling this recently moved earth. It was gratifying to note the greatly increased use of these airfields in just four days.

Above us a single-engine plane was lazily circling the northern tip of the island as it directed naval gunfire at the remaining enemy positions. Our destroyers were laying down a rolling artillery barrage to hasten the advance of our 27th Marines. Without warning, the right wing of this spotter plane disintegrated. The aircraft plunged into a nose dive, and within seconds it burst into a ball of flame only a few yards in front of us. Due to the crescendo of other battle noises, we were unable to hear the moment of impact. A quick check revealed the obvious, there were no survivors. It brought home to us once again that our stubborn enemy still possessed considerable strength.

In just two more hours, our corps command would be announcing to the world that the battle for Iwo Jima was over and the island was secured. The sudden demolition of this spotter plane brought home to us how really insecure we were on this bloody island. Here we were struggling over an impossible terrain simply because a parallel but just passable road a short distance to our north was unsafe to use. Because of his recent experience with land mines, Colonel Robertson would naturally be showing a bit more caution about using Japanese roads. None of us complained too hard about our rugged, up-and-down route but just wished a few of the Marine generals could have joined us as we struggled along under full battle gear.

Because of the semiperpendicular landscape, it took us almost two hours to complete our mile-long journey to the east side of the island.

Lieutenant Familo and the rear echelon of our command post were already established in a small grove of very large deciduous trees some distance east of the main road. Many of the branches of these trees had been shattered by shellfire, but the sturdy trunks, which measured twenty-four to thirty inches in diameter, were essentially undamaged. The eastern border of this woodlot was a precipice that dropped off two hundred fifty feet to meet the sea far below. Two destroyers offshore were firing their 5-inch guns at whatever targets were requested by the advancing 27th Marines.

Familo suggested we set up our aid station on a level, cleared area about one-half acre in size, between the trees and the road. Closer inspection revealed that we were milling around in a recently planted vegetable garden. Between the trampled spots, one could detect remnants of neat rows of radishes, carrots, and beets. Their small size suggested that they must have been planted just before our landing on February 19. After a hurried consultation with my corpsmen, it was decided to proceed with our foxhole digging and not worry about the vegetables. They would be too small to eat for some time to come.

A short time later it became apparent that our new aid station site had a major defect. We had no way to bring wheeled vehicles into our working area. Our location was a considerable distance east of the nearest road. We could not move out to the road because we needed to be tied in with the headquarters company defense perimeter for protection.

Meegan suggested that we divert one of the returning bulldozers that had been engaged in building a road to the north for our tanks. The terrain was so rough farther north that even tanks could not negotiate a passage until a trail was first bulldozed.

Meegan stopped the next two bulldozers without success. They both offered numerous reasons why they could not take time to smooth a path to our aid station. Perhaps some of our medicinal brandy might serve as a useful bargaining agent. I stuffed six two-ounce bottles into my dungaree pockets as I joined Meegan to greet the third returning bulldozer. It was manned by a corporal attached to the 3rd Division.

I said, "Hi, Corporal, we need some help."

He answered, "What kind of help?"

"We need a path smoothed out so we can run our jeep ambulances up to our aid station."

The corporal said, "Sorry, Doc. I've got to get this machine back to the division motor pool for servicing."

As I held up two of the mini brandy bottles, I said, "Would a little dollop of brandy help change your mind?"

He wavered a moment and then said, "You tempt me, Doc, but I'll catch hell if the other two dozers that just went by beat me back with too much time to spare."

As I produced two more bottles, I said, "Shucks, it shouldn't take more than a few minutes to smooth out such a short path."

"OK, Doc, I'll do it for four bottles, but I'll need two more to keep my first sergeant happy."

As I passed over the six bottles containing a total of twelve ounces of brandy, I said, "It's a deal."

It took our 3rd Division friend less than a half hour to bulldoze a fairly serviceable road into our new aid station. For the second time our medicinal brandy had served a really useful purpose.

Our front-line troops were making good progress, but as usual the cost was high. The majority of the wounds were produced by .30-caliber bullets fired at close range. In the early afternoon one of our new corpsmen, who had just joined us four days ago, was brought in from I Company with a disabling leg wound. A replacement would have to be sent up to the front lines. While working on a seriously wounded man, I was aware that Meegan was canvassing the aid station personnel looking for a volunteer to go up to I Company.

Presently Meegan approached me, "Dr. Vedder, for the first time I can't get anyone to volunteer for a stint of duty on the front lines."

"Why won't they?"

"They all think Kramer should take his turn. Everyone else has been up there at least once."

"Has Kramer been doing a good job of keeping the casualty logbook?"

"Sure thing, but that's no big deal. We have a lot of men that could do an equally good job."

"OK, Meegan, tell Kramer to hitch up his backpack and get moving up to I Company."

A little later, while removing bits of twigs and fine gravel from an extensive upper arm wound, I saw Meegan approach.

"I need more help on the same problem."

"What's the trouble?"

"Kramer won't go up to I Company."

"Really! Why not?"

"Says he just can't do it."

"Tell him he's got five minutes to get going, or I'll be over riding his ass."

A few minutes later Meegan returned with a worried frown.

I glanced up from my arm wound and asked, "Now what happened?"

"Nothing!"

"What do you mean by nothing?"

"He just doubled up in his hole and started bawling and shaking."

"OK, let him be for the time being. I'll talk to him as soon as I finish with this patient."

A half hour later I had no trouble finding Kramer's foxhole. Seven men were ringed around it staring down at its lone occupant. The expressions of contempt on those seven faces were actually palpable. Kramer was curled up in the fetal position as he huddled in the bottom of his foxhole. He used both hands to cover his face, a picture of abject despair.

I sat down beside him and told his hostile comrades, "Get back to your jobs. I want to talk to Kramer alone."

They sullenly shuffled over to the aid station area. I said, "Take your hands away from your face, Kramer, and sit up. I want to talk to you."

Kramer complied. His tear-streaked face and red, swollen eyes indicated that I was dealing with a very unhappy man. Sitting beside this weeping hulk made me feel quite uneasy.

I continued, "Do you remember how you panicked on D day when we hit the beach? I had to return to the boat to retrieve our bag of surgical instruments. I told you that I would lower the boom on you if you let me down again. In fact, I did not tell any of our men, including Dr. Hely, about your behavior."

Kramer choked out in an almost inaudible voice, "Yes, I remember."

"Now let's keep your record clean. Throw that pack on your back and get up to I Company."

He dropped his face between his knees as he mumbled in a low voice, "I can't do it. I just can't do it."

While his shoulders shook to the accompaniment of his wracking sobs, I said, "Kramer, I've given you a direct order. Are you going to carry it out?"

It was very unnerving to see this big man weeping like a baby. Over the past two weeks, despite increasing pressure from my corpsmen, I had hoped to avoid pushing Kramer too far. Ever since March 1st when Kramer first refused to be rotated through front-line duty, the tension had been building, either through innuendo or outspoken criticism by his fellow corpsmen.

Kramer was performing a useful function by keeping very accurate casualty records, so I had gone out of my way to protect him from the jibes and taunts of his peers. I had hoped the battle would end before his turn on the front lines became a necessity. Now we were short one corpsman in I Company, and there were no replacements available in the regimental pool. If Kramer would not fill this need, I would have even more trouble getting a volunteer from the rest of our aid station corpsmen.

I grasped Kramer's shoulder and asked him to look at me. As tears continued to stream down both his cheeks, I made an impassioned plea.

"I understand how you feel, Kramer. Just go up there and tough it out for a couple days. Then you can come back to your old job with the battalion records."

As his body continued to shake with slow, convulsive sobs, he answered, "I would like to, I would really like to, but I just can't do it."

After living through three and a half weeks of unremitting violence, I could understand Kramer's state of mind much better than if this incident had occurred earlier in the operation. But the die was cast. He could no longer stay with our 3rd Battalion. There was a certain danger that one or more of his comrades might engineer an unexplainable accident.

Earlier in the operation I might not have been so understanding, but now I had better insight into the problem of failure to perform in the line of extremely hazardous duty. Because we were short of corpsmen, if I sent him to the rear, Dr. Schultz would send him back up to us.

Suddenly, Schultz became the key that would solve the problem. A call to regimental headquarters soon had me connected with our regimental surgeon.

"Hello, Dr. Schultz. This is Vedder calling from the 3rd Battalion. How are things going back there in headquarters?"

He answered, "Things are looking just great. Is there anything I can do to help you out?"

"You sure can. I have a serious problem up here. One of our corpsmen has mutinied. He has refused to carry out direct orders from two superior officers, including myself."

"Who is the culprit?"

"It's Corpsman Kramer. He has refused to replace a wounded corpsman and go up and work in I Company."

Schultz said, "Can you really blame him, Jim? I would be scared to death to be in the company area for even a few minutes."

"I can agree with your feelings, Dr. Schultz. However, his fellow corpsmen couldn't disagree more violently. All the rest of our corpsmen have had at least one tour of front-line duty."

"Why not give Kramer a couple more days in the aid station? He might change his mind."

"It won't work, Dr. Schultz. The danger is too great that he might be subject to a violent death from one or more of his peers. Their nerves really are on edge."

"Well, Jim, what do you suggest we do?"

"Why not take him back with you at regimental headquarters right now? After a day or two you can send him up to one of the other battalions."

Dr. Schultz reluctantly agreed with this course of action. Five minutes later Kramer, with his tear-streaked face, snuffy nose, red, swollen eyes, and all of his gear, was riding the jump seat of a returning ambulance.

Ten minutes later, just before it became necessary to draw lots, Murphy volunteered to fill the empty position on the front lines with I Company.

After Murphy had strapped on his corpsman's paraphernalia and was about to depart for I Company, I called him aside out of earshot of the other men.

I said, "Thanks for volunteering, but take care of yourself up there. Do the job, but don't try to be a hero. You are too valuable a man to lose. We are going to need you back here later on."

Before I finished talking, the usual dimples made their appearance just before his entire face broke into its customary happy smile.

He said, "Don't worry about me. The luck of the Irish will look after me. I'll come back alive."

A few hours later we had a crisis of an entirely different nature. Lieutenant Patrick of the engineers interrupted me while I was plucking debris from a shoulder wound on a newly arrived casualty.

His eyes were blazing and his handsome youthful face was contorted with anger, "Gimme Sergeant Mohr's watch. Your ghouls stripped it from his body."

"Knock it off, Patrick. Sit down until I finish this casualty."

I went back to picking bits of small gravel and twigs out of the shoulder wound with my thumb forceps. Patrick plopped down nearby, but he did not relax. He was soon working out his frustrations against a small shrub surrounded by a clump of grass by repeatedly jabbing at it with the butt end of his carbine. With each blow a small cloud of dust and bits of dried vegetation drifted over in the direction of the open shoulder wound.

"For Christ's sake, Patrick, cut it out. You're contaminating this wound."

This retort got through to him, for he sat quietly with clenched teeth for the next fifteen minutes.

As my patient was being loaded aboard an ambulance, I turned to Patrick, saying, "Start at the beginning and tell me what happened."

"Mohr wore his watch before he got shot; now it's gone. One of your corpsmen has to have it."

"That's cockeyed crappy thinking. I don't recall seeing it on his wrist before he died."

Corpsmen Smith entered the conversation, "It was still on his wrist when we put his body in the ditch."

I said, "Yeah, that could be so, but that was four hours ago."

"Round up your grave robbers and make them cough up the watch."

"No way, Patrick. Many other people have had access to Mohr's body since it was dumped in the ditch."

At this moment three new casualties arrived in the aid station. Hely took charge of the sucking chest wound, Allen and Maloney started working on a lower arm wound, and Rhoe and I started first aid procedures on a bullet wound that had shattered the lower part of the thigh bone. While I was concentrating on the care of this patient, a finger jabbed me roughly on my shoulder.

Without turning around, I shouted, "We're too damn busy. Now get the hell out of here."

As Lieutenant Patrick stalked off, he hurled a long litany of obscenities in all directions. The loss of Mohr's watch was not an isolated occurrence. With the lengthening period of destruction and carnage, the sanctity of the private property of our dead came to have less and less meaning. I never did find out whether or not one of my corpsmen had stolen the watch. In fact, I made no attempt to find out, as there were too many other pressing problems to deal with. It would have taken a naval court of inquiry to ascertain the fate of the purloined watch.

Later, while we were concocting our special stew, Quartermaster Sergeant Wentworth drove into the area with a weasel loaded with provisions. He was a friendly and helpful young man in his early twenties. Lieutenant Jim Gass recognized Wentworth as his most valued noncommissioned officer. He began unloading the usual C and K rations, and both Hely and I importuned him to drop off a case of 10-in-1 rations.

He gave us a wry smile as he said, "I just happen to have one case left aboard."

We both thanked him profusely as he placed these rations beside our Coleman stove.

Hely then said, "Thanks a lot, Wentworth. Grab a cup and have some stew."

Wentworth said, "Thanks, Dr. Hely, I don't mind if I do."

He filled his cup and sat down on a small rock beside Hely. Both men were facing north. I was seated on a small boulder about fifteen feet to the side, on the western edge of our vegetable garden.

Before anyone could taste the stew, a burst of machine gun fire erupted from the south. Wentworth slumped forward with blood streaming down his face. His head was split open like a squashed pumpkin. As I dove behind a boulder, Hely was attempting to cover Wentworth's ghastly head wound with a large battle dressing. Just then a second burst of machine gun fire came from the south. A small bush was clipped off just inches above Hely's head.

I shouted, "Hit the deck, Charlie, and keep your head down. Wentworth is dead. Stay flat and don't move."

Soon scouting parties were sent out to comb the rock outcroppings a quarter of a mile to the south, but they were unsuccessful in finding our assailant. He had undoubtedly crawled back into one of the innumerable caves located in this jumble of rocks and boulders.

During the attack the pot had been knocked off the Coleman stove, and the stew was soaking into the sand. No one seemed to mind; our desire for food had been lost. I had some of the stew left in my cup, but I could not eat it.

I glanced about the aid station area and noted Hely hunched up behind a larger boulder next to mine with his head between his knees. He was obviously brooding over the unexpected death of his friend Wentworth.

I crawled over to him and said, "Charles, it wasn't your fault that Wentworth got it."

"How can you say that, Jim? If I hadn't offered him some stew, he would now be alive and on his way back to the regimental headquarters!"

I asked Hely, "Do you believe in fate?"

He answered, "I'm not sure."

"I believe that if you are going to get clobbered, you'll get it sooner or later, one way or the other. So if you hadn't called him over for the stew, Wentworth might have gotten blown up by a land mine on the way back in his weasel. Or maybe a sniper would have picked him off tomorrow on his way back up here with new supplies."

Hely said, "I can't buy your 'fate' theory, but it is a comforting thing to hang one's hat on."

"One thing is certain, Charles, if they don't get this campaign over damn soon, death will be the fate of every one of us."

March 15   D Day Plus 24

I found it hard to get to sleep this night. To help pass the interminable hours I audited the telephone conversations that operated on an open switchboard during the hours of darkness. The phones were being manned continuously in the battalion command post, Colonel Robertson's foxhole, and by the commanders of the three front-line companies. Enemy infiltrators were making it hot for our men up forward, even though they had the war dogs to help them out. By 0145 they had killed fifteen of the enemy, and estimated that another one hundred were still on the prowl. The good news was that their forward advance on the fourteenth had carried them one third of a mile ahead, which left only a short distance between them and the north end of the island at Kitano Point.

This information concerning infiltration of the front lines would explain the profusion of flares that had been popping off every few seconds for the past several hours. For brief moments we would be treated with daylight visibility.

One blazing hot magnesium flare must have had a delayed action fuse, for it exploded only fifty feet directly above our foxhole. As its parachute lowered it gently earthward, it looked like it was slated to land directly in our foxhole. The magnesium was burning at a temperature of over 1,000 degrees centigrade. If it touched any part of our bodies, we would acquire instant third-degree burns.

I rose to my knees and seized my trenching shovel. I swung the shovel over my right shoulder, waiting for the fiery nemesis to settle down toward us. I hoped the shovel would serve as an improvised bat to knock the magnesium fireball far into left field.

Fortunately, my prowess as a batsman was not to be tested. The white-hot flare landed ten feet from the south rim of our foxhole. I immediately ducked down into the protection of our refuge, for I did not want to be silhouetted by this blinding light and thus make myself a target for a lurking enemy infiltrator. In less than a minute this brilliant light had burned itself out harmlessly.

I must have dozed off momentarily, with the phone lying next to my ear. Suddenly the colonel's steady, confident voice brought me to full wakefulness as he talked to someone at division headquarters. Seizing Kitano Point to the north would be the last mission for our 3rd Battalion. When this task was completed, we would retire to the west beaches for embarkation and our combat duties on Iwo Jima would be terminated.

A medley of excited voices of company commanders broke in on this conversation. All three of these men assured the colonel that Kitano Point would be in our hands by noon on the fifteenth. I hung up the phone and happily jabbed Amrosino in the ribs. Tomorrow was to be our last day of fighting. He only grunted and rolled back on his side to resume his rest, for he was too deaf to understand.

I woke with a start as the bright sun hit me in the face. I popped out of my foxhole; I wanted to be the first to pass the good news on to my men. The war would be over before the day was out. Our front-line troops just had to capture Kitano Point, then we would head for the embarkation beaches. Most of the corpsmen accepted this news, but a few of them were quizzically apprehensive.

Meegan expressed their worries with a question, "You wouldn't be pulling our leg would you, Doc?"

"Never on so important a matter!"

This response caused the entire medical section to burst forth with an impromptu celebration of hand shaking and back clapping as they congratulated each other for just being alive. Our combat role on Iwo would be finished in a few short hours.

I then headed across the vegetable garden to waken Amrosino. As I stopped near my foxhole to drink up the last dregs of my morning tea, I must have presented an irresistible target. A burst of machine gun bullets whipped by my left ear so close I could feel the vacuum that was produced. The bullets had come from the south. As I made an instinctive leap to the right for the protection of some rocks, I noted another burst of fire that was tearing some young radishes out of the ground ten feet to my left. Maybe my assailant had planted the garden and was demonstrating his resentment.

While I was lying flat on the ground sprawled out on my abdomen, Hely peered out from behind a rock and called over, "Jim, they were trying to kill you."

I shouted back, "It's the same bastards that killed Wentworth last night. I'm going over to the command post and get some flamethrower squads to wipe them out."

Hely called back, "Take care, Jim, and keep close to the ground while moving over there."

As I crawled on my belly over to the grove of trees to the east, I felt a rising sense of indignation and anger. The dirty son of a bitch had singled me out and was doing his best to kill me. It was nothing worse than cold-blooded murder.

All the other close calls I'd had during the past twenty-five days had seemed rather impersonal, like getting killed in a plane crash, getting run over by a train, or being wiped out by standing in the path of a tornado. This time it was different. This enemy soldier had planned to kill me and no one else! I not only wanted him eliminated, I wanted to be on hand to watch the extermination.

By taking a well-defiladed route well to the north of the vegetable garden, I attracted no further hostile fire. I arrived in the grove of trees without incident. As usual, Lieutenant Familo was the senior officer available in the command post, for Robertson, Mix, and Knutson were up with the front-line troops planning the final attack to capture the north end of the island.

He was comfortably seated in the far eastern border of the small cluster of trees only a few feet from the edge of the precipice. Far below, the surf could be seen beating at the base of the cliff. Facing Familo were two junior officers with a Coleman stove between them supporting a steaming pot of coffee. All three of them were sipping mugs of coffee as they studied battle maps laid out before them.

I stated my case quite brusquely, for my anger had not cooled yet. I said, "The Nip that got Wentworth last night almost nailed me a few minutes ago. Round up a couple of flamethrower teams and I'll show them where to go. I want to see the bastard wiped out."

Familo laughed uneasily and said, "I'd like to, Doc, but we don't have any of those guys back here. Let me talk to the colonel."

A short time later he located the colonel at the G Company headquarters. Familo turned to me after a brief conversation.

"The colonel says they are short of flamethrower teams on the front lines, and there are none to spare for rear area mopping up. You are to move your medical crew fifty yards to the north, behind that pile of rocks over yonder, which will screen you from the Nips roaming about in our rear."

"Thanks for trying, Familo. I still would like to see that dirty bastard fried."

On returning to our medical section I passed on the colonel's orders to Hely and Meegan.

"Get the men to move all the medical gear to the north side of that pile of rocks. Have them leave all personal gear in their present foxholes. We'll use them again tonight when we tie in with the headquarters company's defense perimeter."

Soon we were back in business caring for a light load of casualties. The drive to the end of the island must have bogged down. Any successful advance always meant large numbers of wounded men. Maybe it would take more than one day to cover those last few yards. At 1330 news from Corpsman Prince came via the field telephone.

"Hi, Doc, I'm calling from H Company at Kitano Point. There are several wounded men lying on the beach fifty feet below me. There is a shaky trail up the cliff. We'll need some six-man litter teams to get these casualties out."

I answered, "All our litter bearers are out in the field. I'll send help as soon as they can be rounded up."

Frantic calls back to Dr. Schultz at regimental headquarters finally produced results. An hour later twelve fresh litter bearers arrived on the scene. After sending them up to the front via two jeep ambulances, I contacted Prince.

"This is Doc Vedder speaking. There are two six-man litter teams on the way up. This is the best I can do."

Prince answered, "I've been trying to call for the last fifteen minutes but couldn't get through. We don't need them anymore because our bulldozers whacked out a road of sorts and a weasel ran down and hauled all the men up here. Some of them are already on the way back to the aid station."

"Glad to hear our dozers did the job for us. Send those new litter bearers back to me as soon as they arrive."

As our Marines had reached their objective and had no need to advance into new territory, the flow of casualties tapered off and stopped by late afternoon. It was time to check with the command post to receive the plans for the following day. As I entered the grove of trees, I noted Familo and Woodward seated a few feet apart on their respective ammunition boxes. Lieutenant Woodward was Familo's assistant in the G3, or intelligence section. His parents were American missionaries, and he had been born in Osaka, Japan, twenty-one years ago. He appeared much younger because three and a half weeks in the field had left his face adorned with a wispy, peach-colored down. After fifteen years of residence in Osaka, Woodward was fluent in Japanese.

Both men were facing a tiny Oriental who was hunkered down on his haunches. As he possessed not an ounce of surplus fat, his weight must have fallen within the 115- to 120-pound range. Except for his breechclout, he had been divested of all clothing. This procedure was routinely used with all prisoners to prevent the concealment of any hand-grenades or other weapons in the outer clothing. Two privates stood guard behind him with loaded rifles.

The prisoner did not appear in the least apathetic or dejected as he carried on an animated conversation with Lieutenant Woodward. The only discomfort he displayed was due to the 50-degree temperature. He kept both arms wrapped about his naked torso as he gently massaged the exposed skin. Several times during the questioning he would repeat a certain routine that consisted of pointing up at our circling planes above, then he would direct our attention to our ships lying offshore, and finally would end up by vigorously thumping on his frail-looking bare chest with his right fist.

After he repeated this maneuver for the fifth time, I broke into the conversation by asking, "What kind of an act is this guy putting on?"

Woodward answered, "He's telling us everything we want to know. When a Nip decides not to die for his emperor and surrenders, he knows he can never return to Japan. So he is ready to join up and be one of us."

"That may be so, but why does he keep pointing at our planes and ships and then beating on his chest?"

Woodward smiled and said, "He feels it is a bad mistake for the Americans and the Japanese to be fighting each other. With the many American planes and ships, plus the superior fighting qualities of the Japanese soldier, we should join forces and together we could conquer the world."

Later on when the interrogation was completed and the prisoner was being led away, I turned to Woodward and said, "Your Japanese friend may have overestimated his own powers a bit, but I will agree with him on his last statement. I sure hope the Nips will be fighting on our side when the next war comes along."

As we settled down for the night, we knew that Kitano Point was securely in our hands, and 3rd Division troops would replace our men in the morning.

Chapter Thirteen

D Day Plus 25 and 26

March 16   D Day Plus 25

At 0215 my telephone rang. Lieutenant Houlmoulka of H Company wanted me to send up an ambulance to get Private Huber right away. Huber had been playing toss-the-grenade with the Nip infiltrators. All the fingers had been blown off his right hand. It was bleeding badly.

I said, "Our drivers don't know the way in the dark. How about sending him back on one of your vehicles?"

Houlmoulka answered, "No chance, Doc. There are too many Nips on the prowl. They would knock off anything except a tank."

"So what would happen to our jeep driver?"

"I guess that wouldn't work too well. What can we do about it?"

"Let me talk to Corpsman Prince. We'll send up an ambulance as soon as it gets halfway light."

I then gave Prince detailed instructions on the proper use of pressure compresses over the mangled hand and the use of intermittent tourniquet pressure over the brachial artery. The active bleeding was stopped in less than fifteen minutes.

At 0545 I dispatched Corporal Wyatt and Corpsman Radford in the jeep ambulance to get Huber at H Company. Ten minutes later they returned empty-handed. Halfway to their destination an enemy machine gun had opened up on them. Two fresh bullet holes in the lower frame of the jeep lent credence to their report. Both men appeared quite shaken by this experience. It was just pure luck that they had escaped injury. A call to H Company brought quick action. Not only did they clean out the machine gun nest, but they brought Huber back in their own resupply weasel. His general condition was quite stable. He obviously had not lost a significant amount of blood. As a result we did not remove the blood-soaked dressings that Prince had applied earlier. We simply gave him another Syrette of morphine to prepare him for the long, bumpy trip to the hospital.

March 16 was a glorious sunny day. The war was over for our 3rd Battalion. We'd be leaving for the western beaches as soon as the 3rd Division troops relieved our men in the front lines. As usual on Iwo, nothing ever really happened according to plan. In making the transfer on the front lines, some of our men inadvertently made themselves targets, and soon we found ourselves encumbered with six seriously wounded men. It would take us at least one or two hours to give them plasma, control the bleeding, and dress the wounds. Captain Knutson stopped by and advised us not to hurry.

He said "The colonel wants you medical people to bring up the rear and pick up any stragglers on the way. Take the main road north of Airfield 3, and head for the west beaches. It is now safe to use this road, as all the mines have been located and removed. You'll find us bivouacked with the rest of the 27th Regiment about three hundred yards north of Kama Rock."

It was 0945 before we evacuated our last casualty and had our gear packed and stowed for the two-and-a-half-mile trek to the western beaches. As we entered the main road, we encountered a unique procession of three Japanese escorted by two privates on their way to the prisoner-of-war stockade. Two of the prisoners walked together behind the third. These two were smartly dressed in relatively clean uniforms, shiny leather boots, and jeweled scabbards at their belts. Their swords were conspicuously absent. Their insignia indicated that they were officers of the Imperial Army. The third prisoner leading the parade was a large man in a ragged, torn uniform. He was at least six feet tall and must have weighed close to two hundred pounds. His long, shaggy, coal black beard would make him distinctive in any group of men. They plodded down the road ahead of us acting out a strange scene. About every twenty steps or so, one or the other of the little men in the rear would take turns stepping forth, and while uttering a phrase in Japanese, proceed to kick the big prisoner in the posterior thighs or buttocks. The large bearded man accepted his punishment stoically and the guards seemed indifferent to this activity.

Later I sought out Lieutenant Woodward to ask him for an explanation.

He said, "That guy must have been one of the Ainus from Hokkaido, the northernmost of the main islands. The Ainus are the remnants of the original inhabitants of the islands that survived the onslaught of the Malay-type people that now occupy Japan. Their present position is similar to that of our Indians back home. I would suspect that our Ainu prisoner must have been serving as an orderly for these officers. What he did to displease them is anybody's guess."

The western beaches had been miraculously changed since we had last seen them two weeks ago. The offshore area was crowded with our ships of all sizes and shapes. The enemy would have blown all of them out of the water if they had dared to venture so close as recently as twelve days ago. The only vestiges of war remaining were several beached and broached enemy landing craft and barges. These wrecks made excellent breakwaters as we gathered on their lee sides to cavort and splash about washing off the accumulated grime of several weeks. Our newly issued salt water soap helped only minimally.

While performing my ablutions on the protected side of a large sunken barge that extended one hundred feet out into the surf, I watched the antics of my frolicking corpsmen. They were all demonstrating uninhibited joy over the simple fact that they had survived. Nothing would stop them now from getting home to see their families and friends. As I scrubbed away with my salt water soap, I felt the same way. A great weight had been lifted from my shoulders, and a similar feeling of joy surged through my body.

Soon my attention was drawn to the horseplay that was developing on the deck of the shipwrecked barge. A number of the men, led by Corpsman Vogt, were lined up before an open place on the deck. They would then make running leaps or dives off the seaward end of the barge into the pounding surf. They seemed totally unaware that the sea bottom in this area was littered with underwater obstructions that could produce serious injuries.

I shouted, "Knock it off, you stupid bastards. That sea bottom is loaded with underwater junk that can cut you up real good."

As Vogt was the obvious leader of these happy young men, I said, "Vogt, come over here, I want to talk to you."

Vogt had joined our group less than a week before. He was an eager, able, and fearless eighteen-year-old who probably should have been a Marine rather than a corpsman. Like a number of our young men, he seemed to be living within an aura of complete invulnerability.

I said, "Vogt, I want to get you home alive. Since you joined us last week, I've been watching you. You've almost got yourself killed several times by doing more things than duty calls for. Now I don't want you to get ripped apart by some underwater obstruction."

Vogt gave me a happy smile and said, "Thanks for the advice, I'll start being more careful right now."

Our seabags, which we had left aboard the SS *Sandoval* on February 19, were all neatly stacked in the regimental supply dump. After locating our own, it was great to climb into a clean change of clothing. Soon my men were speculating about which of the ships lying offshore would take us away from Iwo Jima. They began asking me whether we would embark today or tomorrow. I had to plead ignorance.

At that point a messenger from headquarters informed me that the colonel wanted to see me.

A little later Colonel Robertson said, "Take a motor pool jeep and go back to the hospital and bring back any of our ambulatory casualties that are fit to travel with us."

"OK, sir. When are we going to board ship and where will we be headed?"

The colonel answered, "A specific ship hasn't been designated yet, but we're headed back to Hawaii for regrouping and rehabilitation."

Soon after leaving the regimental bivouac area, I took a heading toward the western edge of Airfield 1 on a four-lane highway. The landscape had been transformed. All the shell holes had been filled in, and the wreckage of war had been hauled away. Both sides of the road were lined with regulation tents or Quonset huts.

On arriving at the airfield itself, I could not get my bearings. Where was our aid station site, where we had spent six bloody days from February 21 to 27? Where was the jutting bank that had protected us from the enemy guns? And where were all the disabled Japanese planes? It suddenly dawned on me that our old aid station site and the wreckage of war had been bulldozed away and was now a part of the roadway on which I was traveling.

A short time later, while parking my jeep at the south end of Airfield 1 at the entrance of the 5th Division hospital, I found the terrain completely unrecognizable. The 16-inch shell crater where we had spent the first night on the island should have been in the immediate vicinity, but there were no shell holes visible in any direction. The land had been leveled off and was occupied by large machine sheds, Quonset huts, and a few tents. The Seabee and Air Force personnel were busily constructing more permanent buildings.

The hospital itself was a huge complex of interconnecting tents used as surgical theaters, dressing stations, and the various wards. It did not take me long to carry out my mission. All of our seriously wounded men would be flown to Guam later in the day. Private Morganelli was the only ambulatory Marine casualty that belonged to the 3rd Battalion. As his flight to Guam had also been confirmed, I did not attempt to bring him back with me to our assembly area.

Because ample time was available, I decided to visit the 5th Division cemetery, which lay at the foot of Mount Suribachi, and pay my last respects to many of my departed comrades and friends.

The cemetery itself was an awesome sight. Over a thousand white crosses interspersed with an occasional Star of David were laid out in neat rows all an equal distance apart. Although the capture of the island had been formally announced two days earlier, the killing was still proceeding at a lively pace. A stack of bodies was lying on a tarpaulin at the north end of the burial grounds. It was in this direction that the cemetery was still expanding.

These bodies were laid to rest with assembly-line techniques. As I watched, a large bulldozer scooped out a trench 8 feet wide, 4 feet deep, and 120 feet long. A sturdy line was then strung lengthwise down the center of the trench. A lead sinker was suspended by a piece of string to the main line at four foot intervals. The grave registration detachment was quite efficient. It took them only ten minutes to fasten the thirty lead weights to the main horizontal line. In another ten minutes, thirty of the stacked bodies would each be placed under one of the plumb lines in the bottom of the trench. At this moment one dog tag would be left with the body, and the other would be attached to the grave marker.

The grave markers were then laid flat on the surface opposite the head of each man lying in this mass grave. Then the bulldozer approached the trench from the opposite side. It took only a few minutes to heap the soil over the bodies. Following the bulldozer came a ponderous, slow-moving steamroller that packed the earth firmly in place. A squad would hammer the respective grave markers into the soil at the site of the vertical plumb lines. Then another squad would stencil the man's name, rank, and serial number on the cross or Star of David. They obtained this information from the dog tag that had been previously attached to the grave marker. So in less than forty-five minutes, thirty men received a burial without benefit of chaplains, flowers, or funeral music.

As I walked along the endless rows of white wooden crosses, it seemed unlikely that I would find any of my recently departed comrades. To my surprise, only four rows to the south I encountered Mule Aarant's cross.

In the center of the cemetery I found a cluster of our men who had died during that bloody battle on Hill 362A during the last day of February. As I stood beside Willis's grave site, I bowed my head in silent prayer and renewed my promise to help him receive a posthumous Congressional Medal of Honor. A little later I thanked Capt. Phil Gray for a job well done. I told him I Company had never been quite the same since he left it sixteen days ago.

A few rows to the north I chanced upon the grave marked with the name Dewolfe. I thought of the long nights we had shared in the same foxhole facing the same terrors and uncertainties. I recalled how hard I had worked to persuade this young man to overlook his fears. In his last days he had been an asset to our medical section serving his fellow men. I was certain that his mother and family would have been proud of him.

And so it went, row after row, until I reached the south end of the burial grounds where the men killed in the early days of the campaign were interred. In this area there were many crosses marked Unknown. Most of these unknown dead had been killed by direct shellfire. Their bodies had either been badly mutilated or their dog tags had been blown away so that positive identification had been impossible. In one row of thirty men, there were nine unknown graves. It was possible that McCahill and Hall occupied two of them; a careful search of this area revealed no crosses inscribed with their names.

A feeling of acute depression engulfed me as I walked out of the cemetery. I wondered if the price paid was really worth it. What if the undersized Japanese prisoner Familo and Woodward had interviewed yesterday was correct? Then the Japanese would be our allies, but would Iwo Jima ever be returned to their custody?

As I slowly headed back north in my jeep, one of the frequently used war slogans came to mind. Our Marines were willingly laying down their lives for their country. This statement was sheer nonsense, for the overwhelming majority of the men felt they would be spared, and that it would be the next guy that would be killed or wounded. They had no intention of laying down their lives for their country or anything else. Each man believed he would be one of the lucky ones to return home. Those that lost or never did have this feeling of invulnerability would sooner or later crack up.

Later as I approached the regimental motor pool parking lot my spirits began to revive. The killing was over for our 3rd Battalion, and tomorrow we would leave forever.

As I was backing the jeep into its parking slot, I was startled by Hely as he hopped into the seat beside me.

His voice was choking with suppressed anger as he blurted out, "Those goddamned bastards at division headquarters have reneged. We'll be wiped out to the last man."

With a feeling of unease, I asked, "What do you mean—reneged?"

"Tomorrow at 0800 we go back to combat on the hill."

"It can't be so."

"Oh yes it is so."

"Who told you that?"

"I got the scuttlebutt on the grapevine from reliable sources."

Hely's unofficial information was just too bad to contemplate. Last night's phone conversation with division headquarters promised us prompt evacuation after capturing Kitano Point. So Hely's information just couldn't be true.

"I can't believe it, Charlie."

"Why don't you check it out with Robertson?"

"That's a good idea."

As we parted a hopeless, sinking feeling churned through me. In the Marine Corps, if a rumor is real bad, it's probably true.

A few minutes later I found Colonel Robertson alone in the battalion supply dump seated on some ration boxes. His dispatch case lay open on his lap. He was not studying the papers in the case. His left hand and elbow supported his chin as he gazed thoughtfully at the distant western horizon; nor did he notice my approach.

When about three paces away, I stopped and said, "Good afternoon, Colonel, I just returned from the hospital. The last of our casualties will leave for Guam in the morning. There was no one left that could be returned to duty."

"Thanks for the information, Doc. By the way, our plans have been changed. All of our staff and line officers will meet right here at 1900."

This statement struck me like a blow in the solar plexus. A twisting, stabbing pain settled in the pit of my stomach that was exacerbated by every effort to breathe. God help us if we had to go back to that deep ravine to fight again.

"Does that mean that we have to go back up to clean out that pocket tomorrow?"

"Save your questions until later. In the meantime, I have to study these new orders."

As he began to sort out the papers in his dispatch case, it was obvious that further questioning would be futile.

Leaving the colonel to study his new orders, I delayed my return to the medical section by taking a detour down to the beach. All those ships lying in the anchorage were not going to do us any good. The colonel must have a lot of bad news to give us this evening. Each step along the wet black sand with these dismal thoughts only increased my feelings of dejection and hopelessness as I trudged along. If we went back up there, would my luck hold out, or would some sniper pick me off, or would a last-ditch banzai charge finish my career? While mulling over these somber thoughts, I returned slowly to our medical bivouac area.

Hely greeted me, "What did you find out?"

"Nothing, the colonel won't talk about it until he meets with all the battalion officers at 1900."

The light was just starting to fail as our officers gathered about the colonel in the battalion supply dump. Similar meetings were usually preceded with a moderate amount of banter and light talk. This evening the colonel was greeted by glum silence from his assembled officers. They had heard the rumors and were anticipating the worst of all imaginable possibilities.

The colonel started the discussion, "I have nothing but bad news to pass on to you men. Don't interrupt me until I have laid it all on the line. General Rocky at division headquarters planned to end our combat duties at Kitano Point, but Gen. Holland Smith, the corps commander, has overruled him. Both the 3rd and 4th divisions are being withdrawn from the island. Our 5th Division will stay until the last pocket of enemy resistance has been wiped out. At present, the 28th Marines occupy the west rim and the 26th Marines the east rim of the canyon. Our 27th Marines will start at the landward side of the canyon 230 feet above sea level at a point seven hundred yards from the ocean. Our men will work down through this draw to the sea and eliminate the enemy. The 26th and 28th marines will lend us a hand from above. The meeting is now open for discussion."

The first shock wave of anger came from the overwrought company commanders, who felt the full weight of the betrayal of their men. I thought that I had heard all the choice expletives, but during the next few minutes I was treated to a postgraduate course in profanity. The colonel wisely sat quietly and permitted his junior officers to vent their pent-up hostility.

After fifteen minutes, the gnashing of teeth and the beating of gums dwindled and the conversation returned to more practical matters.

Lieutenant Nelson, the commanding officer of I Company, asked, "How are the three battalions of the 27th going to attack down the canyon on such a narrow front? It is only thirty yards wide at the upper end and never widens to more than two football fields as it approaches the beach."

The colonel answered, "That will not pose a problem because we don't have many fighting men left. The regiment will consolidate into one battalion of four companies containing 115 men each. The 1st Battalion will furnish the men for Company A, the 2nd Battalion will fill the roster for Company D, and our 3rd Battalion will supply the men for Companies G and H. The headquarters company of the 3rd Battalion will give the combat troops backup support."

Lieutenant MacCumbie of H Company then asked, "When do these troops get fed into the slot?"

The colonel said, "Transport will be ready at daybreak tomorrow; the assault is scheduled to start at 0800."

At this point I entered into the discussion, "I would like to present the problem strictly from a medical point of view. Our 27th Marines landed on February 19 with thirty-six hundred men. During the campaign eleven hundred replacements have been fed into the organization. That means that our casualties so far have exceeded 90 percent at the company level. Besides, many of the men still fit for duty are inexperienced replacements who have had no prior combat experience. On each new push these innocents are the first to get killed.

"Right now our Marines are both mentally and physically fatigued. Will they really fight tomorrow? Are they capable of fighting? How many of these 460 men will opt for combat fatigue? I don't think anyone knows the answer. Maybe the esprit de corps psychology will carry them through, but then again it may not. Doctor Hely and I have agreed that any battle fatigue candidates that arrive in the aid station will be quickly processed and sent back to the hospital."

After this medical opinion had been delivered, silence prevailed among the assembled officers. Some looked dejectedly at their feet, others poked angrily at the ground with sticks, and the rest gazed out at the shimmering sea.

After a moment the colonel said, "If there are no further questions, we'll break up the meeting. I have one request to make. Don't tell the rank and file until tomorrow. Let them get one good night's sleep."

Colonel Robertson appeared deeply troubled as he rose slowly to an upright position and moved along the beach, soon to disappear in the gathering darkness.

After the colonel had departed, some of the young line officers began to conjecture among themselves the reasons for the dastardly treatment we were receiving from our corps commander. It was unanimously agreed that Gen. Howling Mad Smith was a dirty, loud-mouthed bastard, but not a sadistic one. He must have had a reason. After all, he was not a fool.

The assembled young officers finally came up with a reasonably logical explanation for our top commander's unpalatable action. The 4th Division couldn't be used to clean up the pocket because they were shot up worse than we. The 3rd Division was in much better shape. They still had one whole regiment that had not been used in combat. Therefore, the 3rd Division would not be used because it could be restored to full combat readiness in a reasonably short time. The new Army garrison troops would not be used because our glory-hungry Howling Mad Smith hated the Army with a vengeance and would not share this great Marine victory with these lesser allies at any cost. So our 5th Division was selected to receive the black spot.

This wild logical deduction of our junior officers did have a ring of truth to it. Even though I hated to admit it, I felt sure that General Smith had weighed a number of other factors before making his final decision to use our 3rd Battalion one more time.

Almost an hour later, Corpsman Allen asked me to see a young private who had become acutely ill. The symptoms had come on so suddenly and violently that Allen felt the man had developed a ruptured peptic ulcer.

When I arrived, Private Danielson was curled up on his side as he moaned and groaned while clutching his upper abdomen. Examination showed no rigidity or spasm of the abdominal muscles. Although the peristaltic activity was increased, he definitely did not have a surgical abdomen.

Questioning revealed that he was a dispatch carrier for the regiment. His symptoms began only after he had seen one of the new orders concerning our return to combat. These acute symptoms were obviously produced by a psychosomatic mechanism. I sent him back to the hospital for observation and treatment.

I thought the colonel should be informed of this case. He could not be located in the headquarters area. Major Mix had last seen him sitting on the bow of a beached Japanese landing craft a short distance to the north. A short time later I found him exactly where Mix had left him a half hour earlier. He appeared to be in deep meditation as he watched the thundering surf run up on the beach. The colonel seemed impressed with the detailed recounting of Private Danielson's recent hysterical attack.

On concluding my report I said, "With Danielson gone, we now have only 459 men left to clean out that pocket. There is no telling how many more we'll lose when the word gets passed around tomorrow."

The colonel did not answer me. He seemed lost in deep thought.

Five minutes later, as he slid down off his seat onto the beach, he said, "Doc, I'm going back to see what I can do."

He then hurried off southward at a very rapid pace. I did not try to keep up with him.

A few minutes later I crawled quietly into my foxhole so as not to wake Amrosino. I wanted to tell him that he was spending his last night with the 3rd Battalion. I planned to survey him back to the hospital in the morning. Because of his deafness, I did not dare to try communicating with him, for my loud shouts would have roused the entire camp.

While Amrosino snored peacefully, I just could not relax and drop off to sleep. Visions of the countless bleeding and mangled men continued to pass through my mind in an endless single column. I just could not face seeing and treating any more of them.

While these thoughts kept coming to the surface, a deeper dread was forcefully being pushed back into the subconscious. My luck would surely run out when the next sniper zeroed in on me; there were still many antipersonnel mines left to step on; and worst of all, our desperate, cornered enemy might wipe me out on a last-ditch banzai charge. Would I last until the end? Or would I crack up like so many of my comrades?

March 17   D Day Plus 26

When I woke up, Amrosino had two cans of hash warming on the Coleman stove. This would be a good time to break the news to him.

I shouted, "Remus, I have news for you. After breakfast, get your gear packed up."

"What for, Doc?"

I leaned over and yelled into his best ear, "We've got to go back up the hill and clean out that pocket. You're too deaf to be of much help. It's time to get you surveyed back to the base hospital."

Amrosino looked at me with disbelief. His voice was choked with emotion, and tears came to his eyes.

He said, "Please let me stay with the gang. I'll keep a sharp lookout and won't get in the way."

"Don't be a dummy, Remus. You'll be leaving with an honorable diagnosis. Just think, you'll be on Guam in a couple of days."

Amrosino reluctantly accepted this reasoning and went off to say farewell to his buddies. However, the loud conversation had drawn most of my corpsmen over to our foxhole. About a dozen men gathered in a circle about me. Their countenances all registered varying stages of apprehension and worry.

Meegan served as their spokesman by asking, "Dr. Vedder, do you mean that yesterday's scuttlebutt is really true? Do we really have to go back up there to fight again?"

"Unfortunately it is."

There was a babble of protest among the assembled men.

Then Meegan asked, "Do you think the men are ready for further combat duty?"

"Certainly not! Both Hely and I told the colonel last night that our men were in bad shape and questioned whether the men were physically or mentally capable of fighting on the next day."

"What should we do with the characters asking for a combat fatigue evac?"

"Check with either Hely or myself. We'll decide what should be done with each case as they show up."

Meegan then changed the subject, "Who furnishes the corpsmen for our new A and D companies?"

"The 1st and 2nd battalion headquarters companies will supply these men. Some of their extra men will work with us in the aid station until they are needed for front-line duty. I wish you would work out a rotation system so each corpsman is replaced after spending one day in the forward areas."

Meegan said, "I think that can be arranged without too much trouble."

As the bulk of the corpsmen huddled about Meegan trying to hammer out an equitable schedule, the tension seemed to ease appreciably.

I then turned my attention to my overheated can of hash without enthusiasm. The anticipated change of diet to real food would have to be postponed indefinitely. At least we would not starve on these rations. However, anorexia prevented me from eating much of anything. I welcomed Colonel Robertson's request to take a short walk with him.

The colonel seemed much more relaxed as he led me away from the bivouac area. With a twinkle about his eyes and a good-humored grin, he said, "I have good news for a change. After leaving you last night, I picked up Colonel Warnham. We went to division headquarters and had a conference with General Rocky. He got the corps commanders to give us a period of grace for recuperation. So we'll have two or three days off before the fighting starts again."

"Thanks for telling me, Colonel; I think you made the best of a bad deal. Is it OK to pass the word along to the rank and file?"

"You can, but there is no need. Fred Mix is already taking care of that matter."

About an hour later I checked in at the command post. I wanted to ascertain our time for departure back to the combat area. In the midst of the communications section, Private Danielson lay contentedly sprawled upon a tarpaulin gnawing on a K ration biscuit.

A bit taken aback, I asked, "Aren't you the guy with the giant bellyache I sent back to the hospital last night?"

"It was me all right."

"Then what are you doing back here?"

"The hospital docs said I was just another psycho and all the trouble was in my head. They were going to ship me out."

"Then why didn't they?"

"My stomach ache was all gone. I wanted to come back and join my buddies. So they let me go. Besides, I'm no psycho."

Here was evidence that esprit de corps was still a vital working force. I never thought Danielson would pass up a sure trip back to the States. Could Hely and I both be wrong? Would none of our abbreviated battalion personnel opt for medical evacuations? Yesterday I would have bet hard currency that our fighting force would collapse if sent back to combat duty. Now I was not too sure just what would happen.

By midafternoon we were back at the northern tip of the island once more. We were situated at an elevation of 280 feet on the landward side of the deep gorge where the enemy was making his last stand. For the first few yards, the land sloped rather gradually northward toward the sea almost a half mile away. After the first hundred yards, the land dropped off in large rock steps varying from five to fifteen feet in height. As the canyon approached the sea, the width of this narrow valley increased to almost two hundred yards. Bare, rock-walled cliffs lined either side of the canyon as they rose over two hundred feet. Both the east and west cliffsides were honeycombed with many man-made excavations and concrete bunkers.

Our new aid station site proved to be ideal, as we were in a defiladed position and protected from harassing fire from both flanks and the rear. Weasels could travel a fair distance beyond the aid station deeper into the canyon for casualties. From this point, six-man litter teams would be required to retrieve the wounded.

Our quarters for our last stand on Iwo Jima were quite comfortable. The underlying volcano kept us warm during the chilly spring nights. We were situated among a group of abandoned enemy heavy mortar positions. They consisted of four-foot-deep pits cut through the solidified lava, and the margins were almost flush with the surrounding ground. I shared one of the pits with Meegan and Smith. Being eight feet in diameter, it could readily accommodate our three litters and still leave room for our cooking utensils. The previous residents had left interesting inscriptions on the walls that we could not decipher. Neat niches had been carved in the rock near the surface. They served well as temporary repositories for our cigarettes and other personal belongings. Small cactus plants had been planted along the edges of our new quarters by the previous occupants, camouflaging it so well that we often had trouble locating our new apartment again in the broken and rocky terrain, even though the aid station working area was only a few feet away.

The rest of the day was spent meeting with the company commanders and corpsmen of A and D companies. I wanted the company commanders to be aware of our operative and evacuation techniques. Captain Hogan of A Company was a cocky little Irishman who gave me a considerable amount of guff at the time, but he cooperated quite well later on when his men needed surgical care.

After greeting these new corpsmen from the 1st and 2nd battalions, I turned them over to Meegan for their detailed assignments and daily rotations between the aid station and the front lines. I was delighted to find an old friend who had served over a year with me in the Field Medical School at Camp Elliott near San Diego. Arthur Hall had been a highly respected corpsman back there, and he seemed to have survived the last twenty-seven days with the 2nd Battalion of the 27th Marines quite well. He was a very serious young man. He seldom smiled, and I never heard him laugh. Being a very devout Christian, he abhorred the military service, yet I never heard him complain or use profane language.

That night I called battalion headquarters from our volcano-heated apartment to find out how much progress the 26th Marines had made during their attack that day.

Major Mix answered my query, "They didn't do anything. Col. Danny Pollock got plugged in the chest when he tried to lead a charge."

"Will our troops be committed tomorrow?"

Mix answered, "No, for sure."

"When will it happen?"

"I don't know. Even the colonel doesn't know."

"Thanks, Fred, and good night."

Chapter Fourteen

D Day Plus 27–30

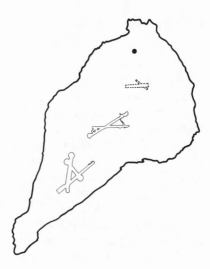

March 18 and 19   D Day Plus 27 and 28

March 18 dawned with rumor and speculation. Maybe the 26th Marines would clean out that pocket today. Perhaps they would put our 3rd Battalion in small boats to enter the gorge from the seaward side and be annihilated quickly by the waiting enemy. Thus an idle mind can think irrationally.

As the day wore on the men became increasingly restless and irritable as they drifted from one group to another discussing the uncertainties of life. They reminded me of the caged animals in the zoo who passed their time pacing back and forth.

Colonel Robertson, recognizing a developing problem that might be helped with a little spiritual stimulation, sent an urgent call to regimental headquarters for Father Calkins and Reverend Valbrecht to visit us later in the day.

March 19 looked like another quiet day on reserve. We didn't know that General Hermle, the assistant division commander, had been sent up to coordinate the activities of the remaining fighting men of the 5th Division.

When no forward movement occurred in the sector held by the 26th Marines at 1600, he ordered them replaced by a company of the 27th Marines. Colonel Robertson selected G Company for the dubious honor of leading the advance.

Within an hour, eleven men from G Company arrived in the aid station with the identical symptoms of diarrhea, abdominal cramps, and exhaustion. They were almost all veterans of the D day landings, and they had fought honorably for the past twenty-eight days. Although none of them appeared very ill, I could not blame them for showing up in the sick bay. Cpl. Jack Stein was one of these eleven men from G Company.

Stein stood before me with an anxious expression as he asked, "What kind of a diagnosis are you going to put on our evacuation tags?"

"You guys are fouled up with several things."

"How's that, Doc?"

"Besides being pooped out with too much combat, you all have had the drizzling dysentery for some time."

"That's so, but what goes on our evac tags?"

"Acute dysentery, that's what's got you down."

Jack gave me a smile of relief as he said, "Thanks much, Doc. Thanks! If you had hung combat neurosis on our necks, most of us would have had to return to the front lines."

I said, "Don't feel guilty, Jack. I don't think I would have lasted up there half as long as you did. Have a safe trip home."

We had sent a weasel along with G Company as they moved up. This vehicle could travel partway, while our jeep ambulances could not move beyond the aid station site. Because they had to evacuate two companies of the 26th Marines to make room for G Company, our men grumbled more loudly than usual. This transfer of combat men produced a new record of sorts. For the first time since the start of the operation, no wounds were experienced by any of the men involved. As darkness settled in, our troops were in place, and the killing would resume when the order to advance was issued on the following day.

At 1910, after we had settled down for the night, I received a surprise call from Colonel Robertson. His voice sounded exuberant and almost carefree as he said, "We have just received some great news. Germany has surrendered. They are celebrating on the south end of the island. Pass the word on to your men. They are to keep quiet and stay put in their positions. We may still have a few prowling Nips in our area."

To attest to the truth of the colonel's report, the sky to the south was lit up by exploding flares, rockets, and crisscrossing tracers. I wished those rear echelon troops would come up here and descend into that pocket. Then they could expend all that ammunition in a useful manner.

A half hour later the colonel called back, saying disconsolately, "That victory report was a false alarm, and we should forget about it."

I asked, "What really happened?"

He answered, "I'll tell you the whole story in the morning. So good night."

March 20   D Day Plus 29

By the next morning the source of the false victory announcement became common knowledge. Last evening while the usual shortwave news report from Hawaii was being received in the corps communications building, an imaginative communications sergeant was standing by outside the building listening in with his two-way radio. At the proper moment this sergeant broke in with, "Hear this! This is a flash report! Germany has surrendered!"

Good news travels fast. Soon ammunition was being expended with great abandon. Fortunately, only one man was wounded during this great display of joy.

The attack on March 20 started a few minutes before sunrise. As the hours wore on, the territorial gains proved to be negligible. However, the wounds received ranged from serious to lethal. A typical example was a young private who was brought in early in the morning. The bullet's point of entry was the lower neck, just anterior to the breast bone. He must have been shot at point-blank range, for the bullet had skewered his entire body and had made its exit via the left buttock.

It was remarkable that he was still breathing on arriving at the aid station. Even more remarkable was the improvement noted near the end of the second unit of plasma. His color revived and his state of consciousness was much improved. But from here on, his progress was all downhill. Before the fifth unit of plasma had been administered, all vital functions ceased and the man was dead. Because we had no time to perform autopsies, it will never be known just how badly his vital organs had been torn up inside.

Corpsman Dolan of A Company also proved that our cornered enemy marksmen possessed a deadly accuracy. A corporal had been shot ten yards beyond the forward positions of A Company. His inexperienced platoon leader ordered Dolan to go forward to see if the man was dead. Before crawling out into the open, a coil of rope was attached to his right leg. The rope could be used to pull both Dolan and the wounded man back, should the need arise.

In thirty seconds Dolan arrived at the casualty's side. His last words were, "He's dead."

Then he crumpled on top of the first casualty. The enemy sharpshooter had been patiently waiting to claim his next victim.

Dolan's color and circulation were quite good on arrival at the aid station, but he had obviously suffered a mortal wound. The bullet had pierced his helmet and had entered the center of his forehead. A large, jagged hole on the top of his head was the point of exit. Fragments of hair, scalp tissue, and bone lined the edges of this ragged wound.

It was unlikely that he would ever recover from his present state of deep coma. However, if a miraculous recovery were ever to occur, he needed prompt treatment at a base hospital. Before shipping him out, the wound had to be debrided and carefully covered. It only took a few minutes to trim back the matted, blood-clotted hair and to snip off the sharp spicules of bone. I did not want the sterile dressings to push these bone fragments deeper into the already damaged brain.

As he was loaded onto the ambulance, I thought, "What a waste. Dolan was a good lad. Why did he have to be the victim of an inexperienced platoon leader's bad judgment?"

The ineptitude of this young lieutenant was not an isolated event. Practically all of the replacement officers and enlisted men had had no previous combat experience and were prone to make tactical mistakes of one kind or another. Usually one error of judgment would be enough to cause the injury or death of the perpetrator or one or more of his comrades. An adage among the older Marines was, "The last to come will be the first to go."

The total ground gained for the day was less than three ten-yard markers on a football field. As we settled down for the night Corpsman Smith said, "It's terrible."

Meegan asked, "What's so terrible?"

"We lost one man for each yard gained today."

"Yeah, but it could be worse."

"How could anything be worse?"

"What if we were Nips holed up in the pocket? They have little food, water, and no hope left."

"They could surrender."

"They'll never do that."

I interjected, "I have a better idea."

Both men in unison said, "What's that?"

"Let the Army garrison troops pitch camp up here, and let the Nips stay holed up in the gorge till the food and water runs out."

Smith asked, "Why don't our top brass do it that way?"

"Maybe they didn't think of it."

Meegan said, "It's getting pretty late. Maybe we should catch some shut-eye."

"Yeah."

March 21   D Day Plus 30

March 21 was a repetition of the day before. We had many serious injuries from rifle bullets fired from very short distances. The low point of the day occurred just before noon when Corpsman Vogt arrived on a litter accompanied by Sergeant Bates, who traveled on his own power as he clutched a blood-soaked dressing wrapped about the end of his penis.

After piecing their stories together, we thought that both men had probably been wounded by the same sniper. Vogt was very eager to engage in combat in addition to performing his medical duties. The day before, he had hauled a sack of grenades up to the front lines and had helped toss them into enemy caves. Today he had been shot in the right lower quadrant of the abdomen while carrying ammunition up to the front lines.

In a reversal of roles, Sergeant Bates had rushed out to drag Vogt back to cover. A second bullet had whipped through between Bates's legs just below his crotch. It missed everything except the tip of his glans penis, which had been neatly carried way. As expected, this blood-filled organ continued to bleed copiously.

I took charge of Vogt's problems after assigning Bates to Dr. Hely. The bullet was of .25-caliber size and had entered Vogt's abdomen very low and quite far laterally on the right side. The bullet must have been embedded in the pelvic bone, as there was no point of exit. I hoped the bullet had not torn open the colon in the region of the appendix.

As he lay on the stretcher before me, my mind harked back to the discussion we'd had on the beach on March 16. I had stopped him from the risky diving off the wrecked barge. At the same time I had advised him to function as a corpsman in the future and avoid activities that required performance by a Marine. If only he had accepted my advice, he would not have toted that ammunition up forward, and he would still be a healthy corpsman. Now his serious wound made it obvious that he needed an immediate exploratory laparotomy to evaluate the extent of the damage and repair any torn or ruptured intestines. I asked Meegan to call the 5th Division Hospital requesting that they stand by to receive Vogt directly into the operating room.

Suddenly Meegan was expostulating, "You won't take him! How can you close up our hospital? We're still fighting a war. You can't do that."

Meegan, usually calm, was obviously furious as he slammed down the receiver and turned in my direction, "They are dismantling the hospital. We should send all patients to the 35th Army Hospital."

I asked, "Where are they located?"

Meegan answered, "They were not sure!"

A short time later I contacted Dr. Chauncey Alcott at division head-quarters. After I complained bitterly about this shabby treatment, he gave me the map coordinates for this newly imported Army hospital.

On concluding this conversation, I noted large tears rolling down Vogt's cheeks.

I said, "Don't cry, Vogt, we'll see that you get taken care of."

He answered, "That doesn't worry me, Doc. It's just that my side hurts like hell."

"That shot of morphine should start working soon."

"Could I have a couple of drags on a cigarette?"

By the time the cigarette was half consumed, Vogt's contorted facial muscles relaxed and he seemed able to cope with his pain.

In the meantime, Hely had finally controlled the blood loss from Sergeant Bates's hemorrhaging penis with several well-placed temporary sutures. Bates's chief concern was not for his own wound. He had over-heard the conversation concerning the closure of our 5th Division Hos-pital and was most worried that Vogt would not receive the best medical care available. He depreciated his own injuries. Everything would be fine if they could just get young Vogt put back together again.

Bates's present behavior was quite a switch from his previous atti-tude. Back in our Hawaiian training camp, Bates was one of our top-rated sick bay Marines. He showed up most every morning for sick call with multiple and changing complaints. Hely and I both thought he would be one of the first men to crack under the stress of combat. His perfor-mance for thirty-one days with G Company had been above reproach.

Corpsman Smith accompanied both men back to the 35th Army Hos-pital. He was not to leave Vogt until he was taken into the operating theater. Smith was to continue harassing them until they performed as requested.

The medical section suffered another loss at 1300. Two bright-eyed and eager young Marine litter bearers had joined us only five days earlier. Carlson was a tall, lean, angular man in his early twenties and Cook was only eighteen. He was short and stocky, almost square. His movements were quick and agile, and his muscles were so well developed that there was not room for a pound of surplus fat on his frame.

Although both men came from the hills of eastern Tennessee, their acquaintance had not begun until they had arrived in boot camp six months before. Ever since, they had remained inseparable friends. When one man went out with a litter to rescue a casualty, the other was sure to accom-pany him. It did not take my corpsmen long to label them "the Mutt and Jeff litter team."

Besides being fearless litter bearers, the two men soon became inveterate souvenir hunters. In only five days, these men had acquired Japanese pistols, rifles, sabres, binoculars, cameras, as well as numerous and sundry flags and emblems.

But they finally ventured too far forward. Shortly after 1300 Cook and two other litter bearers deposited Carlson at my feet. He had received a ghastly chest wound. Two of his ribs on the right lateral side of his chest had been shot away, leaving a gaping opening large enough to accommodate my entire hand. I plugged up the wound as a temporary measure to prepare him for the trip to the hospital, Cook begged me for permission to accompany his friend in the jeep ambulance. He seemed so desperate that I granted permission for him to go.

A few hours later Cook climbed out of a resupply weasel loaded down with all of Carlson's and his own souvenir booty. Contrary to his usual jaunty behavior, he seemed deeply depressed.

I asked, "How did Carlson make out?"

"He died on the operating table."

Cook then slumped down to the ground and allowed his head to sink far below and between his knees in deep despair. A half hour later, after treating a thigh wound, I noted that Cook was still curled up in this same position of dejection.

I shook him by the shoulder as I said, "Sit up and look at me. I know it's tough to lose your buddy. It's happened to a lot of other guys out here. The quicker you snap out of it, the better it will be."

He looked back at me without hope, "My troubles are much worse than anyone else's."

"How do you figure that out, Cook?"

"Before Carlson was hauled into surgery, I promised him I'd marry his wife if he did not make it."

"What kind of a gal is she?"

"I don't know. I've never seen her. Besides, she has two young kids."

"You've certainly taken on a big commitment. How do you know that she will want to marry you? She may have a new friend already picked out."

This suggestion hit a responsive chord. Cook got up, poured a cup of coffee, and began to talk with his fellow litter bearers. He was definitely going to recover.

The flow of casualties did not let up all day. We shipped our last man out at 2200. Checking in at the command post I learned Colonel Robertson and General Hermle were out planning the operations for the following day. Lieutenant Familo said we'd only moved forward thirty yards during the entire day, but these were crucial yards gained, because they ensured enough room so our flamethrower tanks could enter the gorge and lead the advance. G and A companies would be relieved in the morning. D and H companies would mop up behind the tanks as they advanced through the canyon.

I said, "Familo, do you think this plan will work, or will it bog down like all the rest?"

"The colonel seems more optimistic than usual."

"Let's hope he's right."

Familo answered, "I'll keep you posted on how things go tomorrow."

Chapter Fifteen

D Day Plus 31 and 32

March 22   D Day Plus 31

Late in the morning of March 22, Corpsman Maloney said, "Dr. Schultz is on the phone and wants to talk to you."

I started the conversation with a guarded, "Hello, Dr. Schultz."

He answered with a genial, "Hi, Jim. How are things going?"

I said, "Not bad. What can I do for you?"

"You can do me a big favor by sending my jeep ambulance back."

"What for?"

"I need it to pack all my camping gear aboard. They want to load the jeep aboard ship this afternoon."

I answered, "My God, man, don't you people down on the beach know that there is still a war going on? Yesterday they took our hospital apart. Now you want to take our wheels away from us. Maybe we should hand-carry the casualties back to the new Army hospital by litter bearer?"

"Don't you really think you can spare my ambulance, Jim?"

"Not until we get relieved from combat."

"You wouldn't want me to call Colonel Robertson and request its return, would you?"

"That sounds like a good idea. I wish you luck. Goodbye, Dr. Schultz."

The usual stream of casualties continued to flow into our aid station. All our vehicles were needed to handle the load.

An unusual diversion occurred early in the afternoon. A member of the enemy garrison came hobbling into our aid station from the south.

He apparently had been hiding in the jumble of boulders lying two hundred yards to our rear. He was not able to support much weight on his left leg. He was using a section of iron pipe for an improvised crutch. As he entered the outer periphery of our aid station, two of my litter bearers slipped around behind him. They knocked him to the ground and relieved him of his length of pipe, which might have served as a potential weapon.

When one of the men started to prod the disarmed prisoner with this piece of pipe, I shouted at them to stop while I hurried over for a closer inspection. Our disarmed enemy did not present a very formidable appearance. His dirty, shredded uniform indicated that he held a sergeant's rating in the Imperial Army. His scraggly black hair hung down over his forehead and ears. The tint of grayness was due to the powdering of dust acquired from long habitation in the enemy's extensive cave and tunnel system. He did not present a concealed threat. By his simple act of surrender, he had decided to live and join our side rather than die for his emperor.

Closer examination would place his age in the midthirties. He was a little larger than the average Japanese. His weight must have been close to 140 pounds. His muscular development was excellent. My attention was then directed to his left thigh, which was swollen to double the size of the right. The entire left thigh was red and very tender to palpation. In the center of the thigh anteriorly was an old wound two inches long that had recently healed over. Palpation about this scar revealed a soft fluctuant mass beneath the skin surface. From the acute inflammatory reaction, there had to be a large accumulation of pussy material that needed to be released.

Preparing to surgically drain this area, I carefully cut away the tattered trouser leg. Then I gently bathed the entire thigh with liquid green soap, rinsed it off well with water, and then gave the skin a final cleansing with 95 percent alcohol.

While carrying out these procedures, my patient's tenseness and apprehensiveness appreciably lessened. Then, with the help of gestures, I wielded my scalpel about before his eyes and over his thigh in a dry run of the impending surgical attack. My demonstration surmounted the language barrier, for my patient nodded his head in the affirmative. As he did so he opened his mouth widely for the first time. He must have had a conscientious dentist back in Japan, for his teeth had been restored with three bridges and several gold inlays.

The surgery was completed quickly with a wide incision through the old scar, which allowed over a cup of thick creamy pus to exude from the wound. On exploring the depth of the wound with a thumb forceps,

I encountered a solid object that grated with a metallic clink. As I lifted it gently from the wound, I found my forceps was clutching a jagged, three-inch sliver of shrapnel.

After dressing the wound, I instructed Corpsman Smith to accompany the prisoner back to the 35th Army Hospital. In the past ten days we had lost two other prisoners who had been shot while trying to escape from the jeep ambulance. I knew I could trust Smith to see that this man arrived safely at the hospital.

At 2100 that evening, Colonel Robertson paid us a welcome visit.

As he settled down on a carton of C rations with a cup of freshly brewed coffee, he said, "I want you and Hely to be among the first to hear the good news. With the help of the flamethrowing tanks, our troops moved forward a little over three hundred yards into the canyon. Only a small remnant of the pocket remains. General Hermle, our assistant division commander, says the 27th has more than done its duty. The 26th and 28th will stay until the rest of the opposition has been wiped out."

I asked, "What happens to us? Do we stand by as a ready reserve?"

The colonel answered, "No way, after pulling out from the lines in the morning, our men will head for the beach and will board the troop ship later in the day."

"Gee, that sounds great. What ship will we embark on?"

"I don't know. Colonel Warnham will let us know in the morning. By the way, Doc, Dr. Schultz is getting pretty nervous about his jeep. You'd better let him have it back tomorrow sometime."

I answered, "Can we return it when we are sure we've treated our last casualty?"

The colonel said, "That sounds reasonable."

Dr. Schultz did not get his jeep ambulance returned until ten minutes before we eventually embarked on our departing troop ship.

Most of us were too excited to sleep well that night. After tossing back and forth on my litter for over an hour, and after checking my watch for the seventh time, I noticed that Meegan and Smith were doing the same thing.

I said, "Hey, are you guys awake?"

"Yeah."

Smith countered with, "Do you think it's for real?"

"It's gotta be. What do you think, Meegan?"

"I agree. Robertson got the dope straight from General Hermle."

Smith added, "I guess so, but I'll really believe when my feet are planted on our transport's steel deckplates."

Meegan and I responded with, "Amen, amen."

After rolling from side to side for the next hour, I noted that my foxhole mates were doing the same.

"Hey Meegan, how many guys have we treated so far?"

"Got the latest figures in my pocket. They may not be one hundred percent accurate but they are close."

As he said that, he unfolded a sheet of paper and consulted the contents with the aid of my flashlight.

"It says here the number was 794, but only 546 belonged to the 3rd Battalion."

"Where did the other 248 casualties come from?"

"They were strays we picked up from other units."

"Does that count the men killed in action?"

"No."

"Can you tell me how many of the 963 men of our 3rd Battalion that landed on D day were either killed, wounded, or missing in action?"

"That's easy. The number is seven hundred or thereabouts."

"You mean less than three hundred of our original men are still with us?"

"That's so."

"How many of these originals are left in each company?"

"About two hundred belong to headquarters company."

"God, that leaves only a handful for the three fighting companies."

"That's right. The fighting strength of our combat companies would be down near zero without the many replacements."

"Just hope we lose no more men while pulling out of the lines in the morning."

Our desultory conversation finally trailed off at 0300, but real sleep did not come, for the anticipation of deliverance would not permit more than brief periods of dozing.

March 23   D Day Plus 32

My first recollection of March 23 is of Lieutenant Smith of the regimental intelligence section poking me in the back. "Hit the deck, Doc. Get your crew packed up and down to the beach. You will be boarding the SS *Sea Sturgeon* this afternoon."

"You mean we're really moving out? The *Sea Sturgeon*!"

As I slowly crawled to a sitting position, I asked, "Is she a seaworthy bucket?"

"Sure, she is a brand-new victory-type ship, but there may be a problem. She is operated by the Army."

I answered, "So may it be, I'll be happy to take my chances on anything that leaves this godforsaken island."

It took us a remarkably short time to eat a hasty breakfast and to get all our gear stowed aboard our vehicles. Just as we were about to shove off for the beach, we received a frantic call from H Company. "Send us some litter bearers."

One of their men had been shot in the leg while pulling back from the lines.

After dispatching a four-man litter team, we unpacked and sorted through our equipment until we found splints, dressings, and plasma. The casualty was in good condition on arrival. A .30-caliber bullet had made a clean hole through his right shin bone. He had already received his shot of morphine from a corpsman in H Company, so we hastily cleaned the wound, covered it with sterile dressings, and applied a molded plywood splint. In their haste to load the man aboard the jeep ambulance, my men banged the injured leg against the overhead supports with considerable force. The pain caused the patient to utter a howling protest.

I had to chide the men for this unseemly behavior. This was the first time during the entire operation that a casualty had been roughly handled. The men involved were contrite and apologized profusely to the wounded Marine.

Meegan stated, "This raises our total of casualties treated to 795. If our luck holds out, he will be our last one. If any more should arrive, I'm sure they will be handled compassionately."

On our arrival at the western beaches, Lt. Jim Gass met me with two ducks, "The colonel wants you to take these vehicles down to the 35th Army Hospital to pick up our sick and walking wounded." On arriving at the hospital, I was surprised that the Army had not evacuated any of our acutely ill Marines. All the dysentery cases from G Company were completely recovered and eager to leave. Even Amrosino had not been sent on to Guam as I had promised him, but he was not at all upset by the delay. He was very happy to be returning to Hawaii with his buddies. In all, twenty-three of our men were rounded up and loaded on the ducks. They too were glad to rejoin their units for the long voyage back to Hawaii.

As happens so often in the military service, we had been urged to hurry up so we could wait. At 1200 we were impatiently gathered on the beach to board the *Sea Sturgeon*, which lay anchored a few hundred yards offshore. Five hours later, at 1700, an LSM hit the beach with determination and dropped its ramp for a dry landing. Using his public address equipment, the skipper invited all members of the 3rd Battalion of the 27th Marines and the corps evacuation hospital to come aboard for ferry service out to the *Sea Sturgeon*.

Once aboard the ship, euphoria seized the majority of the men as they shed their ragged, filthy clothing, shaved off their thirty-four-day-old beards, and cleansed their bodies under hot showers. By the time they were finally garbed in clean clothes, it began to settle into their consciousness that they were really liberated. There was no longer danger that the high command would again change its mind and send them back to fight again on this ill-omened island.

"We are the minority who are alive and not mutilated. We have survived!" Not many questioned whether or not our survival depended on divine providence or just pure luck. As the 27th Marines waited for their first complete dinner in thirty-four days, they kept the ship's compartments rocking with shouts, loud joshing, and raucous, bawdy songs.

Soon the *Sea Sturgeon* was rechristened the *"Virgin Sturgeon,"* and our troop transport was engulfed in a gala song fest. A lengthy impromptu ballad emerged with countless verses that rocketed up and down the passageways of the ship.

Our transport, the *Virgin Sturgeon,* might still be pure and immaculate, but all the virgins in Honolulu had better be ready when we hit the beach.

Our Last Days at Iwo Jima

We did not leave Iwo Jima immediately, because our convoy could not take off until the 26th and 28th Marines were safely embarked. It took them two more days to complete wiping out the last remnants of that pocket of resistance before turning the security of the island over to the Army garrison troops. As a result we did not set sail until late in the afternoon of March 27. It had required twenty-two crowded transports to bring the 5th Division to Iwo Jima. Now our convoy of eight troop ships accommodated the entire division with room to spare.

I went up on deck to watch the island disappear under the western sun. Colonel Robertson was standing in the fantail leaning on the rail, also apparently having a last look.

After gripping the rail beside him, I said, "Good evening, colonel, it's a great sight to see that bloody island fading from view."

He answered, "Yes, Iwo sure proved to be an even hotter spot than our top command expected."

"Have you heard how many men we lost during the entire operation?"

"I just saw an updated report this morning. The number was a few men more than 24,800 for both the Marines and the Navy."

"Gosh, that's about half our fighting force. Do you think that stinking, sulphur-smelling island was worth this terrible cost?"

He thought awhile and said, "I don't really know. The Air Force people are happy. With the vital airstrips on Iwo in our hands, our bombers now have a safe haven halfway between Saipan and the Empire. Our crippled planes limping home, or those low on fuel, will find a welcome roosting spot in this hostile section of the Pacific. With this additional help, maybe our Air Force commanders can bomb the main islands into submission."

We stood silently at the rail watching Iwo Jima grow smaller and smaller. Soon only the sun-bathed crest of Mount Suribachi was visible on the horizon. At this point Robertson turned to me saying, "I have to go below to fill out some more reports for the V Corps commanders."

I answered, "Good luck to you, colonel. I'll be coming below in a few minutes to finish my report on the medical activities within the 3rd Battalion."

As I stood alone on the afterdeck my thoughts were far away. Soon Suribachi disappeared and nothing but the shimmering, golden waters of the western Pacific lay off our starboard beam. I turned away and descended to my cabin.

INDEX